A
Week
End
in the
Middle
of the
Week

Books by Oliver St. John Gogarty

A WEEK END IN THE MIDDLE OF THE WEEK

START FROM SOMEWHERE ELSE

IT ISN'T THIS TIME OF YEAR AT ALL!

COLLECTED POEMS

INTIMATIONS

ROLLING DOWN THE LEA

MOURNING BECAME MRS. SPENDLOVE

MR. PETUNIA

PERENNIAL

MAD GRANDEUR

GOING NATIVE

TUMBLING IN THE HAY

I FOLLOW SAINT PATRICK

SELECTED POEMS

AS I WAS GOING DOWN SACKVILLE STREET

with an Introductory Essay by Ben Lucien Burman

Doubleday & Company, Inc., Garden City, New York, 1958

A WEEK END IN THE MIDDLE OF THE WEEK

and Other Essays on the Bias by

OLIVER ST. JOHN GOGARTY

The publisher is most grateful to Mrs. W. B. Yeats, the Macmillan Company of Canada, Ltd., and the Macmillan Company, New York, for permission to reprint the verses from *The Shadowy Waters: Introductory Lines* and *Coole Park 1929* from COLLECTED POEMS OF W. B. YEATS. Copyright 1907 by the Macmillan Company, copyright renewed 1935 by W. B. Yeats.

Also to the Executor of the Estate of the late Duchess of Wellington for permission to reprint the twelve lines from the poem *Horses* by Dorothy Wellesley.

Library of Congress Catalog Card Number 58–5939

Printed in the United States of America
First Edition
Designed by Diana Klemin

Contents

Portrait of a Friend from Ireland

BEN LUCIEN BURMAN

He was gloriously irreverent. Neither president, premier, king, or Pope escaped his barbed arrows. I had another friend, far removed in space and culture, and yet the two had much in common. Will Rogers was a Gogarty in cowboy costume; Gogarty was a Mayfair and Park Avenue Will Rogers.

My favorite of all his hundreds of stories and the one that best presents this irreverent phase of his character was the episode of the Pope's medal, which has delighted Catholics and Protestants alike. I can hear even now the chuckle in his voice as he told me the story over a plate of roast beef.

It seems that William Thomas Cosgrave, President of the Executive Council of the newly born Irish Free State, had been invited by the Pope to Rome for a visit, and Cosgrave had asked Oliver to come along. The iconoclastic Gogarty was the last man on earth to invite on a religious pilgrimage, but Oliver, to oblige Cosgrave, agreed. Arriving at the Vatican, the papal secretary told Oliver that the Pope next day would present the chief of the Irish state with a large medal, but in order that his companion not feel slighted the Pope would give Oliver a very small one as well. According to Vatican etiquette, the secretary added, the tray with the medals would be offered to Oliver first.

The papal audience was held next day, and the tray bearing the precious religious tokens extended to the junior visitor. To the horror of the spectators, Oliver, instead of taking the small medal, took the big one and dropped it into his pocket.

A few minutes later the secretary came dashing up to Oliver in the anteroom. "Dr. Gogarty," he gasped, "a dreadful mistake has been made."

Oliver faced him haughtily. "Did I come to Rome to have the infallibility of the Pope questioned?" he asked.

He kept the medal.

Most of my friends I have made on sight. But when I was first introduced to Oliver in the early forties it was like the meeting of two angry dogs. We did everything but bare our teeth.

I had heard he was a professional Irishman and a frightful snob. While he had somehow gained the impression that I was a professional, hundred-per-cent American. Never were two judgments more wrong.

Several years passed and he chanced to read one of my books. He was kind enough to be enthusiastic about it and write an introduction for an edition about to appear in England. I am frank to admit that I am one of those foolish, gullible writers, very susceptible to flattery. If someone likes a book I have written, I think as automatically as day follows night that this individual must have a large measure of wisdom. I met Oliver again, and I learned his real nature. He was the exact opposite of pretentiousness and snobbery. We became friends on the spot.

Oliver was in many ways an imp, a leprechaun in a top hat. Of one thing you could be certain: he would always say or do the unexpected. He tried to have Lloyd's insure him against knighthood; when the Irish banned his books he retaliated by printing a notice in a later one, "Forbidden to be sold in Ireland."

When the plane he was piloting crashed in a field at the time of one of his bitter battles with De Valera and the newspaper reporters came running up to ask if he was hurt, he remarked, "De Valera is right." And in telling the story he always added, "And then I knew I had concussion of the brain."

I wish the Russians had a Gogarty. They wouldn't be nearly so dangerous.

He had an impish remark for every occasion. We were waiting to cross the street one night in New York and he had stepped down from the curb ahead of the light when a taxicab sped past.

"Why don't you stay up on the sidewalk where you belong?" bellowed the driver.

"Elementary, my dear Watson," Oliver retorted.

The driver jumped out of the cab and wanted to fight. He thought Oliver had called him a dirty name.

We were talking one day of a certain feminine literary figure in New York that he detested. "I have lost my faith in the juniper berry," he said.

I asked him to explain.

"Gin is made from juniper," he said. "She drinks it by the gallon. And it hasn't killed her yet."

He delighted in mystification, like the Little Men that lived near his former home in Renvyle. Many times he arranged with me to tell certain friends and his publishers that he was in upper New York State when actually he was in Florida. Or to say he was in Florida when actually he was only across the river in New Jersey.

His elf-like nature persisted even when matters were serious. If he had not been so sophisticated and had come instead from the Ozarks or the Kentucky hills he would have been one of those jovial individuals known in the South as a "card." He delighted in telling how during the fighting in Ireland the English Black and Tans found a couple of rifles on the estate of his neighbor, Lord Dunsany, when the mere possession of a weapon might mean a death sentence. The fact that Dunsany used the guns merely for hunting birds made no difference.

"I spent most of the night telling him not to worry," Oliver would say gleefully. "I reminded him that he was a peer of the realm and, though he would undoubtedly be hanged, they could only hang him with a silken rope. And I demonstrated with a string how he would bounce up and down like a yo-yo."

His devastating phrases gave any casual acquaintance the feeling that he was a complete cynic, devoid of the softer emotions. Actually he was one of the kindest men I have ever met. The moment he received a check for his writing, it evaporated into gifts for those he knew were not "in the chips." When James Stephens, the Irish poet and novelist, lacked money to feed his family, it was Oliver who anonymously arranged with a nearby merchant to send him meat and groceries every day, for Stephens was too proud to accept charity. Often I have seen him carrying a ponderous brief case that when opened contained not books or manuscripts but an expensive steak for a needy friend.

He was, like most great men, a paradox. He badgered and ridiculed the English unmercifully. Yet in himself there was much of the English love of tradition, of doing the same thing the same way. He always wanted to eat in the same restaurant, even though the food had become terrible, the waiters impossible, and everything attractive that had brought us there in the first place had long since ceased to exist. When he came to visit us in the hotel where we stay when in New York I always took care to see that he had exactly the same chair, with exactly the same ash tray and exactly the same glass for his beer. Once we invited another friend, who, unaware of his crime, took this throne sacred to Oliver when it was momentarily vacant. The usually genial Gogarty became tense. Nervously he found a new chair and sat watching and waiting like a leopard, taut and ready to spring. Our other visitor arose to glance at something in a corner of the room. In a flash, almost quicker than the eye could follow, Oliver had bounded into his old place and, beaming like a cherub, triumphantly lit a cigar.

Those cigars were a real problem. I have a supersensitive nose and that of my wife is equally delicate. Oliver's cigars emitted a poisonous fog that reminded me uncomfortably of the gas barrages I had experienced in France during the First World War. I invented so many stories trying to prevent him from smoking on his visits they would have filled the pages of a good-sized novel.

Another problem was his habit of talking in a loud stage whisper about people he didn't like, under their very noses. We were having lunch once in a swank restaurant—not at all the kind we usually patronized. Our host was a publisher I knew who wanted Oliver to sign a contract. He had agreed to the terms when the Duchess of Windsor came in and sat down at an adjoining table.

Oliver shook his head gloomily and said to me in a whisper so loud I am certain the Duchess could hear every word: "Whenever she's around she brings me bad luck. The contract'll come to nothing."

Oddly enough, he was right.

He was extraordinarily modest. For years I had been urging him to write his memoirs of the Irish Rebellion in which he played so vital a part—I have heard many say he was the real brains of the movement. He always refused. "Too much of the personal pronoun," he would answer. And now the story will never be written, episodes like the occasion when an emergency operation had to be performed on the despised commander of the English troops in Ireland and no doctor fit for the task was in the country except the famous Dublin surgeon, Gogarty.

A fiery patriot came to Oliver just as the operation was about to begin. "Here's your chance, Gogarty," he whispered. "Now you can rid Ireland of him forever."

But Oliver's medical ethics were stronger than his hatred of the enemy. As a result of his skill the English commander was made whole again, to fight the Irish another day.

The only story Oliver could be persuaded to put down, and this after years of constant prodding and entreaty, was the account of his kidnaping, happily included in the following pages.

He was the darling of rich old ladies on Park Avenue. Actually his real pleasure came when he was with the simple and uneducated, watching the drama and comedy that filled their eventful lives. Though his drinking was negligible—he had sworn off whisky after some terrific escapades in his youth—he delighted in talking over a glass of beer to the men collected in some obscure bar. I have sat with him until far into the morning, listening as some waiter or floorwalker or truck driver told Oliver of his hopes and desires, or related in great detail his ideas about world philosophy and literature. And Oliver, the most genuinely learned man I have ever encountered, would pay him the same respectful attention he would have given the head of his own Trinity College. By the sheer force of his personality he reigned over these little taverns like a king.

Probably it was his gaiety that charmed the motley customers gathered there, even though his somewhat formal manner and speech were so alien to anything in their experience. It was not merely the superficial gaiety that means only a flash of wit or the quick repartee of which he was such a master. It was the gaiety of one who sees the folly and absurdity in all of us, yet can laugh jauntily and go on enjoying life to the fullest.

I sensed this very early in our acquaintance. I became certain of it in his last days.

We had arranged to have dinner with him one Thursday in mid-September at a Chinese restaurant he fancied. Eight o'clock passed, nine o'clock and ten, and still there was no sign of his arrival. I grew a bit worried, because Oliver was punctilious about his appointments and he had lately been having some trouble with his heart. But I had lunched with him three days earlier and he had seemed in as buoyant spirits as ever. I considered for a moment trying to call him on the telephone. But thinking that he might have dropped off to sleep, and knowing that a tricky heart demands much rest, I decided it would be better to let him go undisturbed. We finished dinner with the friends we had brought along for the evening and went back to our hotel.

Whenever I am working on a book I have my telephone cut off until ten-thirty in the morning. I am given to working late. But before that hour the hotel operator waked me, saying there was an important call. I answered sleepily and found it was an orderly at a New York hospital, informing me that Doctor Gogarty was a patient in an emergency ward. He had collapsed in the street on the way to join us at dinner, had been picked up by a policeman and brought to the hospital in an ambulance. Would I come up as soon as possible?

I went as fast as I could, feeling very melancholy. It's a shock not even two wars can dull to be wakened suddenly and learn that someone close to you has met with an accident. My depression deepened when I entered the hospital. I saw Oliver across the ward, lying in bed. A queer-looking glass flask hung near his head with a transparent tube attached below, dripping some sort of liquid into his arm. Nearby was a tank of oxygen, obviously ready for use. The beds around him were occupied mostly by Puerto Ricans, emergency cases who, like himself, had been brought in during the night.

When I came to his bedside I saw instantly that Oliver did not share my depression. He was talking gaily to his prostrate neighbors. Though they could speak English only with difficulty, they were replying with animation. In the few hours since his arrival Oliver had already stamped the bleak ward with his personality. It was like one of his favorite little bars. Oliver had taken over.

I pretended to be gay as well, though actually as I stayed on I began to grow desperate. The staff of the hospital was unusually kind for a public institution, but the interns were all Latins. Only the chief intern spoke a little broken English. To complicate matters further, his pretty Spanish assistant had acute laryngitis and couldn't utter a sound. She answered my questions by writing in Spanish on a sheet of note paper. Somehow I managed to make them understand who Oliver was, and would they please not neglect him. Between times I tried to reach his personal physician to let him know Oliver's condition. The doctor was out making calls and couldn't be located.

The ward to me was becoming a scene in a grim Italian movie. The wife of the affable Puerto Rican in the bed next to Oliver's brought in a huge television set and plugged it into the wall. It began to roar out a mawkish popular song. Oliver was no lover of any kind of music. But he hated jukeboxes and television tunes with an intensity like that he reserved for his Irish political enemies. Yet as he lay there unable to move away, he smiled benignly through the dreadful cacophony as though he were a Beethoven devotee listening to the Fifth Symphony. I discovered that the owner of the machine could walk about and managed to persuade his wife to take husband and concert to the social room outside. The ward grew quieter.

I was able to reach Oliver's doctor at last, as well as the banker known as the Major who took care of his affairs. It was arranged that he would be moved next day to a private hospital near his tiny apartment. I felt relieved, certain now that he would be well looked after. We sat talking as casually as though we were at our intended dinner. He recited a few poems—his memory was phenomenal—and told me some funny stories he had heard in the last few days. He was so merry and laughed so much I began to worry that it might affect his heart. I tried to talk of something sad in the hope of making him less energetic. It was no use. He was irrepressible.

I left him when it grew dark and found him again next day, still surrounded by the Puerto Ricans. He had a new attack during the night, and the doctors had decided he ought not be moved. But his vivacity was undiminished. At his request I went out and bought him the newspaper that contained his favorite comic strip. We talked about comic strips, and comedy high and low, and Oliver told me another joke.

Suddenly I saw the color leave his cheeks. "I think my trouble is coming on me," he said quietly.

I dashed for the chief intern, whose office was just down the corridor. The hospital staff were alert now. In a few seconds Oliver was under oxygen. Soon the intern reappeared to tell me that he was out of danger for the moment but was too weak to talk to anyone.

Gustav Davidson, the secretary of the Poetry Society, who had been in a little earlier, arrived with his wife for a visit. Instead we stood in the doorway and waved. Oliver smiled through the oxygen mask in answer.

He died next morning. I think it fitting that his last request was for something that made people laugh and almost his last words were the telling of a funny story.

Like Oliver, I pretend to no knowledge of the hereafter. But if the mystical conceptions of most of the Western world are true, I can imagine Oliver coming before the Judgment Seat and asking, "Lord, have you heard about the preacher, the priest, and the rabbi that went to heaven?" And the Lord replying he hadn't but did Oliver know the new one about the passenger in the airplane that wouldn't stop climbing? And I can see them continuing to swap yarns until St. Peter tells the Lord it's late and He ought to get a little rest.

And I can hear the Lord answering patiently, "Sit down, Peter, and listen awhile. I want to ask Oliver a few questions. We've got too many yes-men here in heaven."

I Regard America

You had better know first who is talking. A man from Ireland, an island 133 miles from sea to sea. That is the yardstick that is to measure a continent 3,000 miles across. In spite of the smallness of the measure of comparison there is an advantage in it, the advantage of a fresh outlook and a wonder that is never stale. People born in a country are naturally inclined to take for granted what is marvelous to outsiders. Physical vastness is the first feature that strikes the visitor to America; and as if to accompany that, a breadth of outlook in the American mind.

There is no use in trying to find a comparison for this country in Europe or anywhere else. It is new and unique. In Europe the outlook on things is bound up with the past, that is to say tradition; and tradition is at once the limitation and the guide. In Europe things are referred back. In America they are referred to a future in which every man has sublime confidence. America is confident of its future. Of what other country can this be said?

This engenders a certain restlessness, which is the restlessness of a busy hive, and this in turn influences the American way of life, which is in a state of perpetual flux. There are so many different races in the United States that finding one common denominator for all its inhabitants means that an influence is at work molding the differences and merging them. This influence comes from the country itself, from the landscape if you like; but it comes from America.

The original inhabitants were nomadic. You find traces of this everywhere, even in the short leases of apartments, in the deep-lying similarity of the towns, which are tepees enlarged and luxurious. They are the same no matter how different the latitude and the surrounding scenery is. The atmosphere of America is clear. The complexions of the people are not pink and white, but have the intensity of animated ivory; in fact, a beauty analyst told me that the American skin is not white but of a deeper purity. Brunetism, incidentally, is on the increase.

The trees, rivers, and mountains of America delight me. All smallness was forever driven out. Even though the inhabitants have not as yet dominated the landscape (it is the other way round just now) signs are not wanting that the landscape is entering into American literature. The trees of America are more varied than those of the Old World. Among them is the female yew tree, from which bows are made for the best archers in the world. (These are flat bows on the principle of a spring, not semi-round as the bows of England are.) Of trees in bloom, who can speak? Acre after acre of apple orchard in bloom—a sight that can hardly be sustained, such is the joy it transmits.

There are no peasants in the United States. There are farmers who have a highly technical knowledge of machinery and who can drive their tractors all night to plow or to sow their fields with the help of headlights.

In the country there is no strain. People have time to be kind and considerate; and kind and considerate they are. They have time for everything, and they are devoid of irony of any sort. Their wit is not cataclysmic. If their humor is dry, it is not cynical. Its large tolerance saves it. It is the symbol of large-hearted men.

They say that there are cities in India that are noisier than New York. I doubt it, because they lack the mechanical means for making noise. This noise is barbaric. It seems to be a substitute for or a preventive of thought. The result of all the noise is to raise the pitch of speech and to make people shout in order to be heard.

For a while I imagined that the color of New York was the

counterpart of its noises: yellow, green, white and blue and particolored taxis and men's neckties in the windows of the stores. It is not so. Color is an expression of the country's spirit. There is color in Colorado, in the Grand Canyon, and in the little canyon which I visited at Palo Duro near Amarillo: color on the Rockies and even in the evening sky of Manhattan. When I see the moon hung low between the magic towers of the city, I am spellbound. Nowhere is there such a sight as the electric lights in the countless skyey windows multiplied against the clear calmness of the southern sky.

The first thing that strikes the visitor is the intelligence of the women. Many of the literary reviews, magazines, and poetry societies are run by them. They are more "aware" of the arts than the men. In fact, it has come to be so much their prerogative that to see an "arty" man outside the great cities is to see an oddity. In the United States most of the intellectual societies and social clubs are founded and run by women, and the arts are sustained by them. At the moment, to my knowledge, there is more poetry per capita being written in America than in any country with the possible exception of Scotland, and more poetry is being written in the South and East than in the rest of the states. This is as one would expect. A country which has indescribable beauties should have a society of poets striving until they can express the sentiment of their country adequately. The reservoir is inexhaustible. There is poetry in the very names of the lakes and rivers, even when they are not Indian names. Twilight Lake, Clearwater Lake, Flower Lake, Mirror Lake, Lake Placid: and we have yet to see the appropriateness of Lake Success. The smallest brook in the woods is certain to have a melodious name.

There is another factor for the growth of poetry in America, a factor which is a corollary of expansion and growth, just as in Shakespeare's day and the day of Sophocles, when their countries were growing and hope lit the ways of all men. Therefore I say with assurance that the indefeasible confidence every American has in his future will prove to be the wellspring of new and wonderful minds of modulated expression.

The late Æ used to say that there was no love poetry in America because there were no inhibitions, nothing to yearn about; that Venus was too facile here. This is not altogether true, although now I come to think of it, women write most of the love poetry that is written in the country. This does not arise from the fact that they have to woo the men, but from a circumstance already pointed out: women here are (as Dante said of Florence) "more intelligent in love." When the patriarchal day of the gloomy Puritans had passed, matriarchy was restored to America, or rather, imported; but it developed into a matriarchy different from any known form.

The equality of man and woman is a prerequisite for any balanced civilization. In America equality is the foundation of the state. Here culturally woman achieved more than man. Man is active and wayward; woman is passive and conservative. She took the arts under her care. Her leisure was not dissipated but enriched. Thus, while man was working, woman was fostering everything that made life worth living and justified work. Her societies ameliorated the struggle that was inseparable from production. I have no space to elaborate the argument even if it required elaboration. But I will ask: What would Oklahoma be without its women's clubs—or Dallas on its three hills? Production and profusion are the chief characteristics of the United States; but profusion would run waste were there no women to direct it intelligently and to make it minister to the amenities of life.

There is no mystery in America. America never had a pagan background. There are no fauns and dryads among its trees. So the matriarchy of America is different from that anywhere else. Woman has denuded herself of mystery. She has become contemptuous of her pedestal. She has descended into the arena with man. The American male has accepted the fact and has come to regard woman as of a higher class. Whether she likes it or not, America is upon the brink of empire. And an empire where woman has the say cannot be cruel or oppressive. It cannot be puritanical. The position of woman in the United States is the best augury for its future. It is the one indisputable fact in a world surrounded by uncertainty and threatened by another Dark Age.

A Week-End in the Middle of the Week

Never say, "I have seen all the pictures," for you never know what experience may be waiting for you round the corner. I do not mean that you may find yourself transformed into a sand hog, a Shriner, a crooner, a band president, a missionary, J. P. Morgan, or a milkmaid with a garbage pail under her arm instead of a bucket—a spectacle that Watteau could hardly idealize; but I do mean that within the daily round you may be surprised. So it happened to me.

When my hostess said, "We always take week-ends in the middle of the week," you would have thought that I should have been astonished. I was not astonished because I was so accustomed to making allowances in the (groundless) hope that allowances may be made for me. You cannot tell people that you are making allowances for them unless you are a superior person. I have no intention of posing as a superior person; that is why my hope is groundless—unless, of course, somebody comes along and surveys the scene that includes me and makes allowances for all in it. Any allowance he might make would not be worth much because it would come from a bystander, that is a spectator who regards himself as outside the scene and superior to all in it —a mistake into which it is easy to fall. It used to inveigle me. For instance, when I went into a restaurant and looked around, I found myself making a mental note on the occupants—some were potbellied, some drank too much and in the early noon, some were thin, some were gluttons—forgetting all the time that I was one of them. No; the gladiator is in the arena, not in a front seat.

There is another reason for my not being astonished at a week-end in the middle of the week, and that is the knowledge that I am not the person to decide what is actually the end of the week. There are so many calendars—Egyptian, Babylonian, Caesarean, Aztec, and Gregorian—that for all I know it may fall on Tuesday until Thursday. Ours did.

We were to meet at our host's house at noon. It was Tuesday. We were to go by plane. The plane did not go until one-thirty. What was the noon date for? You may well ask: you could never guess. It was to work you up into thinking that you might miss the plane and with it the week-end. Our hostess had a way of cutting things fine except in cocktails. If you wait long enough there will be a leakage of news; so, when I heard a maid say that a taxi was waiting, I sensed that we would start soon. One of the guests remarked:

"She loves to cut things close. I knew her at school, where she left everything to the last minute. She is getting worse and worse. There's no use in trying to make her change."

"I once made the airport in a quarter of an hour," I remarked.

"Don't let her hear that. We still have time."

She appeared at one o'clock precisely. What she was doing, what any woman does to kill time, is one of those domestic secrets which will never be solved. Not yet! She was not quite ready to go: she had to have a little refreshment. Now you should see me at close quarters with a cocktail shaker. I advanced boldly; but I was not given a chance to show my prowess; I was ordered downstairs and into the taxi. Her man loaded the cab with luggage till there was hardly room for a passenger. Out she came. I determined not to register either surprise or relief. I became nonchalant, which they tell me means not burned up.

"Have you ever seen a more typical town day? Cement mixers are humming; children are escaping; the elevated is running; the poker game of the Fire Department is undisturbed—poker of course suggests a fire, that's why they play it—our driver is sleeping through the Fourth Symphony which is running with the engine."

When it comes to making disconnected remarks I am without a rival. This time I got off five *non sequiturs* in a row. To my astonishment I was taken seriously. That's allowance for you!

"When he wakens he should step on it."

"Beethoven, buck up," I said.

On we scorched, tires squealing at the turns. I began to think of the different worlds in which things live. It would have been appropriate to have included the next world in my reverie; but of that world I have only hearsay. Hers is a world of speed, like the deer flies, I thought; dogs live in a world of scent; birds, sea gulls, and eagles in a world of sight; bats and bartenders in a world of sound; children in a world of illusion; and fellows like myself in a world of ideas. Those five apparently unconnected remarks will illustrate my meaning. They were not disconnected at all; they were summoned up to give the situation and to suggest a day in a city noisy with life. "I am forever grateful to the commissioner who made it easy to get out of New York," she said.

We made it! Oh the relief—not to me, for I was part of the show, but to a guest who was told to meet us at the airport and had despaired of us at the last moment.

"Fasten your belts."

Not yet. Where is the lady? I jumped out. I found her having a last cigarette with the pilot of the plane. She and he were old friends, for she traveled constantly by his line. We got them on board at last and took off into the sceneless air.

It was as she had feared. They had sent her the dumbest of her chauffeurs. She said so repeatedly in French. I hoped that he wasn't a Frenchman or even a French Canadian. He was, appropriately enough, an automaton for an automobile: that is why I don't know where we went or where we came out. The scenery was lost in green; the ground was undulating with valleys here and little hills. What is that quotation from Milton about leaves in

Vallombrosa? What a beautiful name, a valley full of shade. If a field is neglected in America, it is covered with trees, not weeds. Houses now began to appear. By their beautiful proportions they must have been old houses. When Phelps of Yale was entertaining G. K. Chesterton, he asked him what was the feature of America that struck him most. "The wooden houses." "Do you know," said Phelps, "it never struck me that they were made of wood."

"See that salt-box house over there?" Our hostess was speaking. "They say that salt-box houses are made of ships' timber."

"No," I said. "That would require too many wrecks. It is more likely that they are Dutch."

Soon there was a glimpse of sea. Downhill we went and were about to turn left at a house covered with green creepers when someone said, "That's the house that Kipling rented when he wrote *Captains Courageous*."

What a pity, I thought, that it should have been left to Kipling, the professional globe-trotter who had a finger in every pie, to write about Gloucester fishermen. It was Jim Connolly who went to sea with them. Kipling stayed in his rented house and sold Gloucester to America. Kipling who made himself so unpopular that he was forced to leave the United States. He went to Sussex in England and made himself, if possible, more unpopular still: nasty little Kipling, the greatest balladist and jingoist of our time.

"On the rocks at the end of the bay over there the schooner *Hesperus* was wrecked."

I took no interest. I don't like wrecks.

Roses in profusion lined the roadside. Behind the walls were well-kept mansions; at one of the last of these we came to a stop. An unpretentious gate opened on a little path winding and descending. Under large trees we came to the house. And what a house! Pointed gables hidden in foliage, slanting roofs that reached to the ground. A round tower beside the dark hall door; gargoyles in hidden places that grinned down wickedly at the visitor; casements that opened on more roofs. Darkness within.

A maid admitted us.

"Your room is the Paul Revere room. This house was built by

an architect who added a room or two as the fancy took him. One day, for instance, he saw a hearse with wooden shutters pass by, so he built a room with wooden shutters for all the windows." Thus spake my hostess.

"How many rooms are there?"

"Who knows? We have counted fifty-five but there may be more. We never use the same room twice on the same day. We will go to your room by the bathroom, just until the sitting room belonging to it is opened. It is called the Paul Revere room because it once held a collection of Paul Revere silver until the owner sent it to the museum. I will leave you now. Cocktails on the terrace over the water."

The guests were seated beside a table laden with many drinks. They were discussing a statue of a boy with an Elizabethan ruffle round his neck. I, who know very little about ruffles and dislike Queen Elizabeth, was consulted. "Who may it represent?"

"Edward the Sixth, the boy king who died young," I suggested.

"Who is the other statue with the crown and scepter?"

"It may be Edward the Confessor; but does it matter?" The architect may have been collecting Edwards.

Terrace after terrace led to the sea. In the hedges was a blackbird in porcelain, and a squirrel sat up, apparently tame until the shine of the material of which it was made belied its life.

Our hostess appeared in a bathing suit of green.

"Isn't it too cold?" someone asked.

"All the more refreshing."

She dived in backward and struck out. A lady felt the water and cried, "Freezing!"

No wonder the *Hesperus* was wrecked.

Guests were still arriving, among them a good-looking young man. When he appeared a lady said from the depths of a swing chair:

"Rita Hayworth asked three million dollars. I'll settle for a million: you keep out." The lady addressed did not reply. She sighed.

So the talk went on: a medley of princesses. The bather came up from the sea. She put a piece of ice into her mouth "just to take the salt away." She sat in her wet bathing suit until evening fell.

"Dinner in the octagonal room at nine o'clock." She went into the house.

The dining room was large, and the note of it was red lacquer; even the books on the side tables were bound in red morocco; red wineglasses held the wine, which was also red. A raffish collection of ancestral faces with red noses stared from many walls. "They went with the house," my hostess said.

I hadn't plopped down at table before anyone else. When seated, I never thought of manicuring with a prong of the fork. So far, so good. What to do next? I summoned up the shade of my Victorian aunt; but as she was mostly engaged in uttering "don'ts," it wasn't much help: "Don't make food, furniture, or domestics the subjects of conversation." All right; but all negations, when I wanted a positive lead.

During a lull, I should have said that a sudden hush fell on the guests. I started: "Lord Howard de Walden gave a dinner party at his castle of Chirk in Wales. A famous painter was there, seated next to the Bishop of Liverpool. He was dressed as a gypsy, for it was his gypsy period. He had a gold earring in one ear and a dark blue pull-over. A hush descended on the guests, as it is liable to do at a misassociated gathering." (Heavens! what have I done now? I shouldn't have used that word "misassociated." There's no one here misassociated except myself. No one appears to have noticed it.)

"Well?"

Saved, I thought.

"Oh, well, during the lull the Bishop, who imagined that he could be all things to all men, said to the artist beside him something trite, such as: 'Don't you think every man should take unto himself a wife?' 'I've two!' "

Nobody laughed. If they can't see it, what's the use of explaining? I never explain. I am not writing for a publisher's public but for an intelligent one. "Keep the conversation in the middle." That is positive advice. Anyway, I have not monopolized the talk. I will say that for myself. Someone is praising the fish. Leave them alone. I am not the worst after all. Perhaps I should have used my special gambit to dispel the lull. I have never known it to fail: "Do you prefer to be devoured by an alligator or a crocodile?"

It is somewhat odd that no one takes any notice of my good manners. The explanation dawned on me: none of them was born in the reign of Victoria the Vegetable, as I was.

"Nobody is to go into more than fifteen rooms at one visit. If you do, you will lose all sense of proportion, apart from the risk of getting lost."

The ominous house again!

At last the ladies left. "Send a guide back for us."

I was afraid to leave the octagonal room. Suppose I got lost! At length a maid led the way to a darkened living room. A game was about to start. We were not to be told about it. "Silence!"

Awful groaning filled the air. The candlelit room seemed full of moans. Where did they come from? They grew nearer and nearer. Behind that wall. Our hostess had disappeared. Was she the groaning ghost? A candle in a wall bracket began to gutter. One of the party tried to blow it out. This set fire to the molten wax, and soon a flame a foot long leaped up the paneled wall. In fires I am pretty good. I kept my wits about me. I wrapped a wet towel about the blaze. Out it went. Now to return to the ghost, who must be wondering why no one took fright. The reason was that there was no fright left after the fire. One of the guests moved a writing table aside, and the panel went in. Another threw the sodden towel into the darkness. It must have hit the ghost. She appeared, indignant, from the hole in the paneled oak. We were talking about *fumed oak* but the allusion was lost.

"We have seven games. That's one of them. Now we'll play at the missing person. You stay where you are. Alice, come with me."

They left the room. In a few minutes the hostess returned and took us into a room we had never seen before. More groans. It was a bedroom, and I foolishly looked under the bed. Then I opened an antique chest. Too obvious. I tried to open a window.

"No; she is here."

But where? "Do you mean to say that there is a secret stairway in every wall in this house?"

"There is a stairway for every bedroom," was the disconcerting reply. A brilliant idea struck me; when I recovered, I thought of tiring out the missing person. After all, it must be rather eerie in the dark. She'd soon be scared. It did not take long. The missing person appeared from another unexpected opening behind a bookcase.

"I waited and waited all alone in the dark," she said.

The next merry geste was rather surprising; it turned the tables on the jester. What happened was this: Two of the company went up another winding stair hidden in a wall. Then she locked the door and locked them in. We waited for half an hour. Nothing happened; no cries or petitions for release. She opened the door and listened. Not a sound.

"They must have gone out on the roof."

"Which roof?"

"There are about five acres of roofing on this house. Some of it is glass in places. I must light the rooms beneath or they'll fall through."

We looked out where the roof was flat from the Lord Byron bedroom. There was no sign of the prisoners. Our hostess began to show alarm. She went up the secret stairway. She came down looking dismayed. The prisoners had vanished. Had they fallen off the roof into the sea? Just as she was beginning to look for help, voices from a room below brought a reassuring sound. The couple whom she had locked in had found a secret passage unknown even to the owner of the house and had come by it into another room downstairs. That ended the night's amusement.

In my four-poster in the Paul Revere room I lay under a canopy, staring. I was waiting for the wall to open or for my bed to sink through the floor. At 5:00 A.M. the voice of my hostess was still, and sleep fell on the house of many stairs.

Next day I had breakfast in the breakfast room, which was a room with large windows which gave on the bay. On the table was a sphere which reflected in miniature the breakfaster, so that he might not be lonely—his *Doppelgänger* was before him. Except for my reflection, I was all alone.

The arrival of mine host. He was to come by the six o'clock train. The hostess was to meet him with the station wagon; but before that she would have time to call on a widow and to get the services of her maid while she visited. I had to come because the widow had a deep voice which I had to hear because it was unique. Roses in profusion marked the boundary wall. We drove right up to the house and were admitted by a colored man. Yes, she was at home. We were shown into the living room, which looked out upon the sea. The lady appeared. I was introduced.

"Don't come near me. I have hay fever because I played canasta in the hay."

"It doesn't require hay to give you hay fever. It can be contracted where and when there is no hay. You never see a farmer with hay fever. It is only the intelligent or the very nervous who suffer from it."

"I lost my husband, and I will shortly lose my second gardener if this twelve and one half per cent tax goes through. That's enough for anybody's nerves."

Meanwhile, the maid was manicuring my hostess.

"Do you like it on the rocks?"

"No," I said.

"What are you talking about?"

"I thought you were referring to the wreck of the *Hesperus*."

"Nonsense. I was asking you how you liked your Scotch."

It was time to go to the station. The train would be in any minute now. I would walk back. I couldn't miss the way. That shows how little she knew my capacity for missing.

I wandered on until I came to a fresh-water lake. It must have been fresh water, for there were water lilies floating at the side; their large leaves lay like shields on the calm surface. Now what a happy place: sea and lake water so close by.

At last a motor car came along. I asked the driver where was the nearest big house. He drove me back to the Y division of the road. I had lost my way, and it had taken less than half a mile to do it. The sight of that lake was worth it all.

Our host arrived, tall, spectacled, sharp. He wore a canary-colored pull-over. After him other guests began to arrive. They were all to be "characters." That did not mean oddities. It meant that there would be a fancy-dress dinner that night over which our host would preside. She explained in an aside who each new guest was. One was a matinee idol twenty years ago. Another was an attorney and a great whistler and pianist. Two came up from the sea. Their boat had been becalmed. Their unexpected appearance delighted our host. Introductions all round, followed by drinks.

"Take off those heavy sea clothes."

After a while they went into the house. I remained on the terrace over the sea. Up through the house, many attic window lights were flashing and an air of excitement pervaded the rooms. From a dormer a striped dress fell through the night. It was for me.

"You are a quack doctor from Damascus; dress yourself up." It was our host's voice. The instructions were for me. Another voice said, "He must have a turban and a sash."

So I was asked up here to make a fool of myself? Who ever heard of a fancy-dress dinner? I felt as important in an uninspiring situation as an inspector in the Sanitary (Sidewalks) Department.

One of the party appeared. He was a fireman with an antique fire helmet, brass-bound, from the days before power cables. Little Bo Peep sans sheep crook joined our miscellaneous group. Out came our host, a Victorian dandy, peg-top trousers and tall hat which was made of tin or steel. He carried, somewhat incongruously, a unique blackthorn with three branches round the central shaft, recalling Harry Lauder's cane. Our hostess appeared in ostrich feathers and a costume of mauve and rose. It became her well. The ladies, anyway, were spared from the humiliation of dressing unbecomingly. My turban was adjusted by a guest before

I went indoors. Little did I dream that I would find myself an authority on turbans when I set out the day before.

We entered by a living room, past the Jacobean room with its collection of long-necked brown glass bottles shining before a window lit behind, through the octagonal room of the preceding meal, and so on until we came to a longer dining room with two tables. It was decorated by models of sailing ships—the sea room, perhaps. To the flash of many camera bulbs we took our seats. There must have been a dozen of us. Half-blinded by flashing bulbs, I couldn't see the soup; but I saw the lobsters, which were the best I have ever eaten in my life. The food caused a silence which even the Liebfraumilch did not for a while dispel. I am not at all sure that I did not commit gluttony which is a sin I abhor.

A pretty woman sat at mine host's right hand and on my left, but she was more interested in the Victorian period than in Damascus, although it has "The Street Which is Called Straight" —only called, maybe that was why. Obviously she preferred her host to a Syrian, even a pseudo one. She left me alone in my Damascus. I turned to the lady on my right. I remembered Little Bo Peep's remark when she saw the good-looking man who was my neighbor's husband, "Good-looking men as a rule have plain-looking wives." If that was the rule, here was an exception. Another message from Bo Peep, this time in the form of food. It seemed that she could not eat shellfish, so my neighbor passed her portion of lobster surreptitiously to me. I accepted it at the risk of a Seventh Deadly Sin. Ice cream and Indian pie. Then the hostess rose. Mine host shouted, "We'll all meet in the Chinese room."

Yesterday I had come unexpectedly on a large high room which must be the Chinese room. I had opened a door which gave on it from above. The sun was glimmering on the bay outside, and its reflection fell on a river in the landscape on the wall and made its waters live in light. I never confessed my discovery, for I had been warned not to wander about the house. As it was I was nearly lost.

This time we entered the Chinese room from the ground floor. There was a story about the wallpaper. It seems that the architect who built the house heard that some millionaire in the eighteenth century was planning to build a house in Virginia when he went broke. He had ordered wallpaper from China, which duly arrived and was to be found fresh and unrolled in an attic. He bought it and built a Chinese room in which to hang it. It certainly looked fresh. One wall was devoted to scenes of tea farming, one of China's industries; the other depicted pottery making in all its stages. I noticed that the Chinamen's faces were pink: obviously the paper was prepared for the European market.

At one end of the room a grand piano was installed; from behind it a photographer leaped to attention and flashed a bulb or two. A door in a wall was ajar, and voices in a medley came through. Our host sat under the tea farming on an ottoman and stretched his legs and banged the floor with his stick. The voices did not cease. This was disrespectful if not ungrateful; but the noise came mostly from the adjoining room. Again he tried. He was anxious to tell a story and no one seemed anxious to hear it. Could it be that some of them had heard it before and found it long? He was about to begin when Bo Peep asked him to do a step dance.

"I have been in the air, in a car, and in a train today, and I'm tired." But he executed some agile and amusing steps, flourishing his shillelagh. After that the party had to become an audience until his tale was told. He then had the call, and he called on an expert to whistle and to play the piano simultaneously. The whistling and the playing were wonderful; all the more so because I wondered how the artist could whistle after he had wet his whistle so thoroughly. I tried to add to the hilarity, but my costume was somewhat incongruous for an imitation of a Scots accent. In Damascus I would have been arrested for attempted murder of the Syrian language, so I shut up as soon as I could. It was the actor's turn. Actors are seldom vulgar; they possess taste. In his case it was proved by his choice of a wife. His tale may not have been of his own composing, but as it was new to me I will risk recounting it.

An American was traveling from London to Liverpool in a train which was full. He was confronted with the prospect of standing for four hours. He saw a poodle on a seat by the window and a lady, apparently its owner, on the opposite seat. He addressed the lady: "Madame, may I have that seat?" "No; you may not. Queenie does not like traveling in the guard's van so I paid for that seat for her." After an interval: "Madame, if I take Queenie on my lap, may I occupy that seat?" "Certainly not! Queenie is a lady and she does not sit on men's laps." A long pause. The American took Queenie by the neck and threw her out of the window. Whereupon an Englishman spoke: "You Americans do the wrong things; you drive on the wrong side of the road, you hold your fork in the wrong hand, and just now you have thrown the wrong bitch out of the window."

Everyone laughed. Then our host called to a man concealed under the piano to play us back from a wire recorder all that we had said. Good God! Is my nonsense to be recorded? Greatly to my relief, the wire played us back an indistinct medley. The trained and pleasant voice of the actor was the only voice that could be made out. But why try to record anything? Was our host's story to be preserved as an echo forever from the hollow walls? On the Day of Judgment I hope that for every idle word I have uttered there will be but an indistinct medley when the Recording Angel plays it back to me.

As those who were not house guests had to go home, I got to bed approximately early—about 1:00 A.M. I eyed the closed-up fireplace in the Paul Revere room suspiciously. Would it open and reveal a ghost, or should I find myself drawn up a flue instead of a secret stair?

In spite of mine own fears and the lace insertion near the end of the sheet which caught my fingers and my nose alternately, I slept fitfully. I woke to the sound of the word "hobgoblins." I decided that, dreaming, I must have said it myself.

I breakfasted with my *Doppelgänger*. After breakfast I found a copy of Dante illustrated by Gustave Doré in a little alcove. I thought, Gustave Doré never outdid his illustrations of the *Divina Commedia;* and what delightful notes. I was dragged out of my alcove. I had been allotted to one of the guests who was driving nearly all the way back: we were about to start. He had another guest to find. While he was searching for Bo Peep, I wandered into a room within hailing distance of the hall, at least so I imagined. It was devoted to instruments of precision: a radiometer stood in the window, but its black-and-silver diamond-shaped vanes did not revolve, for it was shut out from the sun. I could not be taken away before we said good-by to our hostess. A maid said that we need not wait because our hostess, though she had awakened, had turned again to sleep. Our host was nowhere to be found. I thought that I had caught a glimpse of his canary-yellow pull-over in the garden earlier in the morning. I couldn't be sure. His car was not in the garage. We were told that he was gone on business, although no one in the country except a farmer has any business to be busy.

I was getting anxious. Had I been deserted purposely? Could it be that if I searched resolutely I would find a room that would be in New York? Time was marching on. It would be very awkward if I had to linger on until the lunch hour and if the maid said, "There are no instructions about your lunch." After all, it might be a new method of entertainment not to speed the parting guest: to leave him or her at perfect liberty to go when it suited him. I had been asked for only two days, and this was the second day and it was getting on for noon. Oh, I said to myself, take a pull at yourself. Why should either host or hostess patronize us at the last moment? Isn't it better to be given the run of the house? And what a house, what a run!

There was a room into which I determined not to go. It was a room devoted to the sea: old hour glasses, sextants and log books, and what appeared to be charts lay here and there on long tables. A famous violinist, so our hostess said, had been given the house for a month to practice in. When the hostess returned she was met by, "God damn you, why did you put me in here? I have done nothing but read the logs of old sea captains. I have not done a stroke of work. And they tell me that not to do a stroke is bad for a fiddler."

A maid said, "Your suitcase is in the car." I left the radiometer room and followed in search of him who was good enough to drive me home. He was not as given to making allowances as I. He was disturbed; he could not understand that neither host nor hostess had turned up to say farewell. Bo Peep, who had to be driven to town, was reluctant to leave the house. That disturbed him too: she was not his guest.

Now this is how I made allowances: "Can you not see," said I, "that this is a new form of entertainment? Our hostess does not want to put us under a compliment for her hospitality, so she disappears and leaves us to take off at our own good time. For a moment I thought that I had not entered into the spirit of my costume. Then I realized that the Syrian costume had made me oversensitive; I was not a case of 'a poor player . . . and then is seen no more.' The mind has many mansions, and they are not inhabited at once. This house has many chambers; we are not in them all. Don't you see that our hostess does not want us to know where we have been? If we spoke of our experience, who would believe in a week-end in midweek?"

One Way of Improving Morale

Originally gems were worn not so much for adornment as for the magical properties with which they were thought to be endowed. Bearing that in mind, whenever I am depressed I visit a first-class jeweler. There is a munificence about a jeweler's shop. You need not be afraid or shy. The staff will not accost you, "Can I help you?" nor will they discuss the state of the weather. They are all quietly but beautifully dressed. They move in an atmosphere of wealth and abundance. There is an air of leisure about them, an air that takes "money and that kind of thing" for granted. It also takes for granted that you are better off than any of them. When half a dozen prosperous individuals become deferential in their bearing toward you, depression simply flies out of the window. Millions of dollars' worth are winking at you from the cases. The carpets are deep and silent. If you are dressed poorly it is put down to eccentricity on your part. And when you emerge you feel as elated as though some distant relative had left you a fortune, tax free. If your departure is seen by a friend, it will do you no harm.

I will set down the knowledge of gems I have gleaned on these visits. This knowledge is the result of long talks with the well-informed.

First of all, diamonds take pride of place. I was about to employ a cliché and say that the diamond is the king of gems until I remembered that the word "gem" comes from *gemma,* which means a bud; and you cannot well say that the diamond is the king of buds. Why does it take pride of place? Because of its hardness and its refractibility, which gives it "fire." It is true that paste has great luster, but because it is not hard it cannot bear abrasions that a diamond can bear. This hardness is expressed by 10. All other gems are less hard: rubies and sapphires come next on the arbitrary list, and their hardness equals 9.

The famous diamonds of antiquity must have been Indian stones. America was not discovered and South Africa had not become British. Many legendary accounts of precious stones exist, such as that of Sindbad's Valley of Diamonds and the notion that there was a diamond to be found in the head of certain serpents. It remained for a Portuguese who was physician to the Viceroy of Goa to be the first to describe a diamond accurately. His name was Garcia de Orta, and he lived about the year 1563.

Until the mines of South Africa became supreme, the world's largest diamond was the legendary Great Mogul. It is said to have weighed about 790 carats before one of its owners sent it to Venice to a famous lapidary, Hortensio Borgio, to be cut. And cut it was. Both the Orloff (194¾ carats) and the Koh-i-noor (186 carats) are believed by some to have been parts of this stone, and Shah Jahan, Aurangzeb, Catherine the Great, and Queen Victoria have been among their owners.

A still larger diamond was discovered in South Africa. It weighed over 3,025 carats; but it was cut into nine large gems and many smaller brilliants, and their history, according to books on the subject, is more specific than romantic.

For those who are interested in the late coronation in London, these facts may be of interest. Two scepters are used. That with the cross represents kingly power and justice. Above its gem-encrusted handle is the largest portion of the Cullinan diamond, which is called the Star of Africa. This is a flawless, pear-shaped stone measuring four inches by two and a half inches in thickness and in breadth. It was called the Cullinan Diamond because Thomas Cullinan, afterward (inevitably) Sir Thomas Cullinan, owned the land in the Transvaal where the Premier diamond mine was situated. The stone was found in 1905, and at the suggestion of General Smuts, afterward field marshal, and General Botha, it was presented to King Edward VII as a birthday present. It was set in the scepter in such a way that it could be worn by Queen Alexandra as a pendant.

Why a *flawless* diamond presumably should be cut is to me a mystery. I prefer to think of stones in their original condition, and in this the late Lady Otteline Morrell agreed with me: she clanked with oyster shells.

To some diamonds, sinister histories are attached. I am inclined to believe that these stories were invented to protect the owners from theft.

Jewels play a romantic part in history, too. The *de jure* government of Ireland took the late Czar's jewels as collateral for moneys advanced when none of the great nations would recognize the right of the Russian government to own them. This transaction took place in Paris because the *de jure* Irish government did not wish the amount of money at its disposal to become known. It was feared that if England were to learn of it, she might confiscate the money. So, as Russia was in need of money and as Ireland was in need of some collateral wherein she could bury her wealth, the interchange was mutually satisfactory.

Diamonds may be of any color. Of brown diamonds I have had this experience. During the civil war in Ireland there were instances of robbery under arms for the most patriotic reasons. An English milord who lived next door to our house in the west of Ireland—"next door" being a distance of seven miles or so—had to flee for his life. As he depended (unjustifiably) on the chivalry of the enemy, he left his children and his wife behind. One Sunday morning she rode over to us on horseback, for all her automobiles were "attached." Since we were out at the time, she left all her jewels rolled in a silk handkerchief on the breakfast table. On our return we found a diamond tiara, a pendant, bracelets, brooches, and six or eight brown stones.

Subsequently, when she had left with her family for England, I went to Dublin to have the lot insured prior to being forwarded. Mr. West was the assayer and the best-known of the Dublin jewelers. "These I can insure," he said, pointing to the tiara and the other white diamonds, "but I cannot insure these. They are brown diamonds and I never could match them in fifty years." At the time the rates of insurance, if indeed any insurance could be taken out, were prohibitive. Later, a man of business crossed over from England and brought the jewels to their owner.

"Diamonds may be any color." I learned that during my rehabilitating visits to leading jewelers. I have seen colored photographs of diamonds of a faintly azure hue and of various shades of yellow, like feathers in a light-yellow stone. In another and a harder school I learned that, though it may be all right for a diamond to be all yellow or champagne-colored—appropriately enough!—it is all wrong for a white diamond to have a yellow light. My father wore a large diamond in a thick gold ring on his little finger. As a small boy I did not dare to entertain any idea of its worth. I preferred to think of it as fabulous. After his death, when his ring came to be assessed, the yellow light detracted very much from its value. If a diamond can be any color, see that it is all that color.

The largest diamond belongs to Queen Elizabeth II. It was given to her at her wedding by Dr. J. T. Williamson, who owns the mine at Mwadui in Tanganyika where it was discovered. It is of a pink color and was prepared as a coronation jewel, though she had worn it as a brooch set in platinum and white stones. Its value is about one and a half million dollars.

It may well become the fashion for diamonds to be worn by young women since the coronation of Queen Elizabeth II of England. Hitherto, diamonds have been associated with women who, to the chivalrous, are at least mature. I for one cannot agree that stones distract the observer's eye from the wearer.

Although pearls are produced by an oyster and born of anything but flame, they are regarded as precious stones. Certainly they become the necks of maidens of gentle birth.

I like to let my thoughts dwell on the purity and perfection of young girls curtseying before a young queen.

The lines which I came across the other day from the Persian poet Hafid—it may be Hafiz for all I know—point a moral:

> Forasmuch as the pearl is a product which from an inward trouble and from a fault, produces purity and perfection, it is preferred, for in nothing does God so much delight as in tenderness and in luster born of trouble and repentance.

Tragedies are often associated with gems. One that comes to mind was an occurrence in the United States. This is how it came about. A youthful salesman in a high-class jeweler's happened to be on duty when an important citizen called for his watch, which had been left for repairs. Seeing the address of the customer, the assistant said, "If you are going home, you had better take this necklace of pearls back to your wife." The customer, somewhat astonished, asked, "These pearls are artificial, of course?" "On the contrary," said the youth, "they cost two hundred and fifty thousand dollars." The customer took them. When he reached home, he shot his wife and then himself. He left a note which gave the name of the donor—obviously the lover of the murdered wife. His brother-in-law, who saw the tragedy from the window of an apartment opposite, was the first on the scene. I cannot say what was in the note; but one fact of the matter was that the brother-in-law lived sumptuously until the death of the lover years later.

You cannot be sure that your assistants "burn with a hard gemlike flame" and are forever aware and circumspect.

Rubies at one time during the last war were more valuable than diamonds. They are not becoming in a tiara; but they go well with fingernails colored like pigeon's blood.

When I was very young I used to think that precious stones got their value from being easily pocketed or otherwise concealed. Now I realize that this view was only partial. For one thing, it presupposed a world inhabited by people who were constrained to scoot off at a moment's notice or, at any rate, to be constantly on the run. For another, it did not take into account the fact that diamonds, the most costly of all adornments, required times of peace for their display.

The best diamonds now come from South Africa. The De

Beers company is reputed to be the best of the mining operators there. If you go, as I did, to any jeweler who deals with a company such as De Beers, you will be met with not only courtesy but honesty. You may be told that the price of diamonds is subject to fluctuation. The diamonds remain precious and unchanged (thanks to the policing of South Africa); but nations are subject to fluctuation and there are many countries engaged in the diamond trade.

Something of the old magic is still associated with precious stones. I have recounted how comforting it is to visit the store of a first-class jeweler, one who has an international reputation to preserve. Inside, you will be treated by men more courteous even than bankers, for it is not to them you will come if you are in need of a loan—quite the contrary! And outside you will find the way made smooth for you because the best pavement is outside banks and jewelers' stores.

Incurables

SCENE. *The grounds of a large hospital. A tree, umbrella-shaped like a weeping elm, in the center of the stage. It is about a third of the stage's width. A dense myrtle bush to the left adjoining wing. The floor is a lawn. The background suggests a distant building. There are seats around the tree.*

PAT, *seated under the tree with a rug round his knees, smiles reminiscently.*

Ah, begorra, yes.

A *uniformed porter passes. Pat looks at the sky, then at the porter.*

Them was the days!

The porter looks back wondering.

Aw, Janey Mack!

The porter looks again.

Along the back beach when the wind was blowing and the horses running and every jockey with a different color coming along like hell!

Exit the porter.

Them was the days, and the thunder on the turf! God be

with the times; and God be with Baldoyle! And Red Maurya selling cockles and never troubling to lace her shoes. I never seen her since. Mebbe it's in the workhouse she is. She'd be like a shrunk apple if I seen her now, and her eyes glazed with the palsy like a window in a snug. For God's sake look who's comin'.

MIKE *enters advancing unsteadily pushing a lawn mower to maintain his balance.*

PAT. The auld blackguard that can't balance but has to go chasing himself.

MIKE *retreats and advances balancing. He runs the lawn mower against the seat.*

Up and hooray! Was there ever such weather? Who were ye saying was in the workhouse? Who's shrunk?

PAT. It's a mighty fine humor you're in this morning. You must have been reading *Christian Dying* by Sylvester Stott.

MIKE. And why wouldn't I be merry on a day like this?

PAT. Oh, then you're easily pleased if all you want is fine weather to make ye lep like a flounder. Go aisy now or ye'll cut the toes off me feet.

MIKE. And would ye know it if I did? Hasn't the feeling gone out of yer feet this five years? Usen't you be sayin' that ye had two feet in the grave but that you were all right so long as it wasn't yer head?

PAT. Before ye sit down just roll that up in front of me till I get a whiff of the cut grass.

Sings.

"And the ramble through the new-mown hay."

Mike sets the lawn mower adrift and, balancing, half-falls into the seat.

PAT. Ye'll break your neck if ye keep tripping about like a spavined goat. What the hell has brought you out at all? Don't ye know that if the lawn mower is found here ye'll be kept in like the last time they found you stretched when ye let the roller fall into the greenhouse? If ye can't walk without support, sit still like meself.

MIKE. Whist now. George will be wheeling Mrs. Durkin this way soon and I'll get him to leave it back where I got it.

PAT. He will in me neck.

MIKE. Of course he'll take it back. Many's the chaw I gave him.

PAT. Yer a hard chaw yerself.

MIKE. Cheer up now, me hearty, and give us again.

Sings.

"The ramble through the new-mown hay, Titty fol loll!"

PAT, *surly.* It's a bloody fine ramble you'd take through the new-mown hay if ye couldn't scut behind the mowing machine and then ye'd be likely to overtake it with yer "festination" and trying to catch up with yer center of gravity, or whatever the doctors say is wrong with you, you that can no more walk than a twelve-months' child.

MIKE. Well, I like that from one who can't walk at all. Paralyzed from the hips down. Well, God's will be done. But tell us who was it you were sayin' was in the Union like a withered apple and I coming in.

PAT. I wasn't saying anyone was in the Union. I was only recollecting a walk I had one fine morning thirty good-looking years ago, before you died from the hips up.

MIKE, *humoring him.* You must have been a warty boy thirty years ago.

PAT. I was walking one morning from Weldon's to the Murroch

of Baldoyle. D'ye know the Murroch? And I seen a fine strap of a red-haired woman comin' towards me.

MIKE, *interested.* Red, did ye say?

PAT. Red, begorra, with the sun behind her like the light on a dun cow's rump. "Good morrow," sez I. "Good morrow," sez she, smiling a bit and letting on to be passing but not getting out of my way all the same. "And what might ye be doing in a fine still morning like this?" sez I. "Mebbe it's pickin' cockles I am," sez she.

Nudging Mike.

Picking cockles, mind ye, with her back to the beach.

MIKE, *avidly.* Go on! Go on!

PAT. "Yer done now anyway," sez I. "Look behind ye. The tide's in." "Oh, my!" sez she, laughing with a little laugh as if it didn't matter a damn. "I suppose I'll have to wait now," sez she, "till it goes out."

MIKE. Yes! Yes?

PAT. "That's about the only thing *we* can do now is to wait," sez I. Never letting on

Nudging Mike.

but that I thought picking cockles was the most important thing on God's earth . . .

MIKE, *finishing the sentence.* *We* can do. Were you picking cockles?

PAT. No, you idiot. But I was adapting myself. "If ye don't want to go back empty-handed and lose the whole day, ye must wait now till the tide gives us a chance," sez I.

MIKE, *avidly.* Yes, yes, yes.

PAT. "But where can we wait?" sez she. "In here," sez I, "if the grass isn't damp. There'll be no one to disturb you if ye waited a week, and ye'll hear nothing but the lark singing or mebbe the whistle of a train."

MIKE. Go on!

PAT. "But it wouldn't do if it was damp," said I. "I can put me shawl on the grass if it is itself," sez she.

MIKE, *excitedly*. Yes.

PAT, *leisurely*. "Well, whether it's damp or not, the dew never did any harm," sez I. "When the sun's a bit stronger it'll be as dry as a rick of hay."

MIKE. So it would! Go on!

PAT. So in we went through a hedge, I holding the branches out of her way—I noticed that she had no stockings on—and she spread her shawl under a bush.

MIKE. Oh boy!

PAT, *putting his thumbs in his armpits, sings.*

"Chantez, ma belle!"

MIKE, *impatient*. But what happened then?

PAT, *very leisurely*. "There's one consolation," sez I. "There's no hurry about the tide. It is not likely to go out with a click." "Time and tide wait for no man," she sez, with a little laugh. "That's true," sez I, to keep up the conversation and so on while we were sitting on her shawl.

MIKE, *disappointed*. Aw! What good were ye?

PAT, *bringing his hand down on Mike's hat, revealing a bald head*. Aren't ye the lascivious, evil-minded auld devil to be lookin' for harm under every bush? It's you and the likes of you has the place that it's not worth living in.

MIKE, *sniffing for smut*. I only meant to ask . . . I only wanted to know what ye were talking about while the tide was running out.

PAT. Aye. And when I began telling ye, ye asked me what good was I.

MIKE. Well, what was it about?

PAT. A'll not tell ye! as the Scotsman said when they asked him the morning after his marriage how he was.

MIKE. I only wanted to know.

PAT. Ye only wanted to know. And do ye think I'd tell ye even if your wishes came off?

MIKE. I only wanted to know.

PAT. What? And what do ye want to know?

MIKE. I only wanted to know, is it that that has ye pondering on the past?

PAT. When I had my day I didn't treat it as the future when I had it.

MIKE. Isn't it a pity that ye have not a bit of it left? It couldn't have been picking cockles that turned ye into a mermaid with no feelin' in yer feet.

Laughs, shaking himself.

PAT, *sotto voce.* That'll do ye now.

Enter George the groundsman, wheeling Mrs. Durkin in a bath chair. She is almost completely covered by the chair's apron and her shawls.

MIKE. Aw! Me sound man George!

GEORGE. Good morrow, men. This is a fine sound healthy morning.

MIKE, *raising his hat.* How are ye this morning, Mrs. Durkin?

GEORGE. She can't hear you. She's full of dope.

Moves on.

MIKE, *in an excited whisper*. Eh, George. Whist! Come here a minute. Shove her into the myrtles for a minute and put the lawn mower back for me like a decent man and I'll give ye a chaw.

GEORGE *obeys; then, mockingly sententious*. The matron sez that ye are all to conduct yourselves with due decorum, for the Angel of Death has visited us bringing sorrow in his train. Which means that there's another stiff in the mortuary.

PAT. Who is it?

GEORGE. Auld Bright's.

PAT. Aw. Poor auld Bright's! Who'd have thought that he would be the next, and he as red and as hearty as a forge fire.

GEORGE. Them are the lads that go. They are so full of life that they can't stand the pressure of it. They want to spend it, and they spend themselves. The fellows that go about currying favor with death by looking like corpses, they don't go sudden like poor old Bright's.

MIKE, *sententiously*. A great loss to Ireland.

PAT. Arrah, who?

MIKE. Eddie Bright's.

PAT. For God's sake?

MIKE, *mockingly sententious*. Aye; and a great loss to Gaeldom, the same Eamonn Bright's. There's many we could have spared sooner than Eamonn. The country won't be the same again now he's gone.

Turns up his eyes.

PAT. Well, you may console yourself. Is the country ever the same for two minutes? To listen to you one would think that he had invented Death and went off himself on purpose. For God's sake be honest and sensible and don't be trying to read onto a tombstone more than there's under it.

MIKE. I'd give a lot to have him back for the sake of The Cause.

GEORGE. Well, and you'd lose a lot if he did come back. Wasn't it you who drew him in the sweep on the morning's deaths? How much of yer three quid that ye won would ye give for the sake of The Cause?

PAT, *sits up alertly*. So that is what has you in such unholy good humor this day of our Lord?

MIKE. I didn't know he was dead.

GEORGE. Oh, no. I suppose you thought that the three quid was yer auld-age pension?

PAT. Three quid! Did he win three quid?

GEORGE. He did. He drew old Bright's who went off with the Angel of Death bringing sorrow in his train.

MIKE. Well. Hadn't ye all a fair chance yerselves?

GEORGE. Well, we wouldn't hide it if we won.

MIKE. And who did you draw, Pat?

PAT. That'll do ye. Ye won't draw on me, I'm telling you.

Shivers in disgust.

GEORGE. There's not a shake out of ye yet, Pat, in spite of yer two feet in the grave.

Laughs.

PAT. Mind ye, old Bright's got a long run. He was the favorite this six weeks.

GEORGE. Well he's stretched at last and Mike has the winnings. It'll cost half a crown to get that lawn mower left back. It's confined to the ward he'll be if it's found, as sure as my name is George Daly.

MIKE, *anxiously*. Is the Governor coming this morning?

GEORGE. He's showing the Matron round. He might be here any minute now.

Looks as if to see if they were approaching.

PAT. For the love of Mike give him the half dollar if you don't want to be locked up.

Mrs. Durkin sneezes.

MIKE. For the love of Mike, George Daly, shove her further into the myrtles, and back with the lawn mower quick!

GEORGE. When you part and not before.

He shoves the bath chair in out of sight.

Mike fumbles for half a crown. George takes it and exits with lawn mower.

Enter Governor with the Matron.

GOV., *to Pat.* Well, how are we this morning, Pat? You all right?

PAT. Speaking for myself, sir, it's only half of me that's right. I can't speak for yourself, sir, at all.

GOV. What? What?

MIKE. He's paralyzed, sir, from the waist down. And he's walkin' on wool. So there's only the upper part that can be right.

MATRON. Now how did you get here, Mike?

MIKE, *embarrassed.* I—ah—well, I had to follow me center of gravity. And it landed me here, mam.

GOV., *to Matron.* What is this case?

MATRON. It is a case of locomotor ataxia, which makes the victim keep on racing after his center of gravity. Always trying to catch up with himself.

GOV. Ah, quite. Do you come from the Curragh, my good man?

PAT. No, sir, he comes from Baldoyle, and he may have caught cold in his spine lying under a hedge on the road from St. Doulough's down to the Back Strand.

MIKE, *embarrassed.* Don't mind him, sir. He comes from Moore Street, but I was born in the Coombe.

GOV., *to Matron.* No hope, I suppose.

MATRON. Not the least; locomotor ataxia.

To the men.

When there is no hope the best thing is to be resigned.

PAT. Right, mam. Since we're incurables, it would be the height of ingratitude to get better and upset the charitable institution.

MATRON. That will do, Pat.

GOV. Well, don't despair. We have been so well endowed by the government that something may come of it, something may come of it.

MIKE, *sotto voce.* Now yer talkin'.

GOV. We are already getting results with our experiments. That last experiment, the six hundredth and seventh one, is surprising. Already the Russian experts in the Donnybrook laboratory have revived dogs that have been dead twenty-five minutes.

MATRON. They asked my permission to work in the mortuary this morning.

GOV. You gave it to them, I hope?

Matron nods.

We will take a look into the laboratory where they are working on that elixir of life, or six-oh-seven as they call it.

Exeunt.

Mrs. Durkin sneezes. Pat and Mike start.

MIKE. What's an elixir of life?

PAT. A bottle to buck you up.

MIKE. Didn't you hear him saying they were reviving the dead?

PAT. Aye, a few auld dogs. They're always torturing dogs for our sakes.

MIKE. But this is reviving them and bringing them back to life.

PAT. That's what I'm telling you. Isn't that the worst torture of all?

MIKE. What?

PAT. To be dead twice.

At right side wing as one faces the stage, the lid of a coffin appears and is withdrawn. After sufficient time to engage the attention of the audience, enter Eamonn Bright's. He is apparently naked but screened by the coffin lid. He comes in making growling sounds.

MIKE. Jumping Jehoshaphat!

PAT, *who is sitting to Mike's right and has not a fair view.* What's wrong with you?

MIKE. Bright's!

PAT, *sitting about.* Conistanthu? It's the laddo himself. He that has Bright's disease. Begor, them specialists from Moscow has revived more than dead dogs. Where are ye going, a cara?

BRIGHT. I am going to see my attorney.

PAT. He's as good as dead!

MIKE. They said . . . I thought . . . How are ye feeling? Ye'll catch cold with no clothes on but a plank.

BRIGHT. I'm as good as dead, am I? I'll see about that. I ought to be from the way I was treated for pneumonia. I woke up stark naked on a stone slab, with a hose pipe in me arm and tuppence on me eyelids, and three bearded Sheenies waiting for me to wink them off. And me name spelt wrong on me coffin lid. I'll have the law on the whole bloody place. Nice treatment indeed for an invalid, to be put out of doors with the dead.

MIKE. Sheenies? Is that the way to talk about our most modern scientists? I'd say nothing about it, Eamonn, if I was you. Slip back to the ward and make them give you a cup of G.Y.E. It's vitamins you want.

PAT. It cures pimples.

BRIGHT. Does it, begob? I won't stop until I have the law on them all.

MIKE. You may have been revived, and you ought to be thankful.

BRIGHT. And who the bloody hell said I was dead?

MIKE, *embarrassed.* I don't know. I heard that they were doing a lot with dogs.

BRIGHT. I'm a dog, am I? For two pins I'd give you a clatter with this lid.

Stands behind it showing inscription: EAMONN LOPEZ, AGED 56. R.I.P.

My name is Lopez, an old ancient Irish name. And what have I to do with R.I.P.?

PAT. Aisy now. Don't you expect to rest in peace?

MIKE. No. Nor let anyone else rest either.

BRIGHT. I'll not rest until I get substantial damages.

MIKE. Arrah, for what?

BRIGHT. Indecent exposure.

PAT. If you don't catch your attorney before he goes to lunch, you won't see him for a week.

BRIGHT, *holding the lid horizontally as he goes off, hurriedly.* Begorra, you're right. I never thought of that.

Exit.

PAT, *cogitating.* Ireland's made up now. And Gaeldom's reimbursed! But listen to me, Loco, or whatever you are, there must be great goings on in the Research Foundation.

Mrs. Durkin sneezes.

MIKE. Is there?

PAT. Isn't there? There's your great Gael that you have given so much to see back again. And what about your winnings? What about your winnings? I ask you.

MIKE. Whist.

Enter Gov. and Matron. The Gov., who was gray and past middle age, and the Matron, who was skinny, are much improved. The one is twenty years younger and the Matron aggressively buxom.

MATRON. But if this goes on we shall have no cases for our beds.

GOV. I would not say that. I would not say that. There will always be the poor and decrepit in this country who will be objects of charity. It would hardly be fair to them to make them able-bodied all of a sudden if they were not prepared to work. Have you seen the gardener, my men? If he passes, you might say that the dahlias want watering, or to be bedded out.

PAT & MIKE. We'll tell him, sir.

MATRON. What do you mean?

GOV. I mean that this country is not prepared for this discovery, for the present it must not be released.

MATRON. And that we must keep it in the dark?

GOV. We must not let the elixir get out.

MATRON. May I not have some for my herbaceous border?

GOV. Better not. Better not. Tropical results!

Exeunt.

Enter George with watering can.

GEORGE. Did ye see that auld blackguard?

PAT. He's just gone out with the Matron.

GEORGE. Dammit. I don't mean Verschoyle, but auld Lopez whom we called, because he had it, Bright's.

MIKE. He's gone out too.

GEORGE. Where?

MIKE. To see his attorney.

GEORGE. Coddin' apart, where's he gone? Has he gone at all? The Moscow specialists revived him, and off he goes without as much as by your leave. And they're blaming me for leaving the gates open and letting him out.

PAT. Mr. Verschoyle is blaming you.

GEORGE. Me?

PAT. It seems that there's something wrong with the dahlias.

GEORGE. Let me tell you and him that the Dalys were always decent people and they are all right. What's wrong with them?

PAT. Oh, nothin'. Nothin'. It seems that they want watering and to be bedded out.

GEORGE. Beddin' out?

MIKE. He's only coddin'. It's the flowers he meant. Get the watering can.

PAT. Don't go, for the love of God. Here, George, here. Come here. Listen. You may not know it but it all fits in. This idiot doesn't see it or he'd give you the rest of his three quid and be glad to part.

GEORGE. It's his no longer, now that auld Bright's is not dead.

PAT. It'll be yours, George, if Mike has a spark of sense. For neither he nor me will want it if he does what I'm going to say. Those lads that the government brought over have discovered something good. I'm able to take notice.

GEORGE. And what did you notice?

MIKE. A red-haired woman thirty years ago.

PAT. For the love of God, shut up. This is serious. George, Mike's two pounds seventeen and sixpence are yours if you go into the laboratory and bring us out a bottle marked six-oh-seven. If it isn't in the laboratory it may be in the dead house where they were working all the morning on auld Bright's.

GEORGE. You haven't told us what you noticed.

PAT. Jaysus! Is it necessary? I noticed that the Governor got suddenly twenty years younger and that the Matron put on in half an hour

pointing to his breast

—what d'ye call it?—embonpoint. I noticed that Eamonn Lopez or auld Bright's as we used to call him is up and out and he was dead this morning, and I noticed that the only anxiety of the Gov. and Matron was to keep the discovery dark and in the hands of the hospital. It makes everything grow. He wouldn't give it to her for the herbaceous border. It's too tropical it would be, he said.

MIKE. Begor, if you had it you'd show us something tropical.

PAT. Out with the sweep money or I'll take it off you myself.

Mike reluctantly takes coins from many pockets.

GEORGE. But how the hell am I to know the right bottle? The whole place is full of shelves. Between test tubes and retorts and pipettes I wouldn't know where I was. There are hundreds of bottles and they're all the same.

PAT. Count until you come to six-oh-seven. Or better still, pinch the last bottle on the highest shelf.

MIKE. If he gets the wrong one, do I get me money back?

GEORGE. It's your funeral, not mine.

Exit.

MIKE. I wonder did it really revive Bright's.

PAT. Ye're always thinking about your money. He was dead all right, if that's any consolation to you. And so you won the sweep. Now listen to me. It will be plain sailing if we get the bottle. I'm only half-dead, and you're only creeping.

MIKE. I'm not creeping but sprinting. I wish I could creep. Do you think it will cure Parkinson's disease? And where will we rub it in?

PAT. I'll get George to rub it into the small of me back where the feeling meets the numb. You can have it rubbed into your head for a trial.

Mrs. Durkin sneezes.

MIKE. Or we might try it on her.

PAT. It might be too dangerous.

MIKE. It might be that.

PAT. Well then—

jerks his thumb in the direction of Mrs. Durkin

—ladies first, say I. And I've always said it.

Enter George, excited.

PAT & MIKE. What's up.

GEORGE. Oh, be jabers! Dead rabbits and guinea pigs leppin' all over the place and the auld baboon with the glazed eye gone daft from only just a little rub of it into the butt of his tail. This must be the stuff.

Shows strange phial.

PAT, *reading label.* Poison, be jabers.

Hands it to Mike, in a changed voice.

You paid your money like a man. The first shot is yours.

MIKE. But after you. I don't want to take advantage of a few quid. I'll try it when it has done you good.

PAT. For heaven's sake, don't be flying in the face of science and blocking the progress of modern research. If it were left to the likes of you, we'd get nowhere.

MIKE. But it's labeled "poison."

PAT. Was there ever anything good that came out of a bottle that we were not told was poison? Take it, George, and give him a rub of it like a decent man.

George takes the phial and after some play rubs it into Mike's scalp. Immediately a great crop of hair takes the place of the bald skull. (*A rubber cap is removed, showing the hair it hid.*)

MIKE, *putting his hand up and feeling the hair.* Holy Smoke. Is it crepe that's on me or hair? That's the stuff. What do I look like?

GEORGE. Hairy enough.

PAT, *amazed.* You look like one of them Eyetalians from Abyssinia or a barber's apprentice. Here, give it to me.

MIKE. George, give us a good rub of it into the small of my back.

George rubs.

MIKE. Now let me stretch my limbs and test me equilibration. I'll go backwards first.

He takes two paces backward and then marches in mock military goose-step fashion forward.

PAT. Eh? Here! Where are ye going? If you keep going on like that you'll find yourself in Arbour Hill.

MIKE. And I wouldn't care.

PAT. I suppose not if it were for The Cause, but you're forgetting something. What about me? Give us a lick of it, George.

He pulls his shirt up over his head. George rubs his spine.

PAT, *breathing a sigh of relief*. Test me knee jerks, George.

George taps him under the knee cap. A boot flies off with the resulting kick.

Oh boy!

He stands up in riding breeches with the laces untied and unlaced boot and does a few dance steps.

"And the ramble through the new-mown hay." What do I look like?

MIKE. You look like the Gaelic League. But fasten yer breeches and adjust yer dress before leaving.

Remembering.

What about the old lady under the myrtles?

PAT. Give it to me and I'll give her a dart of it.

GEORGE. But we don't know what's wrong with her or where to rub her.

PAT. Ah, leave that to me.

He goes over and pulls the bath chair into view and pours some of the fluid down the back of Mrs. Durkin's neck.

PAT. That seems to have given her a thrill.

He pours again.

MRS. DURKIN, *wakens slowly. Looks round and at the bath chair.* A perambulator—for the love of God!

PAT, *recoiling in fright.* So it worked.

MIKE, *watching Mrs. Durkin, renovated and comely, throwing off the apron of the bath chair and appearing in apron and shawl as a cockle gatherer.* Well, I should say it did.

PAT. Are ye all right, Mrs. Durkin?

MRS. DURKIN. Who d'ye mean?

She advances slowly and as if menacingly from the chair.

Which of yez called me Mrs. Durkin?

Looking about.

And how did I get into the Phaynix Park?

PAT. We're not in the Park.

MIKE. Hould yer whist.

MRS. DURKIN. Which of ye swiped my basket of cockles?

PAT, *tentatively.* Ye haven't a gray hair on you, Norah.

MRS. DURKIN. And can it be? You're the young fellow that kept sloothering me at the back of St. Doulough's till the tide went out and came in again.

PAT. And you took me up to Weldon's and stood me a few pints.

MIKE. The pair of ye made the most of yer time.

Enter the Governor, running.

GOV., *shouts.* Close all the gates! A great theft has occurred!

Close the gates. Let no one out. Call the police. Everybody must be searched.

Exit.

GEORGE. Now ye see what ye've let me in for. This means the loss of my job. What am I to do with this?

The phial.

PAT. Shove it into the watering can.

George puts the phial into the can.

And pretend that you are watering the dahlias or the grass even. Here, hand us up that rug. Sit down, Mike. Mrs. Durkin, get behind the tree.

Now what do you think of that for scientific research? There's nothing to beat the mind of Man, barrin' the bees.

Noise and loud voices off.

GEORGE. Be jabers, the police!

To Pat.

Now you see what you've let me in for.

PAT. Don't lose yer head, man. Behave as if it was no concern of yours. Water the grass! Pretend to be doing yer usual work. Go on, nonchalant-like.

A SERGEANT'S VOICE OFF. Each patient must be questioned separately and seriatim.

Mrs. Durkin and Pat and Mike are seated under the tree. George waters the grass, beginning at the root of the tree.

PAT, *sotto voce.* Attaboy, George!

The tree grows down gradually; the grass rises up until the trio under the tree are enclosed in the growing greenery. They are gradually obscured. One of them sings, and the song diminishes like the Volga boatmen's song. The light diminishes with the song.

SONG.

It's only a matter of Time
Till grass will cover us all.
Like waves that flow with an undertow,
The grass will cover us all.

The green will win in the end,
And cover us all with green;
On friend and foe the green will grow
And cover us all with green.

We are cured of all disease,
Of Faith and Hope and Strife,
Of Love and legal pleas:
We are cured even of Life.

Fading.

The grass will win in the end
And cover us all with green

fading, almost indistinguishable

and all with green
win in the cover us all with green.

When the light comes on, for a moment, there is nothing but greenery.

Curtain.

They Carried Caesar

AN INCIDENT DURING THE CIVIL WAR IN IRELAND

It is all very well to talk of wearing a revolver. Instead of you wearing it, it wears you. If you carry it in a hip pocket, your trousers sag on that side; one leg becomes longer than the other and you are inclined to trip. If it will fit in a coat pocket, it is liable to become stuck; and as for a holster, leave that to detective stories! Now you will wonder what this is all about. I will try to explain.

I had a friend kept a shop and a lot of red setter dogs behind it. These he took very often for a run. "Last Sunday," he said, "I was taking a stroll along the central road in the Phoenix Park. There was a group of four men in front of me. I heard them say distinctly, 'We'll get Gogarty first.' "

"What does that mean?" I asked. He went on: "Two of them had belted coats like trench coats. The other two were taller. They looked back and saw me, and shut up. I stooped down and patted one of the dogs."

He knew things that I did not know. He knew that something was in the air, and though he told me no more, his manner was meant to warn me. "Remember what I told you and don't forget that you are a senator," he said.

A few days later I met Desmond Fitzgerald, the Minister for Foreign Affairs. Without mentioning my informant's name, I told him what he had said. To my surprise, he took the message seriously. "You must go armed." "Oh, hell!" said I.

"You are not leaving this office until I hand you a revolver." He gave me a Colt with a long handle that did not suit my grip. Just to please him, I took it. "You must promise me to wear it."

The captain of the Government guard saw it as I was leaving. "Let me tell you one thing. You should never put that under your pillow. Wear it between your knees and shoot through the bedclothes if you are surprised in bed."

What had I let myself in for? First I call on my friend, and he tells me what he had overheard in the Phoenix Park. I report this to Desmond Fitzgerald, and he makes me promise to carry a revolver! In fact he gives me one. And now the captain of the guard, obviously an expert, tells me how to wear it in bed!

For a few days I tried carrying it. I forgot it in a toilet in one of the principal hotels and a nervous fellow came shrieking out, "There's a revolver in there!" I had trouble in getting it back from the manager.

I could not sit down with any comfort in a chair. The boys in Kit Marlowe's day wore daggers in their belts, which they had to push behind them and out over the edge of the bench when they sat down. I tried to feel warlike; but it soon passed. The spectacle of an armed doctor was too much of a contradiction for me. At last I threw Desmond's revolver into the drawer of a dressing table, among ties and odds and ends. For that I was very sorry, very sorry indeed.

Many of the more important members of the Government had locked themselves up in the Government Building. They were guarded by a regiment drawn mostly from the north of Ireland. From that I saw how serious was the situation. Civil war, which had broken out, brought treachery with it—which was no wonder, for it began with the basest treachery.

I had no such protection. It was easy to get into my house: a doctor is accessible, or he should be. The selfish, vain instigator of the civil war had caused it under the pretext of personal devotion to a country of which he was not a part, in which he had not been born.

One evening about eight o'clock—on January 12, 1923, if I remember rightly—I was lolling in my bath. The bathroom was near my bedroom, a few steps from it. I was alone in the house but for a few servants. My family had gone to the country for the holidays. I lay in my bath and steam filled the room. I was trying to turn off a tap with my toes when I felt something cold on the back of my neck. I looked around. There was a gunman in a belted trench coat of dark blue material.

"Out and be quick!" He waved the gun.

"If this is murder, may I scribble a few lines to my wife?"

Pale and agitated, he again threatened me with the gun.

"For a housebreaker you seem very nervous," I said. Through the door of the bathroom I could see two gunmen on the stairs. I put a towel about me and cursed myself for leaving my gun in the drawer of the mock Chippendale table in the dressing room. To open the drawer it was necessary to place a foot against either leg; even then the drawer often jammed. Oh, how I regretted that gun now. In the steam of the bathroom I could have blown the head off the unsuspecting and nervous gunman and then rushed at the two guarding the stairs. Who expects a naked man to be armed?

In the dressing room I slowly drew on the trousers of my dinner suit and put on the comfortable old shoes which were down at the heels. The two gunmen and the nervous fellow who seemed to be their leader were now with me in the room while I dressed. I looked in the mirror. My face was almost white. That does not come from thought. Maybe it does. What about "sicklied o'er?" But the pupils were dilated. However, my thinking was unimpaired.

I was thinking that even if I could get my gun out and find the trigger guard unobstructed by a tie or two, I could never beat the gunman who had his gun on my kidney to the draw. He had only to move his finger half an inch and my kidney and probably my spine would be shot through. Besides, if I opened the drawer, it would reveal the fact that I had a pistol and "justify" the already worked-up gunman in putting an end to me. He could discharge my revolver after I was dead. No, I had better leave the drawer alone.

Over by the fireplace I saw a pair of riding boots with trees in them. If I could get one of the trees out, I would have a weapon. But my brain, which was somewhat hysterical with fear and excitement, thought absurdly of Fergus McRoy and his wooden sword. Amusing, if the situation were in accord.

"Put those bloody pumps in your pocket and put on these."

I was handed a pair of skiing boots and an old coat of buffalo leather with the woolly side in. These must have been found on the back stairs. So there was probably a gunman there, and I was counting on those back stairs to make a dash for it. Hopeless now.

Clad in a pair of trousers, a white shirt, a greatcoat, and heavy shoes, I was led down. A hunchbacked woman was in the hall. I noticed that the telephone wire had been dragged out. A large sedan stood at the door, with a fellow bigger than any of the gunmen at the wheel. The little crippled woman got in beside him. Evidently she was used for the purpose of making it look like a social visit if they were interrupted by the guards.

A gunman sat on either side of me; I could feel the pressure of a gun below my ribs. Another sat in my lap and lay back. I was crushed into the cushions and completely out of sight. There were two more in front of me. We started.

"If you shout when we are passing any of your bloody soldiers, you will be blown to smithereens."

Well, Julius Caesar was in a like position when he was taken by pirates in the Adriatic; and he promised that later he would crucify them all. They took it laughingly; but he kept his promise.

"Wouldn't you like to be —— now?" He named the unhallowed name of him who caused the civil war.

"Anything but that," I mumbled, my mouth smothered by the gunman's back.

It dawned on me that I was being taken as a hostage for two men that were held prisoners in Dundalk jail. They had been executed that morning. It wouldn't be a rest cure for me when the gunmen found out that!

To say the least of it, my position was precarious. It lacked humor. One of the corner boys said, "Isn't it a fine thing to die to a flash?" But oh, what a waste: my life for theirs! But if and when I got out of their clutches, it would be my turn. This was a little better than associating myself with Julius Caesar; but there is no accounting for a mind distracted by misgivings.

We reached a deserted house where the river Liffey meets its first weir, that by the Trinity College boathouse. Here at full tide the water can be nine feet deep.

I was bundled through a small gate in the wall.

"Can I tip the driver?" I asked. That made them all angry, the driver most of all.

I was taken to a small cellar, evidently a coal cellar, and made to stand against the wall. Seven men in two ranks stood within and without the door. One of them began to strike matches. Those in the front row evidently did not trust him. He might claim that he had no hand in the shooting if they were caught. There was an altercation. "How can I strike matches if I have to shoot?" he said.

Somebody struck another match. I could see their pistols wavering in the front row. I remember thinking that it was more for the sake of the firing squad than of the prisoner that they bound his eyes. I realized now why a victim gave gold to the headsman to dispatch him quickly. The match went out. I took two steps to the side. When I tried to get back so as not to show the white feather to such despicable little jackeens, my feet were stuck to the ground.

I have seen films where the coward sticks to the ground and is unable to move. It must have been thought, and contempt for the undisciplined rats, that made me able to stare them down.

The captain of the gunmen, the same fellow that pushed a gun against my neck in the bathroom, ordered, "Soldiers, forward and seize prisoner. We are going for a lamp." Five men came forward and led me out.

I noticed that the house lay parallel to the river, which runs west to east. It was in the small cellar at the east end of the house that I was stood against the wall. Now I was being taken to the west end, with the river not twenty yards away. The soldiers took me to what seemed to be a music room. Music books were scattered on the floor, which had been torn up along the wall. The torn-up planks and some music books were piled up in the grate to make a fire, for the night was very cold. The fire soon blazed, but the unheated chimney smoked. "Is it part of your program to gas a prisoner before shooting him?" I asked.

"What d'ye mean?"

"There's too much smoke in the room."

"Ye won't notice it for long, once they come back with the lamp." They were shivering from the cold. I tried a lecture on small arms.

"Those automatics are dangerous. You have to draw the lock back before one of them will fire. Let me show you." I reached for one of the guns; but there was nothing doing. With my ear on a stalk I listened for the return of the sedan with the lamp and the head gunman. Then I would be shot and my body thrown into the flooded river.

I bowed my head and groaned. "You fellows have given me such a fright that I'll soon have diarrhoea." I waited, though every second was precious, for the remark to sink in.

It is a popular superstition that fright produces diarrhoea, whereas the fact is that all secretions of the body are dried. I stamped my feet. "Take off those boots. You can wear the pumps which you have in your pocket."

Whether the remark had sunk in or not, I was terrified that the motor would return.

"Quick, a guard," I said hurriedly. The fools seized me and stuck a gun into each side of my heavy coat. In the darkness—this story will be incredible unless you realize that all was dark—I slipped my arms out of the coat, but I remained inside it.

Up rushed an outside watchman on whom I had not counted.

"What's all this about?" he asked.

"He has to go out."

It was very dark outside, but I feared that the eyes of the

watchman would be accustomed to the dark. By the feel of gravel under my left foot and the smooth cement threshold about an inch above the ground under my right, I knew that I was clear of the house. In a broken voice I said to the watchman, "Would you mind holding my coat?"

With my hand behind me I tore the coat from the gunmen's grasp and flung it in the face of the watcher. I stepped silently away. I did not dare to stand up and dive. I threw myself in on my back, the black water swallowed me.

Oh, how I rejoiced in spite of the shock. Now for the Caesar act! But I still had some swimming to do, and the river was icy cold. I tried to grasp overhanging willows, but the branches passed through my numbed hands.

Cross to the opposite bank? What a fool I would be! The gunmen would rush over there. It would take them only some minutes to drive across the bridge at Liffey Bank and to break into the grounds that went beside the stream. Instead, I floated along and vowed two swans to the river if it bore me safe to shore.

Our good Father Liffey duly received my gift.

The lights of the city began to appear, or were they lights of houses by the river? I was looking and wondering when all at once I felt that I could no longer breathe. I was too young for a heart attack; and I could swim easily. What was the matter?

I pushed my face under and it came up clear. I could breathe freely now. What had happened? A cake of foam had choked my nose and mouth.

At last a submerged willow was directly in front of me. I put my arm round it, and I was immediately swept under. I was prepared for that. When I came up on the other side, I got my two arms around it and gradually moved ashore. After crawling slowly up the muddy bank I tried to stand up. I could feel only my knees; all was frozen from the knees down.

I made my way to a lighted house and looked through the window. Four women and a man were at supper. One of the women saw me, and the table shook. Now all but the man were shaking and moaning. I must have looked a sorry sight, pale and with but one shirt sleeve and with blood trickling down my forehead. But my mind was working like a dynamo.

"I am not dead," I said.

The moaning ceased. I had been taken for a ghost. No one had come into that house from the river before.

The women refused to give me help. Were they afraid of reprisals? Who knows or cares? The man said, "Come along with me." I did not tell him who I was. Least said soonest mended. He took me down a garden and opened a door in the wall. "There is a depot across the Phoenix Park where the troops are."

I crossed the Park, and suddenly I felt very weak. I lay down and brought my knees up. When I rose I was caught in the glare of a searchlight. With my only sleeve raised, I walked along the beam. After a while I came to the depot railings. A sentry asked me who I was, but I could only make hiccup-like noises.

Evidently the sentry feared a ruse; there must have been firing behind me. He would not let me in. Some officer came. By this time I could speak: "I am Senator Gogarty . . . I have been kidnaped . . . I have just escaped." He caused the gate to be opened. The police surgeon, whom I knew, took me in charge. I was put to bed: hot bottles and hot tea.

About two in the morning, after much telephoning and red tape, three armored cars were sent for me. I rode in the middle one, and passed in triumph through a city that saw me going to be shot some hours earlier.

I was taken to the Government Building and given a bed; but I did not sleep. I am afraid that planning retribution kept me awake.

I used to slip out to my house which was but a block and a half from the Government Building. When the Ministers got to know of it, I was given a guard of eight men. The steed had been stolen but was found and guarded now!

My kidnaping would not have been believed had the Government boys not found my coat. A few days later a man called with a bullet, evidently from a .38, its nose somewhat bent. It had been dug out of the spine of the ringleader who had raided my house and carried me off. He had died "to a flash," shrieking (inappropriately) under the wall of the Tranquilla Convent in Upper Rathmines. Later, others were caught.

I did not know what the Government thought of my arrest and escape. I did not like the proof, which depended only on my coat. But when Senator Bagwell was taken from a house in Howth, there was no more uncertainty. It was clear that an effort was being made to intimidate senators and so prevent any laws, punitive or otherwise, from being enacted. Promptly the Government announced that twenty rebel prisoners would be shot if Senator Bagwell was not released unharmed forthwith. He was "allowed" to escape. That was the turning point: opposition was broken. Later, when I inquired why a similar proclamation had not been issued in my case, the President said, smiling, "You escaped."

Butlers I Have Known

There was a great crowd. The Lord Mayor's procession was coming down the slight slope that was Rutland Square, East. In front came the fire brigade in red shirts and brass helmets. Men from Guinness' brewery came next, in bowler hats with a thin strip of patent leather over the crown and the white corduroy trousers of gala dress. They manned shining drays drawn by large horses with hair over their hoofs. Then the band of the metropolitan police with banging drums and blaring brass. Various guilds followed—wheelwrights, bricklayers, stonemasons, plumbers—carrying banners on which their patron saints reeled and glittered in the wind. They proceeded the state coach from which the Lord Mayor and the Lady Mayoress beamed and bowed. Before them on a velvet cushion lay the city mace of shining silver, well-polished for the occasion. Cheers upon cheers!

Suddenly gallons of water descended upon the heads of those who crowded the steps of number 5. The water fell from a cloudless sky. It fell in sheets, for it had not time to separate into drops. Indignation seized the crowd. Their upturned faces beheld a small boy suspended upside down by an ankle from the topmost window out in the air directly above their heads. The small boy struggled with arching back and hands that ineffectually winnowed the air. "That will learn you not to spill water down on decent people who might burst in the front door and wreck the house." There was no doubt about it, for the small boy was I. And the man who held me upside down sixty feet above the street was Whelan, our butler.

He was the first butler I knew. Judge Miller next door in number 6 had a butler who wore red side whiskers; but it was rumored that he was also the crier in his master's court, which diluted him somewhat and degraded him in my estimation, for a true butler should have no other occupation. If they have, so much the less butler they.

This applies to men servants in schools, colleges, institutions, and asylums. You always suspect that they have other jobs, so they are not specialists. Of course there are exceptions; for instance, the provost of a college may have a true butler in his house. When you call or are sent for, he will say, "This way please." Then you know: you know that it is a bad sign. Otherwise he would have said, "What name shall I say?" If he merely says, "This way please," you may be sure that he has been listening at dinner while the provost was discussing your case with your tutor; and the omens are ill.

One of my tests for a true butler is that he makes me feel inferior. He makes me feel unworthy. He makes me feel out of it in some way. He makes me feel that I am not worthy of a butler. I may be oversensitive. I know that I am unworthy. Often have I envied the scion of a well-butlered house who could come bouncing in from the fields and throw his coat *at* the butler, all the while shouting at the top of his voice for a friend still out of doors or for his father. The butler got his own back by calling the boy by his given name, thereby making himself one of the family to the further exclusion of me.

Ah, no! The house from which I came kept a butler only because the public judged the skill of a doctor largely by the servants he employed. The connection between skill and butler is very true. There was a doctor's butler who held the equivalent of an outpatients department later at the hall door of his master's house. "How is your body?" he would inquire before dispensing copies of the prescriptions of the day. His name was John Dunne, and his practice, though considerable, was confined to Ireland, where a doctor still has half-magical qualities. I cannot imagine such a thing happening over the Irish Sea in the Welfare State, which makes a doctor come down to earth and work for his living. Is it any wonder that the nation has become a nation of hypochondriacs?

Butlers have bisyllabic names, all except Dunne and Jeeves; but Jeeves is only a figment of an author's imagination. He does not exist in real life. George Moore was wrong (he always was) when he said butlers should be called Thackeray. That was because he did not like Thackeray, who was as bad a snob as George Moore. Dickens would have been more appropriate. Butlers have names such as Maunder, Jepson, Selden, Burroughs, Bridges, Acres, or Ainsworth.

In lordly houses the denizens of the servants' hall assume the names of their masters. The valet of Lord Derby becomes "Derby"; of Lord Halifax, "Halifax"; and so on. They take precedence according to the rank of their masters; the body servant of a duke is given pride of place.

The official repertoire of butlers is strictly limited. There are only a few phrases which may be used. This is not in imitation of the hunting set, who have got rid of the definite article and hardly speak at all. Extemporaneous speech is nevertheless forbidden. The greatest example of this took place in Ireland during the time that the egregious Mr. Churchill loosed upon the country his murderous irregular troops, locally known from their motley uniform as the Black and Tans. They had raided Dunsany Castle; and as they were driving off shoulder to shoulder in their Lancia lorry, Maunder, Lord Dunsany's butler, framed in the Gothic doorway, inquired impassively, "Who shall I say called?" The convention on occasion can assume heroic aspects.

You may have heard that, owing to death duties, taxes, the ending of old families, and such-like matters, the English butler is a thing of the past. It is not so; not by any means. And from what I heard the other day (it is a top secret of course) this opinion is borne out. I now reveal a fact that I have long suspected. The reason that I did not reveal it before is that everyone took the disappearance of the butler for granted, seeing that his employers had vanished. Another reason is that I have long been suspected of bias. The suspicion is justified. What was it I heard the other day? Close your umbrella and I will tell you. I heard that the butlers of England have taken over the government, and that since the Conservatives have come in this can no longer be concealed. In that I see nothing wrong. It is in the nature of things. When you come to think of it, who is more conservative than an English butler? Who is a greater stickler for decorum? You have only to call decorum "protocol" and you have in the butler a most representative diplomat. Who can be more at his ease in the striped trousers of diplomacy than one who has always worn them? To whom can the English public look with more hope than to the butlers of the families that once ruled the land?

A friend pointed out that the butlers might be exalted to the House of Lords. It was diluted before and it will be diluted again, but if the butlers become lords their conservatism will, if anything, increase.

I have said that in Ireland a doctor has half-magical qualities. He should have physical ones too if he is to be accepted. He should be "the full of a door." Once he is that, he can never be at fault. If things go wrong it is an "act of God" and not his fault, by no means his. He may "indulge," which is a euphemism for being drunk. In fact if he is drunk, he is all the more likely to be inspired. So much for Ireland, which is as everyone knows the Island of Saints and Doctors.

In Germany, in Ober Hesse or near there, I was staying with a German family. They were of ancient stock, and they must have been noble because the Count had at least two children by a morganatic marriage. His wife stayed with him, so it was all right. So long as the estates could not go to the children of a woman of inferior rank, his wife understood; nevertheless, I did not see his morning gift wife around. Their butler was certainly of ancient stock. His beard, which was white, came down half his chest. I was about to quote, "O good old man! How well in thee appears The constant service of the antique world," until I remembered amusedly how my friend Robert Yelverton Tyrrell had quoted the very same lines about the porter in the limerick, "There was a young man of St. John's." He carried in what probably passes in ancient houses for a bath. Then he called me in a language which I did not know. Probably it was some patois of German. At any rate I obeyed, for I thought it an awaking call.

Now we come to the United States. Here the butlers are always foreign. After all, they come from countries that have been feudal. One exception though, and that is Ireland. Ireland has never been feudal. I don't mean its conquerors but the "mere" Irish, which is the English way of saying "pure."

Andy was a butler and proud of it. He was the most extraordinary and incomparable butler I ever met.

Andy was born in Dublin, and like some Irishmen he was very lean. I do not think that I ever saw his full face. He appeared to be always sideways. His face was pale and thin. His eyes must have been put in "with a dirty finger," as the saying is. His orbits were dark, and so were his eyelashes; as for his eyes, they were invisible. Now and then I thought I caught a gleam from them —a momentary gleam, it is true, but enough to make me wonder whether his odd ways were from his outlook on life or whether I was the victim of an elaborate pretense. Even to this day I do not know whether his strange sayings came out of character or were put on.

Riall was his second name, but no one ever called him anything but Andy, and it was very becoming as you will see. He had a good war record. He had served in India as a batman, that is a body servant to some officer. He was gassed in the first "world" war and invalided out of the service. Being a batman, it was easy for him to become a butler when he came to the United States.

I first met Andy when I was living in the northwest of New Jersey. A friend of mine had a country house there, in the grounds of which there was a squash racquet court which had been converted into a studio. In this I lived, and Andy was lent to me to look after the place.

There was an annex in which I slept, and a furnace room off it. One day I got the idea that the furnace was not drawing properly, so I put on a pair of gloves and went to examine it. I found that it had not been cleaned. Andy had put shovelfuls of coke on the top of the burned-out cinders until the furnace was all but choked. I spoke to Andy, who took the sharpness off my remarks by giving me a soldierly salute. Was it to remind me of his military career, to which in comparison mine was very inferior? When he heard me out, "A handy man would do the needful in five minutes and clean the whole thing up." Five minutes indeed! It had taken me twice that long merely to examine it! Whether a handy man was employed or not, the furnace gave no trouble from that time.

I sat at my usual occupation of tapping the typewriter. In order to sit high enough at the table, I put a dozen copies of a popular magazine on the seat to raise me up. I remember that I had had a head cold and had run out of handkerchiefs. I told this to Andy and thought no more of it. I heard water running in the bathroom but paid little attention to it. Half an hour elapsed and Andy said, "Would you mind raising your hips just a bit?" I did so, and he put another copy of the magazine under me. Andy looks after my comfort, I thought. He must have noticed that I was too low on the seat and he put the magazine under me to lift me up. I went on typing. An hour or so passed, and I was getting tired when Andy reappeared. He came over to my chair with, "They ought to be done now. Would you mind just raising your buttocks just a little, sir?" He opened the magazine and there were half a dozen handkerchiefs, folded, pressed, and dried!

Andy was a great hand at polishing silver. When I dined with the family I could not look at it long, it was so bright. One of the family had been an ambassador somewhere and for that reason there was a lot of gilt silver, which Andy thought vulgar. The reason for this was that he could not polish it to his satisfaction without taking some of the gilt off. So he ruled it out as vulgar. Andy was a bit of a judge.

I saw Andy leaning across a fence one day. The fence bounded a little orchard outside the studio. I should have mentioned that the walls of the studio had been pierced for a glass door and two windows. It was through these that I caught sight of Andy. He was gazing across a field. I opened the glass door in order to see what he was looking at. When he saw me he said, "They're very healthy." I asked what were healthy? "Some say they give a taste to the milk." I wondered what he was talking about. I did not like to ask him abruptly, for he might have twisted it into a reprimand for the fact that I had caught him idling; and after all he was only lent to me. So I did not ask. He must have thought that I was losing interest, for he said, "There's some objects to garlic, and they dig it out of the fields where the cattle graze. The result is that all kinds of diseases get at the children and at us too." It was not the season for garlic, but I let it go.

Andy had steered me to a subject that would take my mind off the fact that I had caught him unoccupied.

Then the family went to New York and Andy went with them. New York was too much for Andy, both literally and figuratively. In spite of the indulgence of his employer, who did the best for all her servants, Andy was greatly changed from his New Jersey days. He lost dignity.

He had the greatest contempt for those who with a year or two of soldiering tried to put themselves on an equal footing with him who had spent the best days of his life at it. That was why he had an occasional black eye.

He was allowed to walk the dog, to which he was much attached. One day it did not come back from its walk. Neither did Andy. Next morning a taxi drove up, with the dog on the back seat. There was a label round its neck stating the price of the taxi. Next day he returned himself. He sent for his mistress, who wondered so much that she came down to the hall. Andy spoke: "Behold me now, ma'am, with a greater grip on myself than I ever had before."

On that occasion his absence was passed over and no questions asked. All went smoothly for six months or so, when Andy disappeared again. Four days this time. When he came back, he sent for his mistress, who came reluctantly to the hall. Andy stood at attention and saluted with six inches of her late husband's raincoat hanging over his hand. He had come in for her late husband's coats. "Call out the firing squad, ma'am." He had condemned himself to be shot!

Andy's excuses were unique and amusing as well. One of them was quite subtle. Listen to this. He was absent for the usual few days. Then he telephoned: "Can you hear me, mum?" "Yes, Andy. Where are you?" "I'm glad that you can understand me, mum. Do you remember the bath you told me to take?" "Well, what of it?" "Only this, mum. I was about to do your bidding when I turned the cold water in the shower by mistake and the shock smashed my plates. I am glad that you can understand me, mum." That's a fine excuse. It puts the onus on his employer who told him to take a bath.

Andy had a charm about him. The most suspicious cook, for instance, straight-laced and disapproving, became a friendly supporter of Andy's after half an hour. It worked on elevator men, janitors, and porters, even on the superintendent of an apartment I could name. Even his absences had a charm. Not only were they forgiven but they were expected of him. "Ah, poor Andy; he cannot help it"; that was what was said. As for his employer, she took Andy as a liability and never thought of sacking him. That was her way of thinking, and it suited Andy well. His having been gassed helped: he had a poor chest and he was cosseted as a result. No place suited Andy like the United States. His was service without servitude, and where could you find that save in the United States?

In spite of his lovableness, he came back one night with a broken arm. Andy would not say where he had gotten it. The cook whispered that it was in his club.

His mistress went to see Andy as he lay in hospital. Andy shared a room with three others. The silence was embarrassing, for all had been talking loudly as his employer approached. "Well, Andy, how are you?" At first Andy did not reply. He looked about the room. Then, when he thought that the attention of the others was not on him, he whispered, "There's the makings of a great row in here." Afterward, it was divulged that the others consisted of an Episcopalian, an Arab, and a Jew.

Service without servility. That is the way in America and that is why butlers are foreigners. It accounts for Andy, by the way.

The English butler is nothing without his servility. That is why you are all the more embarrassed when he treats you with disdain. Therefore English butlers are the best, even if they are exalted to the House of Lords. They are accustomed to the peerage: think of what happens downstairs in a lordly house. True, it may have to be diluted on their account. It has been diluted so many times that it is a distinction not to belong to it, for it has now become a place where Labour leaders go when they are spent.

An English butler is born and bred. He has made a tradition out of servitude, and in England everything goes by tradition. You never see a butler "presiding" over lunch; but at dinner with two footmen under him—well, "They also serve who only stand and wait."

Tinted Shadows

How many of those who contributed to their nations' continuance and glory are portrayed in the portrait galleries of their countries? I have a theory that there are both gaps and misfits; so, to put this theory to the test, I visited the National Gallery of Ireland. Here, I thought, of all places there are sure to be misfits, seeing that the Gallery was built and managed under British auspices for the greater part of its existence.

Now the National Gallery occupies one side of Leinster Lawn, one of the pleasantest expanses of mown grass in the city. It is at the back of the house built by a duke of Leinster in what was an unfashionable part of the Dublin of his day. When someone pointed this out to him, "Fashion will follow me," he answered. They tell me that the White House in Washington is a copy of Leinster House; but I failed to find the resemblance. However, that is neither here nor there.

I was right! When I entered the National Gallery the first thing I saw was a large painting of many figures in various uniforms and of two state coaches, on the hindermost of which stood a figure beneath a temporary triumphal arch. It was George IV entering Dublin, August 17, 1821. That he must have entered it "happy and glorious" somewhat earlier is evident from the stance of the blond-headed monarch, who is standing up sideways in his coach of state. His hips are the foremost part of him, while the two curves that the rest of his body makes justify the grip of his right hand on the back of the driver's seat. He wears a red coat regally decorated and white trousers. The artist who was guilty of what amounted to *lèse majesté* was William Turner de Lond, obviously not wholly an Englishman any more than Lord Byron, who was equally disrespectful when he called this miraculously balanced figure "the fourth of all fools." Was it a secret cynicism in the then governors of the Gallery that made them see something appropriate in the entry into Ireland of an intoxicated king? The present manager has preserved the picture, possibly to justify the rebellion of 1916. Here is undoubtedly a misfit.

There is nothing equivocal about the great landscape by Nathaniel Hone, a descendant no doubt of the Nathaniel Hone of the eighteenth century. He lived in St. Doulough's, Malahide, in a great rambling house; and he loved to paint the cattle on his estate. Here are six cows lying in the rain-enriched grass, as if they could graze no more. Another stands by the wood, over which a rain cloud glooms darkly. At the right of the picture the land rises in a gentle slope to where there is a beam of light. The clouds' edges here and there show glimpses of fleeting blue. He had a studio by the estuary of the Swords River, where it meets the waters of the Irish Sea. He was a great bearded figure of a man and one of the greatest landscape painters of his day. I remember asking him once how it was that he painted bright clouds above a murky sea. "Anything can happen in the sky," he said. No misfit here! The day he saw, with its loaded cloud above the wood and the grass that is the wealth of Ireland, has gone forever; but its tinted shadow remains and will remain, a true rendering of the Irish landscape by one who had a heart as rich and as generous as the fields of Malahide.

It is only a few minutes after ten in the morning; let us look at the portraits in the first room. On the left is a three-quarter-length of a delicate-looking man still in his forties, with a golden brown beard, a blue shirt, and a white collar. The portrait is by Sarah Purser, who lived to an advanced age. When she was ninety-six she used to say, "Let me sit with my back to the light so that I may pass for ninety-three." She knew the importance of light! Maybe that is why she has emphasized the beard of her ineffectual sitter, T. P. Gill. He was a civil servant, and he looks it. What he is doing in a national portrait gallery is a mystery. Perhaps he is there to illustrate George Moore's story of his beard. It seems that Gill had a fever in Paris. When he recovered he had a beard. He went to a barber to have it removed; but just as an Irish cattle dealer can see beefsteak in the rump of a bullock, or a Praxiteles a statue in the marble of Pentelicus, so the French barber saw Henri Quatre in Gill's beard. The barber would listen to no entreaties. Henri Quatre Gill had to be; and so his beard . . . but is a beard enough, or a novelist great enough, to have the walls of a national gallery used to illustrate a story?

Next to him is one who made Dublin famous in two hemispheres. He suffered in it too, mostly through the stupidity of a fool who all but ruined the Irish Renaissance, and from the character he inherited from a drunken wag of a father. James Augustine Joyce is portrayed looking forward and to the right of the observer. His right arm rests on a table. He wears the greenish-gray ancestral waistcoat which was a part of his ritual on important occasions, a reddish tie, and a brown lounge suit. His complexion is ruddier than when I knew him, but that may be due to the idiosyncrasy of the artist, Jacques Emile Blanche. His slight mustache is still dark, and his forehead bulges with his mighty memory. There is no unhappiness here. He is full of assurance. He apparently was at the height of his fame and powers when he sat for this very competent artist. The portrait stands up well against the competitions of a better-known Irishman and a greater painter, G. B. Shaw by the Honorable John Collier. Here too is a forehead full of knowledge and self-assurance, with the penetrating blue eyes that were never dimmed by dreams. The portrait is three-quarters-length and one of the most accomplished in the room.

Next to Shaw, as if by way of contrast, there rises from the shades the bearded face with its head of profuse dark brown hair of Ireland's great mystic who used for a pen name the non-euphonious letters Æ. Hence the irreverent Dublin joke about "the Bearded Diphthong." The artist (Sarah Purser again) has proved her artistry by the skill with which she has evoked this apparition from the shades. The head floats with the dimness of a shadow as if seen in the half-light of some séance. What a contrast to the portrait by J. B. Yeats (the father of the poet) which hangs not far away on the same wall. Yeats could see only the organizer in Æ. Perhaps he was set against seeing any other poet but his son. Only Sir Horace Plunkett's eloquent helper is here. So let us give the palm to Sarah. But if the older Yeats failed to interpret the dreamer in Æ, he has succeeded beyond his usual form in his portrait of that pernickety author, George Moore. Maybe he was afraid of his criticism which had he challenged, which would have turned out to be an affectation after all. Here is Moore benignant, with his head held slightly to one side. The full face is rubicund and genial, the forehead domed and full. There is nothing impish here. Yeats was the son or the grandson of a parson, and so born to respect the landed gentry.

It was Standish O'Grady, that enigma, who being a Unionist and so standing for the domination of Great Britain over all the "O's" and "Mac's," loosened the flood of pent-up nationality which resulted in the rising of 1916. His romantic history of Ireland is responsible. The Ireland of the warrior and the poet were revealed. Warriors and poets! But next to O'Grady's is the greatest portrait of them all. It is the portrait of a studious German who, without enthusiasm or romance, brought to light the ancient sagas of Ireland with the interest and accuracy of a scholar; "The tryst after death" and many another grim revelation of the men that warred with each other in times out of mind. And the portrait is a revelation. It surpasses all the rest, just as the fierce spirit that once breathed on the land makes pigmies of us all. Augustus John has painted Kuno Meyer with all the energy of the chieftains whom Meyer brought to life. The scholar sits in his chair turned toward the left. His crippled fingers grasp a stick, the thumb of his left hand is in the band of his trousers. The bearded face is that of a sufferer. You have only to look at the shadows under the eyes and the stillness of the pose . . .

"Did ye see me last night? If ye did, let me tell you it was the one bad half one that did it."

It was Creech! He had been convalescing behind one of the screens. What a place to recover from a hang-over. The taverns had been opened ten minutes ago. Why was he here? I was soon to know. There was a lot of mental spleen which he had to discharge. Creech is a barrister, and so has the time to stroll in galleries and to criticize to his heart's content. He began:

"Now can you tell me how did that old codger contribute to the national life? What is he doing here?" I looked up into the shadows and I beheld the complacent figure of a bishop or a dean with a purple stock and a wide-awake hat. I knew that Creech was a Mason, so I was all the more surprised that he should attack a shepherd of a Protestant church.

"And I'll show you what I call the portrait of a humbug in here." He drew or led me into another hall, where on the wall opposite to the windows there hung the portrait of a round-faced prelate labeled, "Reverend Thaddeus Connellan, Irish Scholar. Died 1851." It was a full-faced man with assessing brown eyes full of cunning and subservience under a domed forehead. His skin was unusually clear, like the face of a child, but it was patched with a pink which was rather blotchy. The fellow was either a teetotaler or a zealot. He was seated in a dark room with the rafter showing. His fingers were folded. Three books at his left elbow. Beyond in an empty marsh lay the sheiling of a peasant. The famine of 1849 had desolated the land. The message of the painting was, "If you accept the Bible you will be no longer a poverty-stricken peasant but a successful man like me."

"I call that a portrait of a humbug. He was the first fellow to exploit Irish, a prototype of all the humbugs of our time."

"What's he doing here anyhow?" I asked.

"There I leave you," Creech replied in the vernacular. "I'm off anyway." And he was gone.

I crossed the room quietly so as to put the wall between me and my uninvited guide, lest he should change his mind and come back. In front of me hung a refined portrait of the grandfather of George Moore. I noticed a hint, faint but still a family trait that could be recognized, of a slight tilt of the head which was more emphasized in the grandson, the novelist, George. Tom Moore, "the sweetest singer of her saddest lay" (Shelley) is here piquant and alert.

It seemed that the "all clear" might be taken for granted. I went into a farther room where portraits of a more remote past were exhibited. Here I saw Lord Edward Fitzgerald and his wife Pamela. George Berkeley, Bishop of Cloyne, the traveler who wrote "Westward the course of empire takes its way," and went West. Is not Berkeley, in California, called after him? I thought of his plans for a school in Bermuda for the noble savage, and of his sojourn in Rhode Island. He was a round-faced, chubby man, hardly the man to invent or to push Platonism, or rather Neo-Platonism, to its conclusion. With his "To be is to be perceived," I wonder that none of his contemporary divines did not see that such a philosophy would leave the existence of the Creator depending on the perception of the creature. But they were not captious in his day. Over him were his wife and himself in miniature, surrounded by a large family. He must have philosophized while he was still young and a bachelor, for few married men, particularly a man as assiduously married as the Bishop, have time for philosophy. You will object, and tell me that Socrates was married and yet he was an outstanding philosopher. I will submit that he kept philosophy for outdoor application: domestically he fell back on resignation. I look at the soft white neck and the dull brown eyes of George Berkeley (don't think for one moment that a dull eye means an unintelligent mind. It is quite the contrary—remember that the aspect of Socrates was bull-like) and I recall the experiment he tried on himself when he wanted to find out what they felt who were hanged, and I think of how that neck was wealed and how the brown eyes bulged before he was rescued.

But here is another contemporary divine, Dean Swift, the opposite of the good bishop. His eyes are blue, so was his outlook on life. Above him is portrayed that enigmatical love of his, enigmatical until Denis Johnston resolved it by showing beyond all manner of doubt that Stella was the half sister of Dean Swift and that the Church of those days held, as did the common law, that a marriage of that sort was incestuous. There is no lack of portraits of the gloomy Dean. There are two of Oliver Cromwell, both of the right side of his face so that his wart is (hypocritically enough) concealed. These men are well remembered by the nation which they served or scourged. Edmund Burke and Molyneux are represented. In the farthest room are those Elizabethans who were connected with Ireland. Sir Walter Raleigh, who "loved a wench well," according to that inveterate gossip John Aubrey, and who was one of the greatest Englishmen of them all. He was unwittingly the cause of the Irish famine by his introduction of free food and low wages, the potato. Ireland grew to a population of eight millions through its production, then in two years was reduced by half owing to the land's exhaustion and the blight of the potato crop. I look at the portrait of his lady and observe the stiff convention that made the artist portray her to look like Queen Elizabeth. I don't wonder when I look at his insipid lady that he "loved a wench well." Does not Aubrey tell how strongly the blood gushed at his beheading, such was the strength of the nature in him? It is futile to speak of the stiffness of the artistic conventions of any period. We are impounded by convention still. Just now it is the convention of ugliness and commonness. Who knows what the conventions of the morrow will be?

I gaze on the silks and satins of James, the first Duke of Ormonde, and as I look across the room I am met by the splendid trappings of the second Duke. I think of the servility, chicanery, and flattery which their state engendered, and I balance this by thoughts of their pageantry and display and the enhancement of the dignity of the human being; and I cannot but regret that for all his loyalty to Charles II, to whom he owed his career, all that is left of the first Duke is a tinted shadow.

Tragedy haunts these rooms as well as mirth (the mirth is but a modicum)—from Parnell who was ruined by a parnel to Raleigh who was betrayed by scheming traitors in London town. They are all well displayed in their historical sequence, and tragedy looms over the greatest number. Joyce died of a perforated gastric ulcer, the result of long anxiety. Tom Moore saw all his children die. Yeats was constrained by love for his whole life long. George Moore died loveless and without convictions. Lord Edward Fitzgerald fell by the machinations of an informer. Dean Swift suffered from unrequited demands and indignation during a long life in a despised town.

Earls and lords in silken robes of state, little joy they derived from lording it here. I wonder do they walk at Halloween, these shadows which the artist's brush has evoked from vanished days. They served their own interests for the most part, and by so doing served the country with which those interests were identified. Was it Ireland that brought them unhappiness? Who can say? But it is not without comfort for anyone who knows that he cannot make the grade and have his image hung on the walls of the nation's gallery to reflect: For happiness, what a poor exchange is fame.

Who Was Dean Swift?

The more we read the biographers of Dean Swift, the more we find ourselves confronted by a person who varies from an oddity to a monster, one who may hardly be included among "the kindly race of men." He differs outstandingly and uniquely from any character in history: all his biographers leave us with is, to say the least of it, an enigma. There is one exception. To a short pamphlet by that most distinguished of the Abbey playwrights, Denis Johnston, who is also a trained lawyer, the solution of the jigsaw puzzle of Dean Swift is due. The theory on which it is based explains much that cannot otherwise be explained.

It is incumbent on anyone who investigates the life of one long dead to bear in mind the fact that in his investigations he is apt to form his judgments by the standards of his own time. It is as hard to get away from this tendency as it is from the notion that our standards are the final word and judgment of an irreplaceable court; whereas the fact is that century repudiates century and civilization civilization: what is sacred in the East may be the subject for comic opera in the West. Yet there are certain standards that are universally valid. We know what Humanity is; but we must take into account the vicissitudes to which it has been subjected, the contemporary customs to which it had to conform, and all that makes it different from our present-day concepts. By making such allowances we should judge Dean Swift.

The investigation falls under three headings. First, his reaction to his own times; second, his attitude toward women; third, the question of his patriotism. When we have examined these, it will be time for a summing up.

Swift was born in number 7 Hoey's Court in the year 1667, the seventh year of the reign of King Charles II. Seventy-eight years later he died in the deanery of St. Patrick's, close by the place of his birth. He was educated at Kilkenny School, the Irish Eton of the day, and at Dublin University.

The strange adventure of his infant years, when he was kidnaped by his nurse and taken to England, and his mother's attitude to what appears to have been a convenient kidnaping, need not concern us at the moment. We are concerned with his adult years, the best part of which were spent at Moor Park, Surrey, in England, the home of Sir William Temple. If you look at the famous picture of the death of Sir Philip Sidney at the battle of Zutphen you will notice a man in whose arms Sir Philip is dying. This is Sir William, grandfather of the Sir William Temple of Moor Park where Swift is working. This grandfather was the first of the Temples to go to Ireland. He was a classical scholar, and he became the fourth provost of Dublin University. His son, Sir John, was Master of the Rolls in Dublin. He wrote a history of the Irish Rebellion of 1641. He was a widower for forty years. His son of Moor Park was a more prolific writer. His works were edited by Swift. This Sir William, after seven years' delay on account of her family's opposition, married Dorothy Osborne, by whom he had seven children, only one of whom survived. To this son he made over his house at Sheen and went to reside at Moor Park, where we find Swift acting as his secretary; but what was fraught with Fate, also as tutor to a little girl, Esther Johnson, who dwelt with her mother in a pretty cottage in the grounds of Moor Park. Her mother had been Sir William's housekeeper.

Swift instructed Esther Johnson with an assiduity as great but incomplete as that of Abélard towards Héloïse. Swift called his pupil Stella.

On the man of the world, Sir William Temple, ambassador to the Hague, Swift depended for his knowledge of the moiling life beyond the quiet close of Moor Park, the world of courts and courtiers and of the struggle for preference and power. He studied for six weeks at Oxford and obtained the degree of M.A. Sir William defrayed his expenses.

After being shuttled to and from Ireland, at last in London Swift became as influential as any man who was not a member of the court or government. He acted as "lobbyist." He was the means of obtaining office for many a friend. Never for himself. This must not be attributed to any neglect on his part, for try as far as his pride permitted, it was not his luck to be preferred. A "go-between" we would call him now; but in his day (as in ours) such activities were essential. Influence was the only way to preferment, that is to obtaining office or a job. That he must have been overzealous, even at a time when every man as a matter of course sought influence, appears from an observation and by no means a friendly one. Bishop Kennett records in his diary for the year 1713 the swagger of Swift who was at the height of his influence or interference in English politics, a member of a kind of inner cabinet with Harley, Harcourt, and St. John:

> Swift came into the coffee house and had a bow from everybody but me. When I came to the ante-chamber before prayers, Dr. Swift was the principal man of talk and business, and acted as minister of requests. He was soliciting the Earl of Arran to speak to his brother, the Duke of Ormonde, to get a chaplain's place established in the garrison of Hull, for Mr. Fiddes, a clergyman in that neighbourhood who had lately been in jail, and published sermons to pay fees. He was promising Mr. Thorold to undertake with my Lord Treasurer that according to his petition he should obtain a salary of 200 pounds per annum, as a minister of the English church at Rotterdam. He stopped F. Gwynne, Esq., going in with the red bag to the Queen, and told him

> aloud that he had something to say to him from my Lord Treasurer. He talked with the son of Dr. Davenant to be sent abroad, and took out his pocket book and wrote down several things as memoranda to do for him. He turned to the fire and took out his gold watch and telling him the time of day, complained that it was very late. A gentleman said it was too fast. "How can I help it," says the Doctor, "if the courtiers give me a watch that won't go right?" Then he instructed a young nobleman that the best poet in England was Mr. Pope (a Papist) who had begun a translation of Homer into English verse, for which, he said he must have them all subscribe. "For" said he "the author *shall* not begin to print until I have a thousand guineas for him." Lord Treasurer, after leaving the Queen, came through the room, beckoning Dr. Swift to follow him; both went off together just before prayers.

All this is in keeping with the times. What is surprising is that Bishop Kennett saw anything reprehensible in Swift's conduct. Maybe he resented his "swagger." By what pretension did an obscure Irishman assume the position of Minister of Requests? Maybe it holds something of more significance than comes to the surface. The Bishop must have had a secret fear that if he were to be dependent on Swift for a recommendation, he might not fare as well as the clergyman who had been in jail. After all, Swift did achieve something. After the long delays of the court, he got the First Fruits remitted. The First Fruits were a tribute to the throne of Queen Anne. Of this success he writes in that confidential diary of his which he addressed in letter form to Stella,

> As I hope to live, I despise the credit of it out of an excess of pride (significant word) and desire you will give me not the least merit when you talk of it.

The getting may have made the gift worthless in his eyes.

This journal to Stella, written in his "little language," has been the subject of much comment. He was not the only one who had recourse to the small or intimate language of a child. We find Sterne using it in his letters to his daughter. Swift may have employed it as a kind of cypher. There is no doubt that he intended

Stella to keep this, his diary, for his future reading. We have his own words for it:

> I know it is neither wit nor diversion to tell you every day where I dine, neither do I wish it to fill my letters; but I fancy that I shall sometime or another, have the curiosity of seeing some particulars how I passed my life when I was absent from M.D. this time.

M.D. was a cypher for "my dear" when addressed solely to Stella. Sometimes it included her chaperon, Mrs. Dingley, a cousin once removed of Sir William Temple.

Always bearing in mind the practice of the time in which he lived (and not unmindful of our own) there is no more blame to be attached to Swift for influencing those in power than there is to Wellesley, afterward the Duke of Wellington, for soliciting his brother in India for preferment—a hundred years after the time of Swift. The remarkable thing is that Swift, a hater of humbug, corruption, and chicane, emerges unstained from the morass of a corrupt court, a perverted king, and a complaisant church and a corrupt one. He was confronted with this last when the deanery of Derry, the richest plum in the Irish Church, was sold over his head by a man called Bush who had already intrigued him out of the secretaryship to Lord Berkeley, to the highest bidder. The highest bidder was Dr. Theophilus Bolton who, in spite of his Christian name (or perhaps because of it) paid one thousand pounds for the love of God.

Now let us turn to Swift's relationship with women. In spite of the precursor of Freud, Krafft-Ebing, who on reading the diary to Stella, pronounced Swift as "sexually anaesthetic," we have evidence to the contrary. Here are two letters concerning liaisons in his youth:—"This woman, my mistress with a pox, left one daughter, Anne by name. This Anne, for it must be she, about seven years ago writ me from London to tell me that she was the daughter of Betty Jones, for that was my mistress's name."

That is one. But:

> I could remember twenty women in my life to whom I have behaved myself in just the same way; and I profess without any other design than that of entertaining myself when I am very idle or when something goes amiss in my affairs. This I have done as a man of the world when I had no design of anything grave in it, and what I thought at worse a harmless impertinence. But whenever I begin to take sober resolutions, or, as now to be thinking of entering the Church, I have never found it would be hard to put off this kind of folly at the porch.

This brings to mind a conversation I had with another famous divine who, like Swift, was an alumnus of Dublin University:

"My dear fellow, I have had sixty-five love affairs. And I have never regretted one of them. Never. But [with a twinkle] they were all before I was ordained."

Here is another letter written to Miss Waring, whom he sued vehemently and called her his Varina after his fashion, only to be refused by her. When afterward she confessed her willingness to marry him, what she got by way of a missive was that, after telling her that he would overlook her shortage in good looks and income, he proceeded:

> Have you such an inclination to my person and humour as to comply with my desires and way of living, and endeavour to make us both as happy as you can? Will you be ready to engage in those methods I shall direct for the improvement of your mind, so as to make us entertaining company for each other without being miserable when we are neither visiting nor being visited? Can you bend your love and esteem and indifference to others in the same way as I do mine?

His letter shows him disadvantageously to us. Then women were more or less chattels. But since we do not know what went to its making, judgment must be reserved. One thing is plain: no one with any spirit could accept a position of household drudge, which was at the time apparently Swift's requirements in a wife. Contrast this with the childish tenderness of his love for Stella.

Now we come to another Esther. She is Esther Van Homrigh, daughter of a lord mayor of Dublin. She herself was given the freedom of that city. We find her living with her mother in London at the time when Swift was at the height of his power. He was familiar with the family. He used their home to change his wig and gown. Very often he dined there. Esther, soon to become Vanessa, was an impulsive, generous, and passionate young woman. She was interested in books and was superior in intelligence to the young bloods of London who frequented the coffeehouses and theaters. Her admiration for Swift and her flattery could not long be resisted by a heart that hungered for admiration. She is never mentioned directly in his journal to Stella.

The condition of the native population of Ireland in Swift's day was unspeakable. Its starving "savages," in the most fertile land in Europe, constituted a blot on the humanity of England that is indelible. For cold callousness England cannot be excelled. "Quite certainly," said the great Bishop, George Berkeley, "there is nowhere so beggarly, wretched and destitute a people as the Irish."

There is not space to go into the horrible details of a prolonged national crime that exceeded the swifter attempts at genocide of our day. The capacity of England's agents for misgoverning is appalling. In one thing they outdo the excesses of any tyranny: their persecutions do not exempt the colonists of their own flesh and blood. It was this injustice, an injustice which included the little Protestant colony in Ireland and not necessarily that against the mere Irish, that filled Swift's breast with *saeva indignatio* against injustice. It could but include, whether he intended it or not, the wrongs of the natives in common with the community of which he was a member.

Swift could exaggerate when occasion rose. He exalted his mother's pedigree from that of a butcher's daughter to a descendant of a family that had fought against the Normans. If Erick was a Norse name, there were Norse in England before the Normans; but there is no evidence that they fought at Hastings. He made his mother a relative of Sir William Temple's wife. This is to account for all the favors he received from Sir William; but it also may be taken as a presumption that he knew he had something to explain.

He was unfair concerning the value of Wood's halfpence. He used exaggeration to help his argument. Most of the fury in Ireland rose not against the token value of the coin, but against the attempt of the king to make the Irish pay for the keep of his German mistress.

His proposal for "The Universal Use of Irish Manufacture" makes him the father of Sinn Fein (Ourselves Alone.) Anent this service of Swift to the Irish, listen to Dr. Johnson, who cannot be regarded as a friendly commentator:

> He taught them first to know their own interest; their weight and strength, and gave them spirit to assert that equality with their fellow subjects, to which ever since they have been making vigorous advances, and to claim those rights which they have at last established.

Here are glimpses of Swift's reaction to the times in which he lived; his attitude toward women and his patriotism. Now let us turn to the talk that still goes on about him in Dublin.

I had been photographing a colored bust of Swift bewigged, which is set above a tavern in Werburgh Street at the corner of Hoey's Court, now a walled-up and dismantled cul-de-sac. I decided to lunch at the Dolphin not far away, where they serve the best lunch in Dublin. There it was my good luck to find two eminent men of letters. One was Denis Johnston, the best of the Abbey Theatre dramatists who survive and an authority on the origin of Swift. The other was Lynn Doyle, the poet and sophisticated writer of many a tale.

Our talk was a causerie of many aspects and incidents in the life of the Dean. "I have always regarded him as a second-rate writer," said Lynn Doyle. I was not surprised, because I knew how exigent the speaker's ideas of great writing were and I had the conflicting opinions of Swift's commentators in mind. For instance, Hume said, "His style contains no harmony, no eloquence, no ornament and not much correctness." Mackintosh calls it, on the other hand, "Proper, pure, concise, perspicacious, significant, nervous." And I remembered my friend Dr. Tyrrell, Professor of Greek in Dublin University, telling how at dinner he sat next to Carlyle and took the opportunity of asking whom he considered to be the best prose writer in the English language. The sage answered without hesitation, "Swift, for his perfect lucidity." With this in mind I asked Lynn Doyle how he came to such a conclusion. "Swift never wrote out of his subconscious," was his answer. To that I had to concede. Had not Dryden testified to it when he said, "Cousin Swift, you will never be a poet." Poetry, in spite of his readiness in rhyme and his multitudinous verses, was as far from Swift as from another great Dublin intellect and master of racy prose, George Bernard Shaw. To neither of them had the vision beautiful been vouchsafed. Think of Shakespeare, Blake, Tennyson, Yeats. I would not have dragged them into such a comparison were it not for Swift's pretensions to the poetic leaf. Arthur Griffith, the father of Sinn Fein and of the Irish Free State, based his incisive writings on Dean Swift.

Denis Johnston was saying, "The Black Book of the King's Inns would repay anyone interested in research of the period. It has not yet been edited. In it we can see the handwriting of Jonathan Swift, who was reputedly the father of the famous Jonathan. Sometimes it is blotted and blurred. The writer was evidently drunk when he wrote in the Black Book. Sometimes there is no entry at all."

I said, "This was the man on whom Sir John Temple wished his mistress, Abigail Erick, when he thought it was time to make provision for her. He was then about sixty-six." Denis Johnston followed, still referring to Abigail Erick's husband, "He disappears from the picture. The entries cease in November, 1666. He died probably during the winter or spring of 1666. On the last day of November following, his widow gave birth to a child—*ten or eleven months later.*"

I thought of how long Jonathan the elder must have been ailing before his death. I thought of the consolation the widow got when she turned to Sir John Temple, her old protector. Enough to make her the mother of his child, who was christened Jonathan to add to the verisimilitude.

Vanessa was the woman of whom I also wanted information. I got it. She followed Swift to Ireland in 1715 in spite of his earnest attempts to dissuade her. She had property in what is now Celbridge Abbey. It was called Marlay Abbey in those days. We do not have to consult Walpole, who was an enemy of Swift, to sense a liaison between the passionate and generous Vanessa and the man who bred true to the Temples. Swift talks of "coffee" in his letters to Vanessa, and we may be sure of its double meaning. And is it not a fact that he never once mentions Vanessa to Stella?

Vanessa wrote to Stella, probably to ask if she was secretly married to the Dean. We know what happened. The Dean came, white with fury, to Marlay Abbey, threw Vanessa's letter upon her bed, and departed. Vanessa left her estate, which had been intended for Dean Swift, to Bishop Berkeley. She survived the incident by only two months.

Stella was not a clinging vine. By no means. She shot a burglar. Undoubtedly she was in love with the Dean (and he with her), but she could not marry him because of the laws of incest, which were strict in both Church and state. It must have been known that they were related. That would account for a lot of things. It would explain why the greatest writer and most devastating satirist of the time and of all time met with no preferment in England where his heart was fixed; and it would explain why he never married.

A Consultation with George Moore

It was not for myself, oh, no! The days when I used to consult the famous author were long past. In the early years he was captious, then he became critical as he grew older. Prejudiced would be the usual word, but it would not be exact. What I want to convey is this: When I came with any writing to consult the oracle, he would put it aside and use the suggestion of literature to open a tirade against far more famous men than I.

Now things were far more favorable. I was informed by telephone that a certain young lady would call on me presently; in fact, she was already on her way. Now don't let me give you the impression that I was not secretly flattered by this visit. I was, to a slight extent; but I could not conceal from myself the fact that it was not primarily to see me she was coming, but to get me to give her an introduction to George Moore. This had been going on for months. Lately the lady was becoming importunate. For a while she would let me flatter myself that she was listening to my literary dissertations; then she would come out with the question, "Then why don't you give me an introduction to George Moore?" Lately it had become, "Why won't you?" I had exhausted all my excuses, the chief of which was, "Seeing that I dare not ask him for an opinion about my own stuff." She had an answer ready, "He is interested in novels. You care only for verse." I remembered that, the last time I consulted him, he laid my manuscript on the table: "I will look this thing over and write to you; but now you must tell me about this fellow Yeats." Thereupon I had to exercise all my ingenuity not to take sides in that age-long rivalry, a thing which I found almost impossible to do. How could anyone give an answer to the question that began, "Now don't you think that is the height of absurdity?" without becoming involved.

So she had arrived. Let me tell you about her. She was just eighteen. She had gone to school in Lausanne. Her father was an American engineer, foremost in spite of the fierce competition in that field. Her mother was French. She was dead, so the motherless girl had been sent off to finishing school in Lausanne. Like many another girl, she was under the impression that her experience was a theme for a novel. It may have been—overlook the pun—it was not a novel experience by any means. One would have thought—I certainly would have trifled with the idea—that the word "finishing" was rather equivocal; but let that rest.

I began—any psychiatrist will tell you that I was suffering from injured pride, "pique" is the word—"You came about that letter to George Moore? Well, here it is. Ebury Street is not far from here. Number 121 is halfway up on your left if you go from Grosvenor Gardens. Don't call until tea time, for he is apt to be irascible if anyone interrupts him while he is writing, 'composing' he calls it. So go along about five o'clock. The lines of strain should have left his face by that time. There's plenty of strain just now, for he has a Greek translating *Daphnis and Chloë* for him."

"And will you be here when I get back?"

Bursting with curiosity though I was, I forced myself to say as nonchalantly as possible, "If I am not, drop me a line." To her letter I owe most of this narrative.

While she was on her way to Ebury Street, I was beset with apprehensions. How would George Moore take her visit? What would he think about my presuming to send him a schoolgirl to consult him about a novel that was not yet written? Would he not think that it was a leg-pull and resent my impertinence for the rest of his life? I took comfort, little enough though it was, in the thought that old men were inclined to be more susceptible to female charms the older they grew: Victor Hugo, for example, who, when he had one foot in the grave, had the other in the housemaid's bedroom. It may be the tendency (modified of course) in the case of George Moore. Let us hope so.

I waited and waited. I thought that she would be unable to refrain from telephoning to me to tell me all about her interview. But the telephone never rang. In a crisis the telephone rings only in detective stories.

It was getting on to seven o'clock. Moore dines at seven-thirty when he is alone. When he is not, he turns dinner into a long diatribe against his cook. So he dines for the most part alone. I could not stand the suspense any longer. I found myself walking down Ebury Street.

I quote her letter:

"When I called the door was opened by a maid. I gave her your note and was shown into a room on the right of the little hall. There were red rep curtains on the bay window. On the mantle piece of black marble stood a bronze French clock with a female figure leaning over the dial. One of the Nine Muses, I suppose. I must have been standing with my back to the door. I heard a soft voice say, 'Won't you be seated?' I looked round and beheld George Moore. His forehead was high and white and large. His hair white and flossy. His . . ." I knew how he looked, so I skipped the description. I am sorry now, for it was a portrait seen through other eyes than mine.

"I was covered with confusion. I must have blushed for his next words were intended to put me at ease. 'You know he's a good fellow'—he was referring to you—'I don't mean *good* in the ecclesiastical sense; but good as a human being. Won't you take off your hat?' I obeyed meekly. When it was off, he exclaimed, 'Ah, you have Kathleen eyes!' How did he know that my name is Kathleen?" Evidently she had forgotten my letter, which of course gave her name.

"'And now tell me what you have come to see me about.' Confusion worse than before, I could hardly speak. What must he think of me. Up to this I had not said a word."

I was getting a little of my own back. Apparently the aspiring novelist was not equal to the occasion. She could not find words to reply.

" 'But you are thinking of writing a novel?' " I must say George Moore was doing his best to help her out.

" 'The important thing about a novel is the story. If you have not got a story, you have nothing to write about. In a novel the story is everything. Now what is your story?' "

In utter bewilderment the aspirant blurted out part of her tale. Moore listened—a thing he never did for me. He even repeated some of her words: "Ah, a finishing school at Lausanne."

He was beginning to appear in a new light to me: patient and encouraging. Suddenly he gave one of his characteristic exclamations,

"Oh, don't use that horrible word! None of us is seduced. We seduce ourselves. However!" It would seem that in her fright my friend tried to amend her story; but that did not help her, for the next utterance of the Master was,

"No, no! A story like that must be written in the first person. You can't have a novel without a story, and you can't tell a personal story indirectly. It must be in the first person. Now let me show you how a story should be written."

She must have found favor, for the narrative proceeds:

"We went to the bookcase in the back room through the folding doors to find the exemplary story; but it could not be found on the shelves, so on our knees together on the floor we searched the lower part of the bookcase; but the book he was looking for was as far away as ever."

"Well, well!" said Moore. "May I get you some tea?"

During tea he talked about his favorite subject, which was himself. And what better subject could he find? *Confessions of a Young Man* and *Memoirs of My Dead Life* were as entertaining and as amusing as fiction should be. Make no mistake about it: no matter what a novelist writes about, the subject is inevitably himself. It may be positively or negatively; but always himself: "*Le style est l'homme.*" Of Moore particularly this was true.

My friend's embarrassment must have eased, for she noticed

that the spout of the Sèvres teapot had been broken in two places and mended with little iron staples. He must have caught her looking at it, for he began by blaming the housemaid. He said that he had sacked her: "A man must be master in his own house."

How I wish I had heard that conversation or monologue. He must have been at his best, as he always was when he had a muse to inspire him besides the one on the clock. He told of his trouble with the Greek who was translating for him. How many times he must have told the Greek in that voice of his which became high-pitched when he became excited, "But that's not English!" That she recounted; but she did not recount the Greek's obvious answer, which he dared not make. I would have made it for him: "How can it be English when it's Greek?"

Perhaps I may have betrayed a mentality like that. It would account for my lack of popularity in Ebury Street.

The situation was beginning to clarify. I could see the pair of them kneeling together on the floor looking for a book that Moore on the floor decided that he wouldn't find. It was in all probability one of the de luxe editions; and his enthusiasm for youth was waning, and the wane was helped by his position on the floor. He had intended to give her something—hence the tea.

I wonder if he read her the first sentence of *Daphnis and Chloë*. It is one of the best sentences he has written and one of the loveliest in the language. How is this it begins?

"The sea flows round Mitylene . . ."

My memory is slipping. So am I. It does not matter. The one thing that matters in this narrative is the result of the consultation. The difficulty of producing a novel must have appalled her. She was not without insight; and Moore was hardly likely to make novel writing appear an easy task.

Nevertheless, it was a fruitful meeting. It showed another side to George Moore, one that never appeared to his male friends. To none else must the credit be given of turning a novice, if not into a novelist, into a lively letter writer to whom I owe an outline of one of the most interesting conversations in Ebury Street which otherwise would have been lost forever.

The Romance of the Tree

The sculptor who was the first to make his statue of the human figure lean more on one foot than the other, and so to introduce a bend or sinuosity into it, made a very great advance in the art of sculpture. He did a thing that nobody had done before him: he outdid all the great sculptors of Egypt. He got away from the original figure, which was nothing but the stump of a tree: you can still see the trace of it in the pediments of busts, and it is significant that no statue of antiquity has the legs crossed. The first statue was the bole of a tree, to which later a mask was attached, because very long ago man in his endeavor to close the gap between all living things held the tree akin to himself. Next he worshiped the indwelling spirit of the tree; and when the tree withered after a lapse of years, he perpetuated its life symbolically by venerating either its bole or a stump fashioned like the bole of a tree, to which a mask was attached. Some of the most venerated statues of antiquity were nothing but stumps. A few exist to the present day, as they existed in druidical times. "Crun Cru and his sub-gods twelve," said Cormac, "are but carven treens." On the life of a tree his well-being and his very life depended:

Tree worship is one of the oldest cults. There are sacred trees flourishing in different parts of the world which, even if they are no longer venerated, are still visited and preserved. Such is the great ginko tree of China, a remnant of the Coal Age.

Primitive man saw in the recurrence of the leaf, the life in its branches, and its outlasting age, something supernatural, and for all we know, a symbol of immortality, in a tree. It may have appealed to some dim sense of beauty within him. Having projected himself into it, he felt a kinship with it. We cannot blame him when we read that Aristotle, "the master of those who know," thought that trees had perception, passions, and reason; and when we see that modern scientists are confronted by phenomena which are forcing them to think on similar lines.

Traces of a tree being bound up with the continuance of human life are not far to seek. The story of Meleager, whose life depended on a beam which his mother rescued from the blazing hearth just before his birth, will recur to the reader. And there is a lovely poem by the too-much-neglected Landor, the poet who wrote the mellifluous verse, "Bees, bees, was it your hydromel under the lindens?" Which tells, though it is somewhat converse to the theme, how a dryad, who as her name reveals dwelt in an oak, died of grief when her favorite bee failed to wing its way back. Dependence of human life on the life of a tree is a lasting sentiment. Lord Byron planted an oak at Newstead, and thought that, as it flourished, so would he.

The oak was among the first of trees to be worshiped. It came before the pine. The druids used its rare parasite the mistletoe ceremoniously. And it was among the last to lose its sacred character; St. Brigid had her chapel under a great oak; both chapel and oak are in the name of what was her shrine, *cella dara*, Kildare. Before St. Brigid and before the druids, there was the oracular oak of Dodona whose attendants slept on the bare ground. It was built into the Argo that carried Jason and his band of heroes in quest of the Golden Fleece.

We are far from the days when consternation seized the Romans because the sacred fig tree of Romulus withered in the Forum; yet the worship of the tree was not done with, for in 895 the Council of Nantes decreed that all trees consecrated to demons should be destroyed. The Council of Nantes contained censors to whom all the gods of old were "demons" and therefore had to be banned. Nevertheless, I could tell of a whitethorn not very far from where I am writing which is bedecked with many colored rags and ribbons, medals and coins. It stands over a well; but as it is a holy well, maybe it is not included in the Edict of Nantes. Now that I come to think of it, there is no need to be overscrupulous about a whitethorn, for the staff of the bringer of the Holy Grail to Britain, Joseph of Arimathea, which was venerated at Glastonbury, was a blackthorn, a shillelagh, which blossoms all white before the leaf.

But what of the Christmas tree, that most outstanding example of all? Neither ban nor proscription can effect it. It has brought more joy to youth than any other emblem in the world. It came from the depths of German forests and its worship spread all over Christendom. *Der tannenbaum!* We hang presents on it. Does it matter whether or not the presents originally represented offerings to the tree or to the spirit of the tree, and then became the perquisite of those who tended it? We exchange presents amid rejoicing that the year's darkness is growing into light; and that life is returning to all that grows. Evidently it was easier to convert the tree than to denounce its celebration. But was the tree converted? If you wish to load this article with cumbersome scholarship, you will find that the tree converted Christmas. The first mention of the twenty-fifth of December is by Theophilus of Antioch, second century, and is probably spurious; and Origen in the third century did not want Christmas, for he denounced as sinful the celebration of the birthday of our Lord, "as if he were a king Pharaoh." The fir tree has come out victorious, and with it the Yule log. It is very hard to think of Christmas without a Christmas tree. It has survived a lot of bigoted opposition, including the worst gang of all, the English Puritans, who in Cromwell's day forbade by law any celebration of Christmas, or any rejoicing (they would) at that time of year. The Scots Puritans sided with them; that is why Scotland is such a sorry place on Christmas Day.

There was a time when I could not look at a shovel with its smooth ash handle without thinking of the great ash spear of Achilles, mountain-grown, the death of Hector. I knew, and I know still, that it takes a fork of witch hazel to divine water, for I failed when the owner of the proper wands succeeded; and I know that a twig of rowan will guard you against the fairies.

But let us now turn from tree worship to the romance of trees in poetry. Spenser was the first in English to catalogue them and to qualify them by adjectives which are commentaries in themselves. Take "the builder oak, sole king of forests all." What an adjective! It says everything. It includes the stately roofs of England as well as the navy, those "hearts of oak"; but I am more attracted by the loveliest of lines,

The yew obedient to the bender's will.

Let us forget Agincourt, Crécy, Poitiers, and all the battles that were won by that special artillery of England, and come down to times more intimate, to the time of the inspired gossip John Aubrey who has included in his *Brief Lives*, lines from the heyday of poetry. It is true that they are *vers d'occasion;* but they are not doggerel—it may have been impossible to have written doggerel then—and they concern a wonderful lady who was an irresistible beauty with eyes wondrous wanton! and

Face she had of filbert hue,
And breasted like a swan;
Back she had of bended yew . . .

That's enough! "Bended yew." It recalls Yeats' "beauty like a bended bow." To a mere surface anatomist it is evidence that the post-Elizabethans and the courtiers of Charles II could see beauty in a back that was not straight as a ramrod but "of bended yew."

One of the best lines of the poet Waller refers to Apollo's pursuit of Daphne, who, as she fled from him, was turned by her mother into a bay laurel:

He catch'd at love and filled his arms with bays.

A line that leaves us with the double thought, the metamorphosis of the maiden, and the metamorphosis of the lover into a poet through his loss. The laurel is sacred to Apollo since then. There is little comfort in that; but then Apollo had other nymphs less coy to console him, for he was the "god to whom all music and song and love are pure." And musicians have a way with them even to the present day.

There was a tree in Persia which grew over the tomb of Tan-Sein, the chewing of a leaf of which conferred the gift of a divine melody of voice; and there are oak trees, including Tennyson's Talking Oak, the leaves of which are melodies in themselves; and in Heaven there is a mystic tree under which the Blessed Damosel dreams of meeting her lover, the leaves of which can utter the Divine Name:

We two will lie i' the shadow of
That living, mystic tree
Within whose secret growth the Dove
Is sometimes felt to be;
While every leaf that His plumes touch
Saith His Name audibly.

In Scandinavian mythology there is another mystic tree, the ash Yggdrasill, which holds together hell, earth, and heaven. Like the apple in the Garden of Paradise, it is the tree of life, knowledge, and fate. Odin hung from it for nine days offering himself to himself. This is not a satirical symbol of a dictator pretending to benefit the people when he is all the time helping himself, nor giving his *all* for his country, which is the same thing. In spite of the myth's coming from the fierce North, the tree sheds honeydew.

My favorite tree is an apple, preferably a mossy one in an old garden which has long escaped the gardener's restricting shears. I like to lie under its boughs with their little branches all akimbo, set anglewise against each other, so that I may dream of the disparity of all philosophies and of the futility of all who would reduce Nature to a rule and prune away its extravagances and its waste. I am not forgetful of the story that it was an apple that made man self-conscious and made him realize what happiness could be, for without something with which to contrast it, how could he know what it was?

It was an apple that caused such discord among the three Graces, and made wisdom and dignity yield to beauty when the shepherd of Mount Ida awarded the golden pippin to Venus.

The letters of the Gaelic language are the names of trees. In the fourth century there was the Battle of the Trees by contending bards in Wales. It was fought to decide whether the secret language which was proper to the higher poets should be revealed to the lesser and more vulgar bards: a war full of mystery but happily limited to jealous professors, like a dispute between dons of the same university. This was a battle that long preceded the *Battle of the Books*, which Dean Swift wrote for his patron (and uncle) Sir William Temple. But let me go back to the Talking Oak that told in our own day of the beauties its old spirit had seen:

The slight—she slips of loyal blood,
And others; passing praise,
Strait-laced, but all too fair in bud
For puritanic stays:

And I have shadowed many a group
Of beauties that were born
In tea-cup times of hood and hoop,
Or while the patch was worn.

And the oak goes on to tell of the days

Whereof the poets talk
When that, which breathes within the leaf
Could slip its bark and walk.

Dryads, of course.

By the elm woods and the oaken
Glades where Phoebus harped of old;
And the wild things gathered to him
And the woods and waters knew him,
As he harped amidst the broken
Dells, his music manifold . . .

So Gilbert Murray in his exquisite verse translates Euripides; but there must be elm trees in Greece, though I saw none. They are abundant in Italy for there they are the supports of the Vine. Anyway, who would restrict a poet's license?

There was no gap between Phoebus and external nature:

The woods and waters knew him.

Of trees in winter, Shakespeare has said everything in that poetry-rammed line,

Bare ruined choirs where late the sweet birds sang.

It reminds me of the subterfuge by which I roused the poet, the late Sir William Watson, from his gloom. It was very simple; I misquoted the line. I said, "Where *once* the sweet birds sang." Immediately he threw off his melancholy. A great line was being murdered. He corrected me. Little did he think that the conversation which followed on his favorite subject and on those who presumed to be poets had been carefully planned.

Sometimes, as of late, we find trees, or rather shrubs, compensating each other, as when the expressed juice of the juniper berry is used in the ritual of Venus. This may be obscure; what I mean is the use of gin in a cocktail to promote an amorous mood, and one not without romance. But this is rather banal—we cannot mix juniper and myrtle. They are shrubs. Let us keep to trees.

Of trees in summer, what gives the sentiment of the green wood in the long English spring better than these lines from one of the ballads of Robin Hood?

In Summer when the shaws be sheen
And the leaves be large and long.

You will search English poetry in vain to get the equal of the eye that saw with Homeric objectivity the leaves as *large and long.*

Sherwood and Barnesdale are the forests behind all the pastoral poetry of England. They merge into the Forest of Arden; they provide all the greenery of the poems of Keats.

The tree is as mysterious and as romantic as life itself; and it is nearer to Nature: "One impulse from a vernal wood will teach us more of Man." Even if this were not so on the sentimental and spiritual side, materially, the tree possesses the essential substance, chlorophyll, on which our life depends; so they were not very far wrong in principle, however odd they appear in practice, who chose trees as objects of their worship.

The World of Robert Flaherty

Revillon Frères got the idea that it would be a good thing to make a movie of the fur industry in the wilds of Hudson Bay. So they chose Robert Flaherty, because the district was well known to him. He was to go there and be back in eight weeks. He was back in eighteen months. Here is what happened: He met Nanook, an Eskimo, and he made a film called *Nanook of the North*. When he returned, it was to find that no one knew him in Revillon Frères, and he was left with the film on his hands. At long last he managed to anchor it to another movie. After a while somebody came along and said that if he could separate his movie from the other one, it would do well. The prophecy proved very well: *Nanook of the North* has been running without a break in different parts of the world since then, and that is near four decades ago.

Bob Flaherty was the father of the documentary film. He was the first to realize its power. It could break through the barrier of language and bring men together as nothing before it had ever done.

This and his faith in human nature made Bob Flaherty great. There was about him something of the innocence of a child, and all a child's enthusiasm.

I have seen geniuses whose presence in a room was like that of a dynamo. They emanated a feeling of power; but power can be an implacable thing. With Bob Flaherty it was different: goodness and geniality shone from him, and his companions shared it. The note of him was joy.

He had a big head and the hair on it was white. His face was pink. His blue eyes were clear as ice. His smile welcomed you. He believed, and you could feel it, that there was a hero hidden in us all. He loved to be surrounded by unmelancholy people, people as simple and as straightforward as himself. That is why he felt the need of scenes where man is elemental and unspoiled. For this he traveled to the unspoiled places on the earth.

He was born at Iron Mountain, Michigan, the eldest of six children. His father was a mining engineer. He spent his youth exploring and mapping uncharted regions of northern Canada. It was during one of these expeditions that he rediscovered an island with a lake and people living on it that was marked as only a pin point on the naval maps. The island is in the Belcher group in Hudson Bay. The Canadian government named it Flaherty's Island. When asked about it, "It has two horizons," he would say.

The abiding cold, the monstrous storms, and great privations amounting to starvation, Flaherty underwent with his Eskimo friend Nanook (Bear). He spent a year, 1920 to 1921, making the picture *Nanook of the North.* Its running is unprecedented.

In *Nanook of the North* can be seen the best photograph of animals ever taken; that which shows walruses coming out of the depths to help their harpooned comrade.

From the frozen North, Flaherty's next trip was to Safune on the tropical island of Savaii in the Samoan group. He made *Moana of the South Seas.* Here he met the most extraordinary character he had ever known, a man originally intended by his father for the German army. But he thought he had a voice fit for opera. So, in spite of his father's wishes, he went to the South Seas. He would come out on his balcony in the evening and sing a whole opera before (he thought) an appreciative audience; while the assembled natives thought it was the devil struggling to come out of him.

Flaherty went to Ireland in 1932 and bought a cottage in the outpost of Europe, the islands of Aran in Galway Bay. He had met somebody on a boat who told him that the natives of Aran had to break stones to make land and they fertilized it with seaweed. They lived on fish and potatoes. He could not rest until he got there. *Man of Aran* shows the struggle for life of a very old and primitive people living on the treeless limestone rock of the three Aran islands. Here men struggle for existence in their tarred curraghs, as they call their canoes, against great seas which crash for the first time against the coast of Europe. "They come against the limestone precipice after their long journey all the way from Brazil," as Flaherty loved to tell.

He won honors at Venice for *Man of Aran;* and he became internationally famous.

Tiger King was the hero of *Man of Aran.* In fact, he was the Aran man himself. Tall and spare, with deep-set eyes under a fine forehead crowned with dark curly hair, he well knew how to keep his curragh's head three points off the stormy waves that had come from so far. He knew how to keep the sweeps by which the curragh was propelled sunk in the sea so that their blades, thin as they were, would not catch the wind. So it was all the more amusing and characteristic when Bernard Shaw was sitting for some sculptor and Tiger King was sent to keep the old man quiet, to learn that Tiger King emerged with a lesson on how to row a curragh! That was in 1934.

He spent a year in London in 1938. Close by the studio he rented in Chelsea, London, was a house in which four Scotsmen used to meet on Friday nights. They discussed molds. One of them was Alexander Fleming, the discoverer of penicillin.

Flaherty and his wife did work for the government in demonstrating the destruction caused by erosion. Farmers were told to plow in circles instead of up and down. Flaherty used a helicopter to photograph the land.

He loved to give an occasional dinner at the Coffee House Club. He would sit at the round table at the end of the room and you did not know whether you were telling the story or he. (I could not help comparing him to Shaw, who used to dominate the table until it was hushed for the oracle to hold forth.) He said—I remember it so well—"When our vices leave us, we flatter ourselves that we have left them." Everyone laughed. "Oh, no," Bob said, "you must not give me credit for that. It was said by some Frenchman. Probably La Rochefoucauld."

He had no feeling for money. Once in a famous restaurant he threw a twenty-dollar bill on the table and said to his companion, "Let's get out of this. Oh, the pressure of the waiters." Afterward they both settled for sixty-five cents' worth of ham and eggs.

He had two chances of becoming rich and missed them both. Once, when surveying for the Canadian government, he came across a rocky outcrop of an unknown formation. He left his sleigh and with a hammer broke off about a score of the crystals, which he put in a little bag. Twenty years later he found the bag in the drawer of a desk; and the incident came back to him. He took the crystals to a lapidary who worked for a world-famous firm of jewelers on Fifth Avenue, New York. The lapidary told him that the crystals were unique. They were both dextrorotatory and levorotatory; that is, they could turn a plane of polarized light to left or right. But they were too rare to be salable.

On another occasion he was present when a Polynesian diver came up with the largest pearl ever seen. Unfortunately, it was not round but pear-shaped, so it could be bought for a few dollars. While Flaherty was hesitating, a French buyer got ahead of him and bought the pearl. He had a client in Paris who would give anything for a pearl that was unique: the largest pearl in the world.

Though not concerned with enriching himself, he took care to enrich us all. No one can see the beginning of his last picture, *Louisiana Story,* without feeling endowed, as it were, with a glimpse of a byway in Paradise.

His ability to make an untrained child act and respond meant that he had something of the child in him, a child's wonder, a child's interest in things we take for granted, the quality of water for instance; an eye that looked with a child's freshness at the world.

When someone brought up the subject of diplomacy, he would

say, "If they only told the truth." That meant he would sweep away the "language of diplomacy," the language of double talk that leads to war. Think of what it would mean: the training of a diplomat would be the first thing to go. And to train a successful diplomat is a matter of a lifetime. Then the language of diplomacy, a language that it takes years to learn. A language that so sickens people that they prefer war to it. Perhaps that is the achievement of diplomacy.

Now it takes a particular gift of pomposity to make a successful diplomat. Lord Curzon in the old days was peculiarly suited to diplomacy. Even in Oxford, where he wasn't thought much of, there was a rhyme about him: "George Nathaniel Curzon, A most superior person." There was only one road open to him after that and he filled it well. Anthony Eden fits well into the picture, as the recent threat to Egypt so well bears out. But give him his due, he should have stuck to soldiering. He was mentioned in dispatches, and for a diplomat that is not done. The newspapers, yes, every day; but dispatches, no. And Winston should have stuck to politics, for which he was pre-eminently suited, instead of imagining, as Lord Alanbrooke said, "That the mantle of Marlboro had fallen on him."

Yes; Winston should have stuck to politics.

Diplomats get a lot of traveling. They meet ambassadors, generals, and dictators. It is a good way to take advantage of dullness because dullness is the larger part of diplomacy. Brains should not be mixed in it. That is why I don't recommend it to Churchill. But it's rather late.

Flaherty's home in lovely Vermont was simple and very well kept: thanks to Mrs. Flaherty, very well indeed. "It is about twelve hundred feet up on a mountain shelf and there is a pine wood three hundred feet higher still." That is how he described his home to me when he invited me to spend a few days with him. After lunch, someone asked him how long I was staying (as if it was any business of theirs). "For the summer," Bob said.

The great living room looked out west to Mount Stratton, forty miles away. Between, the intervening mountains undulated, wooded to their crests.

"He was a difficult man to live with—he was so restless, so full of ideas," Mrs. Flaherty said in the recent telecast, "The World of Robert Flaherty." I remember his restlessness. We were flying from London to Dublin. We were about an hour out when Bob said suddenly, "I can't stand this!" and he started to rise as if to get out. Jokingly I said, for I did not take it seriously, "Watch your step! It's five thousand feet down and it's sloppy underfoot."

Peter Freuchen, the winner of a "$64,000 Question," who helped to make the telecast, said of Bob, "You people are film makers. To me Bob Flaherty was an explorer. His name is legend in the North. He is right there on the maps. It may be a fine thing to make a movie. But show me the first white man to cross Labrador on foot. That's a man!"

Memory is linked to sadness at the departure of great men. From that sadness we refuse to be divorced, because with it lies the memory of greatness, and the memory of greatness renews our faith in human nature.

Over the fireplace in Vermont is engraved, in Gaelic characters, WANDER NO MORE, a fitting sentiment for the man of many wanderings now that he is at rest.

The Rehabilitation of Abington Talmey

"For a mathematician he is almost a gentleman."

Jan and I followed Professor Talmey's gaze as he looked out upon the College quadrangle that was bounded on two sides by the gray buildings of Trinity College, each with its little separate front lawn on which stood a great holm oak with spreading branches. The third side was open; in its center rose the graceful Campanile. Beyond it and its larger lawns, a rose-red group of houses built in the days of Queen Anne closed the perspective. The quadrangle was paved with cobblestones. Across it, as we gazed, a stumpy figure came striding; his blown-back gown exposed striped trousers. On his head, above a stout nose and an undomed forehead as high as Bernard Shaw's, a mortarboard rested. Its texture was of velvet. The wearer was the Provost.

Our gaze returned to our friend. For my part I had some misgivings; for it is, to say the least, an undiplomatic if not a dangerous thing to criticize the head of a college adversely. What Jan thought I could not tell, but his silence suggested surprise from which I deduced that his feelings were similar to my own.

"The Greeks had no mathematics, which, as you know, has come to mean 'science.' They had a smattering of Phoenician jugglery. The Phoenicians were businessmen, so whatever they added up added nothing to the humanities. They were prototypes of those who think that by gazing into a microscope they will find good manners, or by working a dynamo, culture."

Dr. Talmey smiled and, sighing slightly, buried his face in his glass again. It seemed that he had had a hard day. His appointment as Registrar was beginning to weigh upon him. He had been appointed nearly a week. The discovery of thirteen forgotten bottles of Bass, implemented by two flagons of Marsala found behind the shutters as he was preparing for a nap after lunch, alleviated for the moment the cares of office.

There was yet an hour to spare before the Board meeting. Now it seems that the older the university, the less the work of the Board. Oxford and Cambridge have no Board meetings, though every college which forms the university may have a Board of its own. Dublin University has only one college, that is the College of the Holy and Undivided Trinity, hence its concentration on its Board. But why cross your bridges before you come to them? We had yet an hour to kill.

"As I was saying," the Professor continued, "this wine comes from the southwest corner of Sicily, where the grape is so abundant that the natives never think of fortifying it with the cheap and trashy brandy that is put into so many light wines to help them on their journey overseas. It has a somewhat sulphurous aroma; but on the whole, it is not unpalatable. I would rather discuss it than any subject with Tom Thompson Ney." He smiled indulgently on Jan.

Now Tom Thompson Ney was, like the Professor, a member of the Board; otherwise they had nothing in common. His prejudices had formed his face, thus illustrating the Platonic principle that "soul is form." He was tall and gaunt and black-a-vised. He made me think of some mute, inglorious Pilgrim father, with an accent on the "grim." He was a personification of disapproval and social severity. If any proof were needed, let it suffice to say that his portrait by Orpen was the chief distinction, boast, and camouflage of the Friendly Brothers' Club. Tom Thompson Ney—could anyone with such a character have an apter name?

I took it that he was another mathematician. I could not help feeling that the lack of sympathy this implied made him all the more formidable as a member of the Board.

Again I gazed through the window. A tall, leaning figure with a colorless face, nondescript mustache, and chalk-blue eyes as opaque as those of an electric eel came hurrying. My tutor! After an interval another figure, taller and far more distinguished, appeared and leisurely entered the small door that led to the Provost's House. I knew it at once. Who could mistake the great Mahaffy, that sweetly cynical man? "The Greeks never hurried." He was acting on that aphorism now. The philosopher without effeminacy! I recalled the plaque recently presented to him, in the rooms of his friend the Professor of Moral Philosophy, with the Greek quotation under it: *Philosophoumein aneu malakias.* I thought of his pupils, J. B. Bury, now Professor of History in Cambridge, and the more widely known Oscar Wilde. They both lacked the authority and large urbanity of their master. Now comes a tall figure dipping gently to one side like a yacht in a light breeze—Fitzooth, Professor of Moral Philosophy.

Behind me I could hear the pleasant drone of Dr. Talmey's voice. He was talking about a system; and Jan was acquiescing in that hesitating way he had.

Suddenly the significance of the appearance of these men bound for the same goal dawned on me. We had *no* hour to kill. There was *no* time to spare. The Board was about to meet. How time flies! I spoke to Jan and tapped my watch. That brought him to his senses. We broke the news to the Professor. "Remember, sir, you are secretary to the Board," Jan said. "Dear me," he sighed, "I suppose I must yield myself up." We helped him into his gown. There was some difficulty with the sleeve. There would be when every minute was important. Together we went down the stairs. We were hardly in the hall when Jan said, "We have forgotten his cap. Go back for it." I was prepared to return, but then there came the question of the door key. The Professor, wrapped in his gown, with difficulty searched his pockets. He found nothing but some loose coins and a tram ticket. He stood undecided in the entry. "I think we'll pass crownless," he said. Jan hesitated. But the Professor began to move. "Some on boards, some on pieces of the wreck," he quoted.

We watched the portly figure with the magnificent profile as he walked along the wall. His full-skirted gray frock coat was hidden by the gown he wore. Hidden too was the gold oval ring, ornamented by a four-horse chariot, that contained his dark red tie. His back was turned, his left hand was laid across it palm outward, as he ambled purposefully along. Then he entered the little door and passed out of sight.

"Why did you not think of his cap?" Jan asked. "He'll walk into the boardroom without a cap; and you know what sticklers for decorum the Senior Fellows can be."

"I never thought of it," I confessed. "Only for me, you would have kept on talking until long after the Board had met. It was I who was watching the time."

It was not exactly true. I was watching the Fellows crossing the quad when it dawned on me that they were foregathering for the meeting. Yet that the situation was saved was due to me.

"Another thing. If we had not brought him back after lunch, he might have had his usual nap and missed the meeting altogether."

Jan thought awhile. Then he said, "At lunch he had several whiskies with his lobster. Don't you think that the bottles of Bass, not to mention the Marsala . . ."

"Nonsense," I said. "You may remember the answer he gave you when you drew his attention to whisky with lobster, 'I always let my stomach fight it out.' That should reassure you. There was Porson in Cambridge, also a professor of Greek, who invented Porson's pause in spite of the fact that here was one thing at which he never paused. His '*oude tode, oude talla*' when the candle fell into the empty whisky barrel has gone the rounds. A few drinks are nothing unusual for a scholar and a gentleman."

"All right! All right! You are always optimistic," said Jan.

We walked in the direction of College Park—past the great Library, past the Engineering School of which Jan was a member, full of "science" though it was, and out beside the spreading green which extended to the Back Gate.

"Did you hear of his 'system'?" Jan asked.

"No. Tell me," I replied.

"Well, it seems that now that he is Registrar he puts the letters which require an answer on one side of his desk, those which do not require an answer on the other side, and *the rest* there." Jan pointed his finger at the center of an imaginary desk.

This plunged me deep in thought. I did not like to give up the problem at once. I knew that there was no mathematical catch in it, for it came from Dr. Talmey. Nevertheless it was disconcerting not to be able to solve the riddle of letters which remained after those that required an answer and those that did not.

After a long pause, "I give up," I said.

"I gave it up too," said Jan, "until I thought that 'the rest' referred to the letters he had answered and forgotten that he had answered, or those that he had not opened at all."

The solution was so simple that I was, I must admit, a little rattled; but then Jan was an engineer and to him such problems were easy, negative values and so on; Yogi stuff like the invention of zero: all below the belt, so to speak. I changed the subject, retired to a neutral corner, which is the only thing to do when you are all but down and out.

"Why do they have Boards at all? I can understand that the College wishes to keep track of its Senior Fellows, otherwise they might be dead from sleeping sickness and nobody would be any wiser. But otherwise one might think that a college as old as this would run automatically by now. A hundred years ago it must have been deadly dull, with church going from morning to night to herd them together; and Tom Thompson Ney all over the place. And then, of course, the frantic, spasmodic reactions to so much discipline."

Jan mumbled and hesitated, stuttered a little. At last he spoke.

"That's just it," he said. Again he muttered in a way that made a statement ominous.

"What are you talking about? Your muttering is enough to make anyone self-conscious. No wonder that the Professor of Moral Philosophy feels guilty at the very sight of you. Explain." I was getting short-tempered with my friend's manner. He could not help it. That I knew. But sometimes he could get on my nerves.

He shut up for a while; and I feared that I had offended him until he said, "What I meant was that you were right about the reaction to discipline. Do you know what this Board is meeting about?"

I was interested immediately.

"It's sitting on the conduct of the Professor of Romance Languages, and of Theocratis, the Greek who lives in the corner of the Queen Anne Building."

"Oh!" I exclaimed.

"Yes. It seems that the parents of some lady student wrote a letter complaining angrily about the way the Professor of Romance Languages illustrated the performances in Provençal Courts of Love . . ."

"It's a pity that Dr. Talmey was not the recipient of that letter," I suggested.

"It was a week before his appointment."

"Why did she take Romance languages if she couldn't take the romance?"

But Jan went on.

"The Greek student, I hear, was astonished. He explained to the Provost, who had him up, that it was not unusual in his country to have one if not two girls in his rooms to comfort him before any trying emotional experience such as an examination."

Ho, I thought, it will go badly with him. The rules against bringing women into College are pretty strict. There was only one Greek student in College. There were many students of Greek; but only one from Greece. I knew him.

"It will go hard with him," I said, "if he is the fellow who unintentionally nonplused Mahaffy at an examination in Greek, when he was asked with characteristic sarcasm, 'Where did you come by that pronunciation?' 'In Athens, sir.' "

However, I took heart for, as I told Jan, there never has been an expulsion of a don from College, at least in our time. What they did with themselves in the days of old, I know not; but I think that they had to avoid scandal then even more than at present.

"The usual reprimand for the Romantic; and rooms outside College for the Greek."

"Let us be fair," I began. "It must be an anxious thing for the Board to preserve discipline and keep up the name for probity and respectability which parents expect from the College. The Board has to preserve the good name of the institution, for on that good name the value of a degree depends . . ."

For a while there was no comment from Jan. It would not have mattered, perhaps it would have been just as well had he not spoken at all, for his answer was somewhat frivolous.

"Respectability and dullness are so alike that I often wonder if they are not twins."

We sat and waited where it was pleasant to sit and wait; but night fell and our dinner hour approached. Before we left Mr. Murtagh, the proprietor whispered, "You have heard, of course, that the Board meeting is to be resumed tomorrow?" We had not.

"Extraordinary!" I exclaimed.

"You are right. It is an extraordinary session," said Jan.

It was four days later, for the week-end had intervened and the week-end does not count, when we found Dr. Talmey again. He had been absent from his usual haunts; and we had grown anxious. The hall porters were concerned too. Did they look askance at Jan and me? After a good deal of reticence, for theirs was "the constant service of the antique world," it was conveyed to us that we might find him in his rooms.

The rooms were gloomy, and so was the Professor. At first we thought that he was asleep until he spoke dejectedly.

"Well, my friends, won't you sit down?"

He had not even been reading, for his gold-rimmed eyeglass hung down on his waistcoat, and there was not a book on the table at his side though on it fell the only light that was in the room.

"You may as well open the shutters," he said.

The light seemed to clear the room, though it failed to dispel the gloom that surrounded Dr. Talmey. We were both loath to ask questions, though for my part, I was full of curiosity. It was all I could do to stop myself from blurting out, "What happened?" Jan's habit of muttering as if to himself apparently affected the Professor, for he volunteered to tell us of the proceedings of the Board.

"The first day was a blank so far as I was concerned because, after reading the minutes and listening to a long harangue from the Provost and Tom Thompson Ney, to tell you the truth, I fell asleep. When I awoke there was a diatribe from the Provost, which it seemed was directed against myself.

" 'No minutes,' he roared, 'and our whole meeting has gone for nothing. Talmey, you are the Registrar, and you were asleep. Your conduct is inexcusable.'

" 'I don't like listening to scandal,' I remarked. But instead of placating him it only made him worse. 'You call a plenary, a disciplinary meeting of the Board, scandal?' "

So he did fall asleep and Jan's anxiety was warranted, I thought.

"Now I don't mind the Provost. After all, he is chairman of the Board; but I do mind Tom Thompson Ney, who could have let the Provost get it off his chest without putting in his spoke to injure me personally. He is a vindictive and a mean creature. 'Talmey,' he said, 'if you cannot keep awake at a Board meeting, you should resign. I do not intend to let this dereliction of duty pass. I will frame a motion for our next Board meeting to that effect.' So you see I may have to resign, and you know what that would mean to my family and to me . . ."

"Of course it had to be Ney," Jan said.

"Mathematics is the science which draws necessary conclusions," I quoted B. Peirce. "And like Ney, he is one of them. You fell among scientists, sir," I remarked, hoping to rally him into his old form. He smiled only faintly. After a pause, he brightened and with a sign of his hand toward a cupboard under a bookcase, "We might float our intellects into sunnier waters." Jan brought out the decanter, hemming and hawing as he did so. When he had served us, he lifted his glass and said, "There cannot be another Board for a fortnight. Here's to the confusion of Ney." To that we drank. The Professor became confidential.

"The Board, adopting the motion of the Reverend George Bellows, have decided to install an organ into the rooms of Theocratis." He smiled delightfully.

"To exorcise the rooms, no doubt," I suggested.

"To me it seems a homeopathic procedure," he said.

"Inverted, surely," Jan said. "They would drive out the effects of the smaller by the larger, if you see what I mean. Usually it is a hair of the dog. In this case they are introducing a mastiff to cure a hair."

For my part I did not dare risk a pun.

Dr. Talmey continued, "Mahaffy, though there is no love lost between us, stood up for me when he saw that Ney was determined on victimization. He was more than usually sarcastic.

" 'Ney would murder sleep,' he said.

" 'But he has left us without minutes!' Ney insisted.

" 'Have we not reached decisions without them? We do not want every peccadillo that occurs in College recorded in black and white. He who makes an occasional mistake does more for truth than the pedant who spends all his life trying to appear infallible.' If that wasn't a slap in Ney's face, I would like to know for whom 'trying to appear infallible' was intended. Nevertheless, if Ney perseveres in his motion against me and the Board supports him, I shall have to retire . . ."

Jan counted on his fingers: "But you have Mahaffy, and the Professor of Moral Philosophy, Smithers, is a gentleman. How will Wilkins vote?"

"Oh, for goodness' sake, Jan, don't let us take it for granted that it will ever come to a vote," I said, for I wanted to keep our friend's mind from revolving things to come. We had a long way to go before the next Board; and there were many wires that could be pulled, provided always that Jan and I kept out of it. We were much younger than the Professor; and we could not say whether he was, like Socrates, regarded as a corrupter of youth, or whether we were regarded as "bad companions" for "encouraging" him.

Together we took the tram. Dr. Talmey sat near the door. He paid for all three. When the conductor gave him a handful of pennies in change and turned away, "But, oh! the heavy change, now thou art gone," the Doctor quoted. His old form was returning. We got out at Stephen's Green and left him on his homeward way.

"The estimation of the public is everything," I said to Jan; but he was alert. He recognized the symptoms; and he turned a deaf ear, so I had to go on cogitating to myself:

"A certain aroma still lingers about learning in the mind of the people, the same mind that of old looked upon grammar as a kind of magic, grammarie. It surrounds universities and endows them with a romance that is more magical the farther it goes back and the dimmer it grows. That is why there is such a value in Tradition; the older a university is the more reverence it gains in the eyes of the public, and the more influential are its degrees, for Tradition stands for culture. Without this tradition, a university is no better than a big school or degree-confirming syndicate, the degrees of which are not respected by the majority of men. I see a paradox on the mental horizon—tradition can become more important than a degree. Otherwise, that collection of examining booths called The Royal University, which holds stiffer examinations than any of the old three, Oxford, Cambridge, and the Silent Sister, which is Trinity College, Dublin, would take precedence. It comes to this, then—the degree is not as important as Tradition. Scholarship without culture can be a form of vulgarity."

It was soon over. I stopped cogitating, so I was able to converse with Jan.

It was agreed that he would find out from his Professor how the voting on Ney's motion versus Dr. Talmey was likely to go. Meanwhile I would have a few words with my friend Fitzooth.

The Professor of Moral Philosophy received me blandly. "Sauterne," he said, "is more suited to the morning than Guinness' stout."

When the bottle was finished, I broached—not another bottle, as you might in your haste think—the subject.

"I am afraid that the venerably dull members of the Board have agreed to support their fellow Tom Thompson Ney in this matter. Very much afraid. I do not wish to disappoint you, my dear chap; but I can hold out no hope, no hope at all. It is the culmination of much resentment."

Despondency fell upon me. I was more despondent because of my friend than I could possibly be about myself, and yet I am not by any means an altruist. Strange that I could be sorrier for a friend than for myself. Was it because I could not believe that circumstances could possibly affect me?

I remember gazing stupidly at the wall of the philosopher's room. A colored print of a marriage feast and the newly presented plaque to him who philosophized without effeminacy, though he could be sarcastic in a genial way when the spirit moved him. I recalled his crushing question to a man who was urging the respect due to a *descendant* of Dean Swift: "By whom? Stella or Vanessa?"

Mahaffy was superior to the chances and changes of this mortal state; not so Dr. Talmey.

"Who did that?" I inquired, pointing to the plaque on the wall.

"Some little *émigré* sculptor called Brissac, who lives in Stephen's Green. We gave him the commission because he was recommended to us as a promising artist. He is still in the promissory stage, as you can see for yourself." The Professor smiled his sad and gentle smile.

Jan had a smiling face when I met him. He made me think of the Frenchman who said, "There is something not altogether unpleasing in the misfortunes of our friends."

But Jan was, in spite of his intermittent way of speaking, sincerely concerned. We exchanged notes. It was evident that there was no hope for our friend.

What goes on in the mind; and what has time got to say to

it? Is it because it is immortal that it takes its time? Why should there be such a thing as a doorstep witticism! That is, something that you think of when the opportunity has passed.

The opportunity for putting my plan for saving Dr. Talmey into immediate execution was almost lost. It came to me suddenly: not too late, thank goodness!

"The problem is as good as solved," I said.

"Oh, is it?" Jan answered incredulously.

"Listen, will you? You know that plaque which his friends presented to Mahaffy on his birthday? Very well. If we can get one like it done of the doctor and get a splurge into the daily papers and build him up in such a way before the Board meets that it will think twice before putting a petty domestic, splenetic quarrel before world-wide publicity, the thing is done. Any board would be disgraced, and so would the university that persevered in calling for the resignation of such a distinguished scholar. Why, man, he is Honorary Doctor of Literature in Cambridge University, Doctor of Common Law in Oxford, L.L.D. of Edinburgh, Doctor of Literature in Queen's University, and Fellow of the Royal Academy of Letters, and something else in the University of Durham."

Jan was not carried off his feet; but for an engineering student he was quite flexible. He said that he would be round to see me. I told him to fix the commission up with Brissac while he was on his way. No time to spare. This was Wednesday, and the Board would meet on Tuesday. Yes; yes, I would take care of the publicity. But we would have to keep well out of it. Consent? Of course we would get the Doctor's consent. It was tantamount to consenting to be saved.

Jan was quite right. I am thoughtless. He pointed out that we could not present the case to the Doctor as I had presented it to him, Jan. We could not expect the Doctor to enter into what was more or less a conspiracy without loss of self-respect. No. We would have to proceed as if the idea cropped up in the ordinary course of events. We would have to get a few names to preside over the unveiling and the presentation, including the editors of the dailies and the London correspondents of the same. I was to see the Doctor as early as possible in the morning. Jan would drop in during our talk.

When an idea impinges on me, I am at first exalted, then the impact of the idea causes me to pass into shock. As a result of this I felt listless when I called on the Doctor. I found him in a state of dejection, if not of despondency, and in an irritable mood which with him took on a sarcastic phase.

He was reading some comments that Mahaffy had sent to the daily paper about some poor old woman whom the superstitious villagers had buried alive because they thought that she was a witch. Little did I know, though I might have guessed it, that the village in question was the village in which the Doctor's father had had his parish.

"After all," he said quietly as he laid down the paper, "it is only a question of premature burial, which is not such an obnoxious thing as delayed burial, which Mahaffy so obtrusively represents." His bitterness doubtless came from his trouble.

"Well, you cannot say with Shakespeare that she is one of those inhabitants of earth who 'yet are on't.' Perhaps it was she who 'set the ministers of hell at work.' I am thinking of the obsession of Tom Thompson . . ."

But the Doctor was more interested in the source of the latter quotation than in its application. I told him that it was from Rowe's *Jane Shore*. I thought of Jowett's definition of a scholar as one who could point to his references. That is why the Doctor had to get my quotation right.

"By the way," I went on carelessly, "there are certain friends of yours who want you to sit for a portrait bust. Later, it can be cast in bronze." Then I added—and I thought that this was the height of diplomacy; it was as far as I have ever risen almost to Talleyrand form—"Sir, if I may make a suggestion, don't be too hard on Mahaffy. At any rate, not until you have had a better plaque than his cast in bronze."

The Doctor took thought for a minute or two. At last he asked, "You don't mean to tell me that Mahaffy approves of this?"

Now I was in a real quandary. What would Talleyrand have done, or rather, Machiavelli?

Fortunately, Jan appeared at the door. "May I come in?"

"Come in, come in!" said the Doctor. I caught what sounded like a note of enthusiasm—not for Jan, of course, but for my suggestion. He wanted to tell it all to Jan. I rushed to anticipate him, for Jan could not yet know what we had been saying or how far the project had developed.

"Jan," I said, "you know the quotation at the base of Mahaffy's bust, *Philosophoumein aneu malakias?* What would you suggest for a bust of the Doctor here?"

Jan hummed and hawed and spoke intermittently. But as it turned out, eloquence would not have got him half as far as his halting suggestion, for it made the Doctor take the bust for granted and jump to the consideration of the quotation that was to go on the plaque.

What Jan said was this:

"Isn't there? It seems to me that there is . . . I can't recall it accurately though . . . some remark of Dido when her city was being built . . . It could be used to refer to the walls of the Classical School which the Doctor has founded in College . . . if you see what I mean. *Meos murus vidi.* Those may not be the exact words. My Latin is rather rusty . . ."

The Doctor groaned. Then he softened, out of his affection for Jan. "*Murus* means a partition wall like the wall of a water closet; the word you want is *moenia.* And the quotation which you quite rightly attribute to Dido is *Mea moenia vidi:* I have seen my walls arising . . ."

"I cannot imagine a more suitable legend for a plaque of the Doctor," I added hastily. So it was arranged!

Before the Doctor had time to ask himself why this should be left to his most irresponsible friends, we had to rush the sittings through. I saw Brissac at once. He was delighted. He would do it for nothing. That was out of the question. What we wanted was a plaque the same as the one he did of Mahaffy; and we wanted it completed in two days, so that it could be unveiled and photographed for the daily papers. The deadline would be Friday. Saturday for the ceremony.

While Brissac was seeing himself elected as official sculptor to the university, Jan was entertaining the Doctor at what was a "holding lunch." Jan was to engage the Doctor until I engaged Brissac. When we got the Doctor back to his rooms, Brissac was to begin. The floor had already been covered with tarpaulin, the dais was in place and the plasticine prepared. Brissac was instructed not to insist on the dais but to start on the head, whether the Doctor posed deliberately or not.

Very few would be interested in a description of a sculptor in action and of a sitter in inaction. It is enough to say that all went well. We had a scratch audience for the well-chosen words that we got the Public Orator to say at the unveiling.

The photographers from the various dailies were enthusiastic: they imagined that they had made a scoop. "Publicity" had been foreseen; and printed matter, explaining the occasion of the presentation to Dr. Talmey, had been made available, for obviously neither Jan nor I could pose as the "onlie begetter" of the plaque idea. So let us pass over the unveiling. Suffice it to say neither the plot nor its purpose was unveiled.

It was at the beginning of the week after the meeting of the Board that Jan got a word with the Doctor. He did not allude to the Board meeting. He refused to dine with Jan and me. He was dining elsewhere.

Jan looked at me. I looked at Jan.

"It must have gone well," we said together. It deserved a celebration to itself. What a pity that the Doctor could not be let in on this.

When I did see the Doctor in his rooms, I thought that his manner was somewhat distant or rather lofty, as if he had turned himself into an examiner again and I was "up."

He sat at his table under the window, and he was writing. The table was crowded with letters. The wastepaper basket was full of envelopes.

"You must excuse me. I have a considerable amount of correspondence to deal with. I am trying to explain to the Master of Balliol why I did not give him timely notice about the presentation of my plaque."

I felt superfluous. On tiptoe I withdrew. I regret to say that I was not missed.

Anyway, I knew where to find Jan. His hours were his own. He had drunk himself into the Local Government Board and was a treasured fixture, for he had not been found wanting during the prolonged initiation. Old history, ours was new.

He gave the order, and I took my seat.

"I saw the Doctor," I began. "He was answering letters, of which there was a pile on his desk. He was so busy that he did not ask me to stay."

"I hope that he did not 'put the others there.'" Again Jan made a gesture with his finger as if pointing to the middle of a writing table.

"I only know that he was rather short with me. Not a word about the Board. Not even a hint of a drink; not a 'Won't you be seated for a while until I get this letter off my chest.' Not a thing. I slipped out."

Jan hawed a little.

"When I saw him, he was rushing off to dine with the Provost."

I could see that Jan was trying to read a real excuse into that, rather than confess to himself that he had been brushed off.

We sat silent. How long I could not say, but it must have been for at least five minutes, and that is a very long time if you follow it on your watch; but it was at least five minutes because, when I did speak, the outlook had changed completely. I am a slow thinker. That is why when I say five minutes, I am not exaggerating.

"Do you know what has happened?" I asked.

Jan made one of his inarticulate sounds which was meant to show that he was surveying the situation in all its aspects.

"Nemesis has interposed. When we undertook to draw a red herring—no, a red gurnet—across the track of the Board, we little thought of the factors which were out of our control . . ."

"Such as?" Jan asked in a hushed way.

"The stature (not the statue) of the man, for one thing. How were we to know what an inundation would follow the publicity? Then how were we to know that we would have to keep out of the whole business for the obvious reason that if our scheme were found out, it would stultify its object and render the Doctor suspect as an accessory to a trick? I did not realize, but you did, that we could never tell the Doctor that the only thing we could think of to save him was this publicity. When you remember the abject state he was in before the Board meeting and compare it with his present state when the Provost asks him to dinner, you will realize how successful our scheme was. You will also recognize that the greater the success, the greater the need for the preservation of our secret."

"We have started an avalanche," said Jan.

"If we could only get him out of the way. To take a holiday, for instance," I suggested.

"We may have to get ourselves out of the way before very long."

When I met Jan next day he had an air of reserve about him, something withheld, aloof. It was not until, rather cheerfully, I told him that I had a letter by the morning's post asking me to call on the Doctor.

"What hour did he happen to mention?" Jan asked.

"Four-thirty," I said briskly, though I was far from feeling comfortable.

"Same here."

"Rather formal, this letter writing—disconcerting, what?"

"You know he never uses the telephone," said Jan.

"Oh, so we're both up before the Board, so to speak, only that it is a one-man Board consisting of the Doctor?"

I interpreted Jan's grunts to be equivalent to a more eloquent person's, "Well, I'll be damned!"

"Well, young men," said Dr. Talmey, "when I consented to sit for that plaque I was surprised by the haste and the suddenness of your arrangements. I have still to see the reason for such a stampede; and many of my friends also have been taken by surprise; and they have written in no uncertain terms to complain to me about their treatment, as if I were responsible. Why was it so clandestine?

"As for the artist: no one has ever heard of him, and, though far be it from me to suggest it, there are those who state that I was his most important subject."

Jan looked at me. I know that he wanted to ask "what about Mahaffy?" I wanted to ask that question myself; but how could we?

"Nevertheless," the Doctor proceeded, "he modeled me with my eyes half shut or altogether shut. One might think that I was asleep. Then there was the publicity, for which there was no discernible reason. It was little short of indecent: my picture, or rather reproductions, in Monday morning's papers of that fellow's (what do you call him?) bust that purports to be me. Then there is all this huggermugger about the donors. At first, when Ney congratulated me, I thought that the portrait was being presented to me by some members of the Board; but when I thanked Mahaffy he was astounded, genuinely so, I will admit. 'My dear Talmey,' he said, 'is it not enough to immolate myself to a wretched artist to please Fitzooth without adding you to the sacrifice? I am thanking my stars that the artist is not another Pygmalion and that my statue is not likely to come alive.' His attitude left me feeling that I had become the victim of a practical joke . . ."

"Sir!" we expostulated in unison.

"I won't go as far as to say that; but I cannot rid myself of the suspicion that the invitations to dinner that have been pouring in on me are not free from a touch of condolence; that they are intended to comfort me. I am dining too with the Archbishop of Dublin, no very intimate friend of mine. It is the only way I can account for it. Who can tell how deserving an object of pity I may appear to such as he?

"On the other hand, you have always seemed to be good friends of mine. You have been indiscreet in this matter, though I have little doubt but that you both meant well."

The Doctor rose. And even though I may have gazed down microscopes and Jan worked a dynamo, we had sufficient manners to take our leave.

Later, when Mr. Murtagh had filled our glasses and we were left to ourselves, "Well, I'll be damned," said Jan.

"You are already damned; so am I, in the Doctor's opinion at any rate. Let me tell you this"—Jan could not escape me this time even had he wanted to—"it's the last time I will try to save anybody. There are too many saviors in this world: saviors always come to a bad end."

"True." Then, as emphatically as his hesitating speech permitted, "The idea was yours," said Jan.

"*Et tu, Brute,*" was all I said.

The Big House at Coole

Concentration and continuance of life about a spot on the earth's surface are necessary for civilization and culture. It was such a concentration that struck that writer of pleasant prose, Gerald Johnson of Baltimore, when he visited Dublin and wrote about the Ely Place of George Moore, which was a *cul de sac* closed in due season by lilacs, laburnums, and apple blossoms in the heart of the old town. Here were Georgian houses colored like warm roses and houses with gables like the top half of fiddles from the reign of Queen Anne, houses before the Duke of Wellington was nursed off down the street and houses built in 1800 that were as shabby as the Act of Union of the time.

Out in the country great Palladian houses derived from the genius of Vincenza stood nobly in their parks. Each was a center of civilization with a village at its feet. Afar in distant Galway, sporting ground of the famous fox-hunting Galway Blazers, stood Coole Park, lessened as it were by distance from the mansions of the east and richer side of Ireland; but large enough to be called by the cottagers "The Big House." Around for miles spread its influence, cherishing the old people who were the last repositories of the customs and legends of the land.

Here Lady Gregory lived for fifty years. George Moore mischievously describes her dressed in black going into a cottage and emerging after a while chuckling like a jackdaw with a silver spoon, having salved some precious phrase in the Gaelic speech.

Here came scholars and poets who, like Lady Gregory, were busy saving the remnants of an older culture from which their own literary renaissance was to spring. Other big houses were more interested in fox hunting, race horses, guns, and rods.

The Big House at Coole was unique, in that it was devoted to the culture of the country people, and in the traditions of politeness which image the manners of courts and courtiers who passed away in the times out of mind.

Once their innate suspicion was at rest, the country people were well disposed to the Big House, which is more than can be said for the country people elsewhere near houses of greater size.

Sir William Gregory, owner of Coole, had been one of the many proconsuls who ruled India for Great Britain. When he retired, he filled the friendly rooms of Coole with mementoes from the East. Coole became the concentration point for the families around it, families of Galway who covered shortcomings by tradition and family pride; families like the Martyns of Ballinahinch Castle where "Humanity" Dick Martyn, author of the bill that punished those guilty of cruelty to animals, was born; the Goughs of Lough Cutra (and of India); the Dalys of Dunsandle; and the Persses of Roxborough, the dark blue range of low streamy hills beneath which Lady Gregory, the last owner of Coole, who was one of the Persses, grew up. That was almost a hundred years ago, when her brothers changed into "Roxborough" the ancient "Echte of Streams."

When Lady Gregory became a widow, goodlier company could be seen at the Big House, not so cheerful and boisterous perhaps as the pink-coated, top-hatted horsemen who met to hunt the fox over the mortarless walls which fence the fields of East Galway; but more significant men. Coole welcomed genius.

Looking over his half door of a morning, the cottager might behold a tall, red-bearded man striding in high boots like buskins for a health-giving walk before breakfast, for, vegetarian and valetudinarian, he was pedantic in all things and especially about his health; and learn from the gossip of the servants that George Bernard Shaw was staying at the Big House. Over from London with him had come that lover of the ballet, Arthur Symons. Douglas Hyde, Gaelic scholar and native speaker, would be there in quest of a fragment of a poem in the Gaelic of Blind Raftery, who sang of "that calm and easy woman," the lovely Mary Hynes, the story of whose beauty so moved the poet Yeats. Credit is due to Douglas Hyde, for, by his researches, preservation of the old culture and creation of the new resulted. Walking alone deep in the darkness of the Seven Woods of Coole might the gloomy Synge be seen, dim as a shade in the underworld, or the taller and darker Yeats, murmuring the most melodious movement that is to be found in the blank verse of the present day. After lunch, Edward Martyn would drive over from Tilira Castle with the yellow-haired and Dresden-china-faced George Moore, who would soon be found walking with a lady in his peg-top trousers which recalled the Champs Elysées to the woods of Coole. He would be talking and gesticulating peevishly, expostulating against anyone who held any author but himself in esteem. He would stop to gaze at the lake of Coole for a moment and months after would write like this:

> I forgot Yeats and everything else in the delight caused by a great clamour of wings and the snowy plumage of thirty-six great birds rushing across the water and striving to rise from its surface.

But Moore never forgot Yeats. Yeats was always on his mind, for Moore's instinct, which was unerring, felt that the poet's fame would outlive that of the novelist. With all the perversity and peevishness of a spoiled child, he resented his rival and never missed a chance to lampoon him: "Yeats, standing in his dark cloak like an umbrella forgotten at a pic-nic."

Meanwhile, Yeats was making the Seven Woods of Coole immortal beyond the reach of ax or the frost of years. He called them by the sonorous Gaelic names recovered for him by Douglas Hyde. Listen to the gentlest blank verse in the English tongue, where half of its sweetness is due to the Gaelic names:

I walked among the Seven Woods of Coole
Shan-walla, where a willow-bordered pond
Gathers the wild duck from the wintry dawn;

Shady Kyle-dortha; sunnier Kyle-na-no,
Where many hundred squirrels are as happy
As though they had been hidden by green boughs
Where old age cannot find them; Pairc-na-lee
Where hazel and ash and privet blind the paths;
Dim Pairc-na-carraig where the wild bees fling
Their sudden fragrances on the green air;
Dim Pairc-na-tarav, where enchanted eyes
Have seen immortal, mild, proud shadows walk;
Dim Inchy Wood, that hides badger and fox
And marten cat, and borders that old wood
Wise Biddy Early called the wicked wood:
Seven odors, seven murmurs, seven woods.

The enchanted eyes were those of that visionary seer George Russell, who wrote under the nom de plume Æ. He and his wife stayed for two months at the Big House. He would brood for hours in its library, gazing with his childishly blue eyes over his glasses into quartos of gold-tooled calf or morocco and carrying fixed in his memory whatever he found therein. He was the greatest inspirer of his time.

All, all are gone, and the Big House is demolished. Not one of the Seven Woods remains, woods where on a tree you could find the initials G.B.S. or W.B.Y. or J.M.S.; but the tree may now be on a railway wagon going to supply the demand for building material, though it makes one wonder what can be worth building in a land where there is no reverence for great times and great men. A land run by a cultureless gang who are as incapable of respecting the past as of improving the present: little bureaucrats as busy as a swarm of hornets, and as productive.

The De Valera government took over the Seven Woods of Coole for a forestry school. The Big House had been demolished by a "contractor" to provide materials with which to build, during the shortage of such materials, an ecclesiastical house on the grounds of the empty jail in Galway. Of the forestry school, only a sawmill was visible. Its engine was going strong; but there was no sign of any lumber. It recalled another famous engine at

Mount Bellew. Colonel Grattan Bellew applied to the government for facilities to provide boxes for the nation, regardless of the demand. He did his part by appointing a manager, and the government did theirs by sending him an engine and, after the proper interval, an inspector. The inspector asked, "Where are the boxes?" The manager said that they had not come to making them yet. The inspector gazed around him at a sea of derelict tree stumps. "Where are the woods?" he asked. "Sure, they went to feed the engine." Which is an excellent symbol of a nation which devours itself.

The life that centered about the Big House is no more. The singers are mute and the audience has walked out. Factories and slums have taken its place.

With prophetic vision the poet Yeats saw the trend of things. He knew that Periclean periods of civilizations are less than fifty years. He caught sight of the puny men with their "mandates" from Oblivion. In an "In Memoriam" which he wrote of Lady Gregory's only son, who was killed over Genoa while serving in the Royal Air Force, he wrote:

Here traveller, scholar, poet, take your stand
When all these rooms and passages are gone,
When nettles wave upon a shapeless mound
And saplings root among the broken stone,
And dedicate—eyes bent upon the ground,
Back turned upon the brightness of the sun
And all the sensuality of the shade—
A moment's memory to that laurellèd head.

The "household of continuance" has gone now. Two years is the average length of a rental. Mansions are no more. The very apartments in which we live are hardly stationary. They, with the times, are on the move. All are caught in the eddy of ever widening circles and of ever lessening intensity. Dignity has given place to discipline. The solitary man, the individual, is no more. The masses everywhere are moiling to tyrannize over themselves. Whither is all this leading? Who knows? But wherever it is leading it is not leading back to the Big House.

Dirty Drawers

It was 7:00 P.M. when the girl announced there was someone to see me. Now as a rule I did not see patients after five o'clock. She could easily have said so, or that I was out; there were two stairways in my house in Dublin, and so the front of it could be closed off after five.

"Who is it?" I asked.

"He didn't give his name, sir."

"Go back and ask it."

She came back to tell me that a man who said Tom Kelly would do was there waiting for me. So I went into the reception room, and on the far side of it, in the bay window, I saw Tom Kelly. He was standing up. His cap was on the table and his hand on his cap. He spoke in a whisper, so I asked if his throat hurt. He shook his head and stared at me desperately. Then he said, a little bolder, "Cocky Meade, sir," and corrected himself: "Mr. Meade" had said that I was a good sport and would see him right. He stared me straight in the face, watching for the effect of his message.

I saw a man in his early thirties. He was dark, with flaggy hair and a broad face with brown eyes widely separated. He stood about five feet six or seven. The wrists and legs were thin, like an Arab's. But what really amazed me was his great cage of a chest. He was built like a miner who works where the air is as thin as in the heights of Peru.

"What does Cocky Meade want me to do?"

"It's like this, sir. I am late with my entry. It's the four-mile cross-country race at the Police Sports. Mr. Meade said you would make it right for me . . ."

"How much is it?"

"Five shillings."

Five shillings was less than a dollar, and it did not seem extravagant. But what did seem extravagant was my visitor's rather desperate desire to be entered in the race. Still I knew Cocky Meade would not send me a dud. So I produced the five shillings.

"Sit down, Tom," I said, to put him at his ease.

As he moved to a chair I noticed that his shoulders were high. It was not the clothes; he was built that way. Now high shoulders can bespeak a runner. They give him more breathing space, just as a pregnant woman becomes high-shouldered and for the same reason.

"How did you know Cocky Meade?"

"He lives in Bath Avenue. That's where I live."

"Have you done much running?"

He hesitated. His eyes brightened. He started to rise on his toes as if he could address me better that way. When at last he did speak, the shyness or whatever it was that had made him whisper had gone out of his voice.

"I don't get much time for much, sir; but the little I get makes me think I can knock hell out of the crowd coming over for the Sports. It's four miles cross-country, and eighteen laps and the four jumps they use for the horses in Ballsbridge."

"It used to be four laps to the mile in my day," I said.

"That's all right for the cycling track, but the running track is inside that and they calculate eighteen laps for the four miles."

I nodded. "What work do you do that gives you little time for training?"

"I'm a scavenger. I work at night."

A scavenger belongs to the Sanitation Department of the Dublin Corporation. I have often watched them shoveling liquid mud into large semicircular metal containers drawn by one horse.

He rose to go. As we were leaving the room, I asked what made him so sure that he could lick all comers, men who were famous athletes from the foremost English clubs.

His voice dropped to a whisper: "I clocked twenty on the four miles last week."

"But how did you get into Ballsbridge?"

"I know the man on the Anglesea Road side of the grounds. We were having a few drinks and he asked me in. I lepped the jumps for half the distance, then I ran outside them—it's the jumps that kills—and when I had finished I went into his cottage; and when he pulled out his watch, there it was: twenty minutes exact."

I stood dumbfounded. I heard him take his leave with, "You may put your shirt on me. I wouldn't tell that to a living soul except the boys that are in the secret." Then he was gone, to take up his work for the night.

I was dumbfounded, as well I might be. I knew that five minutes a mile was about the average for anything above three miles on the flat with ditches and jumps, and here was an unknown man clocking twenty for four miles, half of which were over very trying jumps. And what a timekeeping! He went into the cottage and they pulled out a watch! And they had been having a few drinks before the trial!

It was over two weeks when the day for the Metropolitan Sports came. There were eight thousand people at Ballsbridge. They kept the four-mile almost until the last because they knew that not many people would wait half an hour to watch men going round and round in a continuous grind. I for one sat in my seat. I had to see Tom Kelly do his work.

There were no bookmakers about with whom to bet my shirt even had I been inclined, but there were two stout men in bowler hats and raincoats—though the weather had turned fine after the rain yesterday—who had evidently crossed over with the English team and who looked like men who could make a book. If they did, it would have to be in the dressing room, for betting, though legal enough at horse-race meetings, was frowned upon at athletic sports.

Out they came. There were tall men with "H.H." in large red letters. These were the Huddersfield Harriers, whose prowess had put fear into the hearts of the home teams and all the other athletes—with the exception of Tom Kelly, of course. They were well turned out, and they had brought their trainer with them. They were tall men and they shone with fitness, all pink and white. Beside them the local talent looked scrawny.

I looked down the program. Shelbourne Harriers, Bohemians, Al Fresco, etc. Where is Tom Kelly? Ah yes, here he is; Thomas Kelly, private. Casually they filed to the starting place. Then I spotted Tom. He came out the last, and he was barefooted. All the others wore running shoes, and the Englishmen wore short socks with red tops.

There was a hush before the pistol went. It seemed a long delay. Some officious idiot with a tall hat was gassing with the runners as if they had never competed before they came to Ballsbridge. Tom hid himself in the group, or his low stature concealed him. I did not catch sight of him until the gun went off. There he was! He took the first jump, a stone wall, in his stride, and his stride was leisurely.

There were five jumps: the stone wall, about four feet six inches high; a hurdle covered with brush; a double bank well over six feet, on the top of which a horse was expected to change legs before he jumped down; a jump with a broad sheet of water on the other side of it; and lastly a gate.

Tom kept up his leisurely pace. He hardly seemed to be running; I mean that he did not appear to hurry. Anyway there was a contrast between him and the others. He rounded the last curve, and the white legs and the white shorts stood out.

When they came to the double bank all the runners jumped up on it and then jumped down. But not so Tom. He climbed up and slid down, and he was just as quick as if he had jumped, but his white shorts were smeared in the back with black mud.

But what is this? Tom had stopped! I could hear yells coming from the cheap seats opposite; the crowd was hooting and shouting, "Go on, Dirty Drawers!" and Dirty Drawers had stopped to shake his fist at them and answer back. Then he remembered he was in a race, turned and spurted ahead, and caught the leaders before they had rounded the upper curve.

For a moment they were all hidden behind the brushwood fence. The first through was Tom, and before he came to the next jump he was fifty yards ahead. The experienced men running behind him seemed to think the pace would kill him, for not a man started out to run him down.

There was silence when again he sped past the cheap seats. By the second lap he was a hundred yards ahead and not a sign of fatigue.

The field was struggling now. Some were getting their second wind. But Tom had them panicked. Suppose the pace didn't kill? After all, he had set it himself. It wasn't just that the shouts of derision had goaded him on, for he was running well within himself.

Now the field was spreading out halfway round the course. The stragglers were already being passed by Tom. At this rate the tall men with H.H. on their chests would soon be lapped.

It happened before the fifteenth round. Tom had kept behind the laboring runners. Then when a little fellow from the "Shels" drew shouts from the crowd for a sprint he made and held past the tallest Englishman, Tom pursued him. Surely, having lapped the field, he might let the man alone. But no. Tom began to sprint as if he were competing in a hundred-yard dash instead of a grueling four-mile race. The bell rang, and he sprinted on until he threw up his arms at the tape!

The crowd went mad. Nobody cared about the others in the race, and I never knew what teams came in first or second. Tom Kelly, private, had done it.

About a week later the maid announced Tom again, and this time she was smiling. "Show him up," I said.

"Well, Tom, you kept your word!"

"I've come to pay you back, sir," he said.

Now it would be easy to say, "Forget it," but you had to make allowance for a man's self-respect. Silently I took the proffered coins, and I rang the bell for drinks. The maid appeared again and Tom said he would have Guinness. This time it was easier to get him to talk.

"What was the idea of your final sprint?" I asked.

"Well, sir, it's this way. You see you never know what the lap counters are doing. How did I know I would get the credit for lapping the field when they were so spread out? It came over me like that I had better make sure and win it straight as if I hadn't a lap to my credit."

"The pace was terrific," I said in awe, for never before had I seen such a turning of the tables on the high and mighty.

Tom ignored my praise.

"I brought you a little present."

He produced from his pocket a pawnbroker's ticket.

"That's the suitcase I won. It has silver brushes and a looking glass and a flask and a shoehorn and a buttonhook. All I could get for it at Weldon's was two quid, though Cocky Meade hocks all he wins and he says it's worth twenty-five."

"I don't want to deprive you of this. Some day you can redeem it."

"And where would I be going if I did?"

I thanked him again and changed the subject.

"What was it that stopped you on the first lap? My heart was in my mouth."

"Ah, that. It was some jackeens that made remarks about what happened to my pants when I slid down the bank. It's the leppin' that kills, and I reduced it, and some ignorant sooners in the half-penny place hooted at me. I let them have it and no mistake."

"I didn't see you until the last when the boys came out for the start."

"No. I was in the gateman's lodge. He gave me a parting pint of porter and wished me luck."

Good God, I thought. Why, a horse does not get a drink before even the shortest race, and here is a fellow who runs on a pint of Guinness.

"On what did you train?"

"On scallions, bacon and eggs, and strong tea. Cocky says it's the meal the day before that does the trick. So I like to run on an empty stomach."

An empty stomach and a pint of Guinness! Or was it just a pint? I remembered the story of a gillie in Scotland who at the age of a hundred and one could direct a stag hunt and never drank less than a gallon of whisky a day!

"Is it any harm to ask how many you had with the gateman before you were clocked?"

"We had half a dozen pints apiece, about. To me it's eatin' and drinkin'."

Tom Kelly stood up to go.

"The Corporation's promoting me now. I'm going on day duty."

"Congratulations, Tom. You well deserve anything you may get."

"Ah, sir, it's yourself I owe it to, for giving me the chance."

The Romance of the Horse

What are the gifts most beneficent to man? That was at one time the question, and it was then that the horse enters our history. The legend tells that when Poseidon and Athena disputed as to which of them should give the name to the capital of Attica, the gods decided that it should get its name from the deity who should bestow upon Greece the most useful gift.

Athena represented wit and wisdom, Poseidon natural force. Athena caused an olive to break out on the hill, and Poseidon struck the ground with his trident, and lo, a horse!

I know not if this story be true or false, but I have seen the marks of the trident on the Hill of Athens, which as everybody knows is called after Athena, because the olive was held to be more useful than the horse. And the city proved worthy of the goddess, for its citizens never lacked for wit, which may be due to the olive which simply bristles with vitamins.

Apparently Poseidon left his gift behind when he departed in a rage; or, perhaps, inspired by their tutelary deity, the Athenians found a way to compromise. At all events, the horse was not withdrawn. Compromising has been associated with horses ever since. Howe'er it be, the horse remains and figures largely in Greek song and story. Homer is full of horses. He tells of the divine horses, gifts of Poseidon to the father of Achilles, who drew the chariot of that hero and prophesied his death, and how Achilles rebuked them. The greatest of all poets knew more about horses and wrote more about them and their chieftains and charioteers than all the rest. The last word in Homer's great poem is that title of honor, "horse-taming." Horses were associated with aristocrats from the beginning. In ancient Irish history, as in Greek history, none but an aristocrat could be a charioteer. It is to Homer we must go if we are to get a parallel to the horse races of ancient Ireland, for the Homeric age lasted in Ireland down to historic times. The Twenty-third Book of Homer should be in every racing stable, so well do its bright lines full of youthfulness and the joy of life portray the sympathy between man and horse. And the sympathy of the god-given immortal steeds for their mortal masters.

It is a far cry from the days of Homer, you will say—days when horses and horsemen were in the ascendant and the rest of the people were mere fans—to the poet Pindar, who sang to princes the ambition of whose lives was achieved if the chariot they had entered came home first in the Olympian, Pythian, or Nemean games. For all their fame in connection with horses, no one has thought at Newmarket or at Ascot of having medals or their city arms stamped with a horse's head, as the coins of Syracuse in Sicily were stamped when Hiero, the ruler of that

nursing place divine of horses and steeds that rejoice in speed

immortalized his horse Pherenikos by portraying his head upon a coin. No. And maybe it is just as well, for where can the artist be found to equal that marvelous portrait of a horse on a coin of Syracuse?

Here are the famous lines of Homer touching man and horse which are so full of a mysterious strangeness, of a pathos with all its wistful and unanalyzable charm. The immortal horses had been given, as I said, to Peleus, and he left them to his son Achilles to draw his battle chariot in the war of Troy. Poseidon who gave them speaks:

> Ah, unhappy pair, wherefore gave we you to King Peleus, to a mortal, while ye are ageless and immortal? Was it that among wretched men ye too should have sorrows? For in sooth there

> is naught, I ween, more miserable than Man among all things that breathe and move upon the earth.

A god pitying Man, and the immortal steeds touched with mortals' woe through sympathy with mankind!

Where are those immortal horses Xanthus and Balius gone? Have they fled away from earth and from the men whose lot they could only mourn? They have gone away with the minds that imagined them and wherein they dwelt. Theirs were the days when horses were the companions of heroes. The immortal horses, the gift of the earth-shaking god, are gone with Homer! But before we leave him, let us hear of those horses once again, when they are so grief-stricken for their charioteer that they could not be entered in the race while grief was on them. Achilles their owner is speaking to the competitors:

> For ye know how far my horses twain surpass in excellence, seeing they are immortal, and it was Poseidon that gave them to my father and he gave them to me. Howbeit I verily will abide, I and my single-hooved horses, so valiant and glorious a charioteer have they lost, and one so kind, who full often would pour upon their manes soft oil when he had washed them in bright water. For him they stand and mourn, and on the ground their manes are trailing; and the twain stand there grieving at heart.

It is delightful to read about these steeds, the friends of men. And to read about heroes who had no nobler title than to be "tamers of horses," and to learn that there is nothing new in racing under the sun since the time Nestor gave his lad "instructions" just before the race and bets were offered during it. And this is all as it should be, for the tutor of Achilles was the centaur Chiron, who was half a horse.

I suppose that one of the most famous horses in the world was Bucephalus, the war horse of Alexander the Great, that bore him through all the wars which brought Greek civilization to the Near East. How Alexander cherished his charger Plutarch tells us: "He rode up and down the ranks reviewing his troops on a palfrey to spare Bucephalus, who was growing old." Bucephalus, that bull-headed stallion who suffered no man to mount him but the King of Men. And no horse, save the horse of Caligula who was made a senator by that Emperor, has been honored more than the horse of Hiero above mentioned who won at the Pythian games.

It is fitting that that great nurse of horses, Ireland, should show some pride and affection for what is now perhaps its chief contribution to civilization and claim to fame. True, its horses are not immortal, but they have brought the only immortality of a kind to many a millionaire when he led in a Derby winner foaled in limestone fields of Ireland.

Horses, if we are to believe Dean Swift, are superior to men, not to millionaires only but to mankind. That, however, is a Gulliver story. If the Irish horses are not immortal, they have the advantage of not sharing in the sorrows which make Irishmen such adepts at nursing their own miseries.

Horses brought sorrow to the men of Ulster because of the curse of Macha upon their king who matched his steeds in a race against a woman. This is an account from the famous Irish collection, the Dinnsenchas, a compilation of the sixth century. As no man can equal the pathetic simplicity of the old poem, I quote from it at some length.

One day there came with glowing soul
To the assembly of Conor
A gifted man from the eastern wave,
Crunn of the flocks, son of Adnoman.
It was then were brought
Two steeds to which I see no equals,
Into the horse race, without concealment,
At which the king of Ulster then presided.
Although there were not the peers of these
Of yokes of steeds upon the plain,
Crunn the rash hairy man said
That his wife was fleeter, though then pregnant.
"Detain ye the truthful man,"

Said Conor chief of battles,
"Until his famous wife comes here
To run nobly with my great steeds.
Let one man go forth to bring her" . . .
She was the sun of woman-assemblies.
When she had come, in sobbing words
She begged immediately for respite,
From the host of the assemblied clans,
Until the time of her delivery was past.
The Ulstermen gave their plighted word
Should she not run—no idle threat—
The king should not have a prosperous reign,
From the hosts of swords and spears.

Then stripped the fleet and silent dame,
And cast loose her hair around her head,
And started without terror or fail,
To join in the race, but not its pleasure.
The steeds were brought to the eastern side,
To urge them past her in manner like:
To the Ulstermen of accustomed victory
The charioteer was a man of kin.
Although the monarch's steeds were swifter
At all times in the native race,
The woman was fleeter with no great effort,
The monarch's steeds were then the slower.
As she reached the final goal
And nobly won the ample pledge
She brought forth twins without delay,
A son and a daughter together.

Few languages have suffered as much as Gaelic from inept translators. James Stephens the poet is one exception; but he reincarnated the dead poets as well as he could, rather than endeavoring to turn one idiom into another one that was unreceptive. But to continue: This poem does little credit to the men of Ulster, superstitious and savage as it shows them; but what comes down through the ages, barbarous as they are, is the Irishman's pride in the horse.

This long-descended pride is not the attribute of any one race. Rather is it a sign of race: a race warrior-founded, conquerors or conquistadors who rode upon horses.

You will have noticed that this account so far deals with horses that were not ridden, for in the early times no one rode upon horses. They were yoked to chariots both for battle and for racing. It was not until we come across cavalry in war that we find horsemen in the modern sense. Of course no one knows for certain what went on in China, for to us China was non-historical, non-existent, until Marco Polo brought back to Venice his incredible tales. There are little statuettes of unglazed clay found in Chinese tombs of an early date which represent women playing polo. These go to show that horses were ridden and that women had an honored place in society, more by far than was conceded to them elsewhere.

There is evidence that horses were ridden in Japan in the year 550 or thereabouts—with what is very important, the stirrup, which became one of the greatest war engines ever invented. When the stirrup first appeared, it must have had the effect of a tank or a bomb, for actually it could convert the mounted warrior into a tank of sorts and give him a fulcrum for his blows. To Europe the stirrup was introduced not from Japan but from the steppes. Up to this we see—in the famous equestrian procession of the Parthenon, for instance—youths bare of limb riding without stirrups.

It was the stirrup that enabled Richard Cœur de Lion to cut a charging Saracen captain literally in two. The stirrup made chivalry possible—in the very word there is a horse—chivalry with all its joustings and its tournaments. That English substitute for Homer, Malory's *Morte d'Arthur,* is full of jousting knights and fair ladies.

Fair ladies were associated with horses, as they are now more than ever; but we will discuss that later on.

Obviously, it is impossible within these limits fully to cover all the romance of the horse, from the steppes of Russia where the wild men rode drinking mares' milk and sometimes drawing blood from their horses by way of sustenance, down to the "horse of brass whereon the Tartar king did ride," to the white Arab on which Napoleon rode at Waterloo, where he was thoroughly trounced by Wellington on his bay horse Copenhagen.

The romance of the horse is long. It has been the most engaging of all the influences on man from the animal world. The horse's effect on the intelligence of Europe would require a treatise far beyond the scope of this. Here is one instance of how the story of the horse that drew a cart in Paris before he became one of the best sires in the stud book inspired a poem by the present Duchess of Wellington, a poem which had only to be shown to the poet Yeats to be at once included by him in the *Oxford Book of Modern Verse* which he edited. As well he might, for he recognized the mastery of the meter that could use proper names melodiously.

That stallion, teaser to Hobgoblin, free
And foaled upon a plain of Barbary:
Godolphin Barb, who dragged a cart for hire
In Paris, but became a famous sire,
Covering all lovely mares; and she who threw
Rataplan to the Baron, loveliest shrew;
King Charles Royal mares; the Dodsworth Dam;
And the descendants: Yellow Turk, King Tom;
And Lath out of Roxana, famous foal;
Careless; Eclipse, unbeaten in the race,
With white blaze on his face;
Prunella who was dam to Parasol.

That white blaze reminds me that the charger of Alexander had a white star on that bull-like head of his from which he got his name. That white spot is important as a sign of breeding.

As I have said, there is no space here to investigate the effect of the horse on the mind of Europe. But lest it be thought that I am carried away by enthusiasm for the subject, I will weight down the pace of this narrative by an admission. Among animals the horse is far from being first when it comes to an intelligence test. The I.Q. of the horse is pretty low. This may be the reason that those who take delight in horses either have naturally little intelligence or have deliberately dowsed their brains. In rare cases this is necessary. That is why at the two universities any evidence of learning is bad form. In fact it is not good form to have a copious vocabulary. I do not mean that you must reduce yourself to neighing or whinnying, but you simply must set a limit to your speech, imitate the best people, who are always to be found in the hunting field or in the paddock. And get rid of the article "the." Do not take this as sarcasm, direct or implied. It is necessary if you are to be worthy of the horse, because it comes to this: that the Horse is a form of religion to a great mass of mankind. He is a substitute for a church for those who are not churchgoers. He happens to be also an antithesis to a true church, for all the dishonesty, dodging, and chicanery of the world are associated with his cult. He cannot help that; but it explains the taciturnity of the better classes, who don't wish to be suspected of having a vocabulary efficient for cheating.

The horse has done more for mankind than reduce their vocabulary. He has introduced a deity in which Julius Caesar and Napoleon believed, the goddess Fortune. He has given his votaries assurance and a certainty in all the walks of life except the finish. And who knows about that? No doubts assail men who follow horses. They may not be educated, but then they are exempted from the uncertainty and the ignorance of the learned in their special fields. If for instance the question of the identity of Shakespeare should arise, any racing man can tell you unhesitatingly that he was the son of Hobgoblin by Aleppo and he covered the dam of Eclipse. He won't say for certain that he was the sire of Eclipse. You may object that you are at cross-purposes; but you cannot take a man out of his world for the sake of an argument.

From the days when knights carried their ladies' favors in the jousts and defied the world to say that there was a lovelier than their love, ladies have been associated with horses. Who would go to Ascot were the ladies of fashion not there? Very few. And it is the King's Master of the Horse who decides who is worthy of being admitted to the Royal Enclosure.

The horse has been gripped by the thighs of kings and conquerors from time out of mind; and from time out of mind he has been associated with chivalry and beauty. Maybe when everyone has been leveled down, mankind may owe its salvation to the horse.

The Contribution of Mr. Theopompholyx

The telephone rang in Mr. Theopompholyx' delicatessen. Mrs. Theopompholyx listened, replaced the receiver, turned to her husband, and, smiling, nodded her head. "A dozen quarts of Ballantine's," she said.

It was just six o'clock. Mrs. Idoneus, the widow who had just telephoned, would be entertaining her friend, Dr. Theodore McWilliam. It was to cater to him that the particular brand of beer was ordered. He was particular; Mrs. Idoneus was more catholic in her taste. Mrs. Theopompholyx was happy; her business was prospering. She was lucky to have such a customer as Mrs. Idoneus.

Mrs. Theopompholyx never regretted her decision to stay near the Grand Central Station in New York. It seemed less than a year since the couple had stood on the lofty gallery of the Grand Central and gazed at the moiling crowds beneath.

On that morning Mr. and Mrs. Theopompholyx had just arrived, after many changes and delays, from one of the islands of Greece. The heart of Mr. Theopompholyx grew heavy as he looked. He turned to his wife to cheer her, for he was sure her heart was as heavy as his own; but to his astonishment, he saw a rapt look on her face. "We will stay here," she said. Instinctively, she saw a use for the crowds; to her they meant buying power. The pressure of wealth she confined to cities; and here, literally under her feet, was the richest and most compact city in the world.

"But . . ." said Mr. Theopompholyx.

"And sell them things," said his wife.

She never regretted making that decision. That is why they are now dispensing good cheer from their little delicatessen near the Grand Central Station. That is how they are contributing to the civilized existence of an appreciative and paying clientele.

On the ground floor of one of the largest apartment buildings on the Avenue, Mrs. Idoneus dwells. She is fancy free and full of interests and enterprises. Her energy is remarkable: in three years she has mastered four widely different subjects—social service, remedial reading, canasta, and child welfare. She is now studying ceramics, not because it happens to be fashionable at the moment and the thing to do, but because it permits her to make lovely forms; and everybody knows how wonderful it is for a new form to appear in the world. Also, it provides an outlet for her energy. One of the rooms in her apartment is filled with clay, not dry and dusty clay but clay of a puttylike consistency, clay which has to be slammed down on her best table to dispel air bubbles. While she is waiting for the clay to dry, she sends out for beer, which Mr. Theopompholyx personally delivers and places in the icebox. He is a favorite of Mrs. Idoneus because his opinions of art have the long tradition of Greece behind them. As one of his perquisites, he is permitted to keep the proceeds of the empties for himself.

Dr. Theodore McWilliam is a frequent visitor to the apartment of Mrs. Idoneus. They are old friends, in spite of the fact the doctor has not the subtlety of mind nor the manifold interests nor the power of adjustment and application of the widow. Yet it cannot be said that he is slow on the uptake.

One evening the doctor, having picked his way carefully through many shining examples of the widow's dedication to art, subsided into an armchair and watched. Mrs. Idoneus, dressed in sculptor's overalls, shapely arms bare to the shoulders, was busily molding wet clay. The doctor buried himself in a newspaper and smoked.

"You will not disturb me if you talk," said Mrs. Idoneus.

"Don't let that beer get hot," said the doctor.

"Talking of beer," said Mrs. Idoneus, "do you know how I flatten my modeling clay?"

"No," said the doctor, hoping to hear something new on a subject older than Praxiteles.

"By using one of Mr. Theopompholyx' empties."

It has been remarked that the doctor was not slow on the uptake; and the association of an empty bottle with the hallowedness of Greece and her glorious sculpture, as Mr. Theopompholyx' contribution to the revival of art, sent spasms of laughter echoing off his diaphragm.

Mrs. Idoneus ignored the ill-timed outburst.

"My instructor, a temperamental fellow by the way, advises his pupils to work with the left hand like this." She demonstrated by holding a lump of clay up to the light. "He says that you should be able to model with your eyes shut."

"But . . ." the doctor interposed.

"That gives you facility. When you can work by feeling only, you and your material may be said to co-operate; that is, the clay will help you to model it as if it were sentient and fearful of being turned into a vessel of ungainly shape."

As she spoke, a snakelike object wriggled from her hands and dropped to the floor. Mrs. Idoneus opened her eyes. "Where did that handle go? Did you see it?"

The doctor was about to assert his innocence when Mrs. Idoneus found it at her feet. "I am making a pitcher and that's the handle. I hope it won't come off. You see, you must smash down the lumps of clay as hard as you can so that all air bubbles will be expelled. I have banged this down the forty times which my teacher says are necessary, so it should stick on."

Mrs. Idoneus resumed her work. The doctor returned to his newspaper. He was awakened from his reverie by an exclamation of delight from Mrs. Idoneus.

"Now! It is finished."

By one of those coincidences which are so common that they have passed into the proverb, "talk of the devil," the doorbell rang.

The doctor opened the door and admitted the little Greek, who, having hailed him politely, passed with his burden into the icebox. When he emerged from the kitchen, Mrs. Idoneus said in her most inviting tones, "Would you like to see what I have been doing since you called last?"

Mr. Theopompholyx inspected the works of art with the silent appreciation of a connoisseur. His silence became somewhat enigmatic to Mrs. Idoneus after a while, and she was about to exclaim when Mr. Theopompholyx lifted a vase, one of the largest on the table, turned with it held as reverently as if he were about to put it in a bag of brown paper, and exclaimed, "Oh, my!"

Mrs. Idoneus was all dimples. "It is strange that you should have picked out that. Perhaps not so strange after all. Instinct, of course. It happens to be one of my masterpieces. You notice the bright red glaze? Isn't that a lovely color? And then the blackish blue coming from underneath, as if someone had laid the vase in a bed of leaves. You can never tell what will happen in a kiln. A thing may go in one color and come out another, and one that you never intended . . ."

Dr. McWilliam sighed. It sounded like a groan. He was running out of beer. He dared not break into the explanation of the vicissitudes of kilning by by-passing artist and connoisseur on his way to the icebox, so he sighed. Mrs. Idoneus, interpreting the sigh as questioning her accuracy, turned on Dr. Theodore McWilliam.

"How do you know what goes on in a kiln?"

"Oh, nothing, nothing," said the doctor.

"On the contrary, everything," said Mrs. Idoneus, her voice rising. "The strangest things can happen in a kiln. You never can tell when you put in a model how it will come out."

Mr. Theopompholyx, who did not like to interrupt old friends, took the opportunity which their conversation afforded to grasp the empties and flee back to his store.

"See what you have done now," Mrs. Idoneus accused the doctor when she found herself left without an appreciator. She seized a lump of wet clay and smashed it down on the table, calling, each time she hurled it, the name of an enemy.

"Jim!"

"Leslie!"

"Stalin!"

The doctor intervened, relieved not to hear his name mentioned, "Let me help." Reluctantly, Mrs. Idoneus yielded the clay. The doctor threw it with great force.

"You are not doing it hard enough. Throw it down on its edge. You have done it only six times; there are thirty-four to go.

"You can release all the venom from your system if you bang the clay down hard enough."

"I've already released all the breath from my lungs."

Beer has a sudorific effect: the doctor began to perspire.

He began to pant at about the twentieth throw.

"I know very little about art," he confessed; but that did not make her relent. "Ten more," she announced.

"Can't I stop and have a little beer?"

"Nine to go," was the implacable answer.

At last his heavy task was at an end.

"Now, see here," said the widow. "Since you showed such ignorance, I will explain what goes on in a kiln. First, you wait until the clay you have modeled dries. Then you give it the first firing. The result is called 'bisque.' That is the French for baked, 'bisque,' baked, biscuit—the cracker we eat or the biscuit, it's only a derivative, it means 'twice baked,' but it will help you to remember 'bisque.' When you get to the bisque stage, you then apply the glaze. You can paint it on or pour it on; if you pour it, you will have to pour it off. Do I make myself clear?"

The doctor nodded. It was about all that he could do. The widow noticed his exhaustion and sympathetically went to the icebox and returned with two fresh glasses.

After an interval of silence in which the doctor was expected to recover, the widow resumed her work. She explained that it would never do to permit the clay which she had taken such pains to "smash down" to dry before it was modeled. She dipped her fingers daintily into a bowl of water and started to turn an amorphous lump of clay around on a revolving wooden disk. In the silence the doctor's strength was returning.

Very sweetly Mrs. Idoneus inquired, "Where do the McWilliams come from?"

"I do not know," said the doctor, who feared to be drawn into an argument, this time on genealogy.

"Surely you know your own family?"

"It is not necessary. I always took them for granted."

"What do you mean—it is not necessary?"

"I mean that there never was any question about our antiquity."

"The 'Mc' sounds Gaelic; the 'William' is probably from Wales. At any rate from some country not distinguished for its sculpture."

"I see what you mean," the doctor said meekly.

"Now how different you are from Mr. Theopompholyx. He has a natural instinct for the beautiful. That is why he picked out the vase which I consider one of the best things I have done. His instinct was unerring, and no wonder, with all that Greek art behind him."

It began to dawn on the doctor that the widow was much influenced by Mr. Theopompholyx.

That was his contribution, and not the empty after all! This gave Dr. McWilliam food for thought. He had laughed when he thought of that empty. It would be a laughing matter if it were all, but now the widow was taking Theopompholyx' opinion seriously, though she in turn had laughed at the thrill he was supposed to be getting from being consulted. "It may well be subconscious," she had said. Was the appeal of Mr. Theopompholyx addressed to the widow's subconscious—subconscious calling to subconscious? Mr. Theopompholyx' background to Mrs. Idoneus' dream of herself as an artist? All Mr. Theopompholyx had said when he picked up the vase was, "Oh, my!"

What was all this about his lack of an artistic background, all because he had not a Greek name? After all, his forbears had been great travelers; the doctor himself had been here and there.

"In the Museum of Athens," he said suddenly, "there is a beautiful chryselephantine statue of the Snake Goddess. She wears a shirt with floor flounces, perhaps to represent a snake, but it looks quite modern; that is the astonishing thing, although it was sculptured in the sixteenth century B.C. It came from Crete. The goddess is represented standing with closely plaited hair and a miter-like headdress. She is extending two snakes which she holds in either hand. They are curled around her arms."

"What is chryselephantine?" asked Mrs. Idoneus.

As if bored with her lack of knowledge, the doctor drawled, "Made of gold and ivory."

"Oh!" exclaimed the widow.

The doctor thought that he had gained a victory, but the widow was merely remembering something. She went to the telephone. Could Mr. Theopompholyx come around at once? There were more than half a dozen empties she wished removed.

"Do you know," she said, "I forgot to show my pitcher to Mr. Theopompholyx?"

The doctor's reply was lost in his glass.

When the ring came, he let the widow open the door herself.

The little man came in, eyes bright and expectant. He had accepted his role as an art critic. Mrs. Idoneus led him to the table. She pointed to her latest achievement.

"Oh, my!" said Mr. Theopompholyx, and he made as if to take the newly made pitcher in his hand. The widow was just in time.

"Don't touch it! It's wet," she shouted.

Abashed, the little man drew back. However, he was awarded with nine empties. When he was gone: "He seems a bit of a dumbbell. I thought he had more sense."

"You ought to be highly complimented," said the doctor. "To him it appeared a pitcher; and it was so real that he couldn't keep his hands off it. Have you ever heard of Zeuxis, the Greek artist who painted a bunch of grapes so realistically that the birds came to peck at it?"

"Oh? Won't you stay to dinner?" she said.

Swords and Singers

The question is: How many of the poets who have sung of war were ever in one?

Take Homer first. If he were blind, as tradition says he was, then we ask if it is necessary for one "who sang of battles and the breath of stormy wars and violent death" to have seen them? And though no one ever sang more heroically, we also know that he was not at the seige of Troy because it was five hundred years or so before he was born. Obviously he could not have been blind all his life, for his was the clearest eye that ever beheld life in its simplicity and beauty: the Homeric eye! He saw the clash of tempest-tossed trees, rivers in flood, lightning from dark clouds; and, in his milder similes, trout rising, wasps issuing out, the long, flowing manes of horses in their pride, the glory of young men in burnished helmets and gleaming armor, and the far-seen splendor of light on the sea. His are the greatest battle scenes that ever were painted. Does this mean that the best descriptions of battles were by bystanders or poets who imagined them? Here we have the old question again of the artist as opposed to the man of action—"Ung has not stood to the aurochs." It is a question as old as art: the contrast between the rhapsodist's and the eyewitness' account.

Aeschylus, the father of Greek drama, fought in four great fights—Marathon, one of the decisive battles of the world; he fought at Plataea; and he was in both sea fights, Artemisium and

Salamis. His brother Cynaegirus fell at Marathon in a heroic deed of arms, and yet only here and there in his plays is a soldier's knowledge apparent, and then only indirectly. Does this mean that the real soldier is inclined to be reticent? Yes; it does. We have but to meet a present-day veteran to realize how true this is.

Before we leave Aeschylus, let me interject the remark that the legend of his death cannot be true. He is said to have been killed in Sicily by an eagle that mistook his bald head for a stone and dropped a tortoise on it. The objection I have to this story is far more cogent than that of any scholiast, for an eagle does not make any mistake about a stone; and there never was a poet yet who was bald except two; but they were moderns.

I read of a Spartan who was lame and he wrote war songs that inspired men to fight. He could not join the army, and yet the songs he made gave others enthusiasm for war; and this is agreeable to my argument.

Sophocles, the poet, perfect man in mind and body, served as a general in the Samnian war. He certainly "saw life steadily and saw it whole," for, like a playwright of the present day, he lived to be over ninety, and until he could tell his friends, when they asked him about love, that he had escaped from an unconscionable master. Our nonagenarian playwright was born free. Sophocles, in spite of his acquaintance with war, does not write of it with relish.

Pindar, the greatest lyric poet of Greece, was older than Sophocles and a little younger than Aeschylus. Though he celebrates the battles of Artemisium, Salamis, and Plataea and calls Athens "the bulwark of Greece," there is no evidence that he was a soldier; his lot was a far happier one. Perhaps it was the happiest of all lots that fall to men: he celebrated chariot races, boys' boxing and wrestling matches and foot races, and he sang processional songs. The men of Rhodes are said to have preferred an ode of his, which they caused to be inscribed in letters of gold, to the extinction of the national debt. In his eightieth year he died of joy in the arms of his favorite Theoxenus of Tenedos. "To be happy is the chiefest prize," said the great lyrist who preferred sport to war.

Let us turn to the Latin poets. We do not hear much about war from Horace, and the reason is not far to seek. He ran away from the battle of Philippi and left his shield behind. He had taken the side of Brutus, who was defeated, and yet Horace suffered little harm, for he was like Chaucer without fortitude. He was a trimmer, a surf-rider, a political tightrope dancer. And as a singer was he not right? Who wants every poet to be a warrior? A man of Horace's temperament had more to give by being true to that temperament than any military tribune could offer.

While Horace was escaping from the battlefield, Virgil was "cultivating the woodland Muse" with his friend and patron Pollio near the Italian Lakes. He sang of battles; but his breath was gentle. His nature was amiable, candid, and retiring. And yet he wrote the greatest enconium on empire that the world had ever heard. His description of a boxing match with the iron-weighted glove is far different than Pindar's, who knew more about sport and sportsmen than the gentle "Parthenias," the maid, Virgil. This raises the question: What would become of our sports writers if they had to experience the things about which they write?

From this pillar of European culture we turn to another one, to Dante, who lit the Middle Ages with his paradisal light. He fought at Campoldina, but there is no more than a soldier's reference to and no enthusiasm for war in Dante's great poem. His courage was as unconquerable as his pride. Exiled under pain of being burned alive,

He found
The unpersuasible Justice, and he found
The most exalted lady loved by a man.

There is but one more mighty example before I come to the English writers. It is Miguel de Cervantes, warrior, poet, playwright and novelist, and man of extraordinary fortitude. He fought at Lepanto, and though sick, he came from his cabin and asked his captain to place him in the forefront of danger. How he fought is well known. He gained a pension for his wounds, one of which maimed his left hand for life. He was given letters of honor to his king; but this is not the place to tell of his capture by the Moors and his great fortitude; but rather to tell how he could in laughing at himself make the unwitting world laugh with him in that crown of his life's achievement, the novel *Don Quixote.* For who else but Cervantes is the Knight of the Rueful Countenance who, for all his unselfish chivalry, finds himself beaten by boors? His courage and self-sacrifice availed him naught. What a farce this fighter makes of war.

In taking now the English poets of battle pieces some might welcome the slight conjecture that during the six obscure years of Shakespeare's life he may have been a soldier; but he, like Homer, knew too much about battles ever to have been in one. His was a Muse of fire. That imagination of his could summon up war and the horrors of war with more intensity of feeling and suffering than the most bloodthirsty soldier could experience.

The cannons have their bowels full of wrath,
And ready mounted are they to spit forth
Their iron indignation 'gainst your walls.

Or that description of Marc Antony's heart

That in the scuffle of great fights hath burst
The buckles on his breast.

The master of the adjective supplied words that made war more real than the warriors felt it.

Of Milton, what shall be said? Like Homer, he was blind; but his blindness came on in later life, as we may safely conjecture Homer's did. He was never in Heaven; yet he made a battlefield of both Heaven and Hell. He lived in warring times. What he projected beyond the flaming walls of the world was more than any of the wars he lived through. He had no lack of courage. It is still a mystery how he, who was Cromwell's secretary, escaped being hanged, drawn, and quartered at the restoration of the son of the decapitated Charles I. Maybe he was spared for reasons like those which moved Alexander when

The great Emathian conqueror bade spare
The house of Pindarus.

If so, it is one of the redeeming acts of Charles II's reign.

But look at this; you might as well have been at Agincourt!

When down their bows they threw
And forth their bilboes drew
And on the French they flew,
Not one was tardy;
Arms were from shoulders sent,
Scalps to the teeth were rent,
Down the French peasants went,
Our men were hardy.

This fervor is rather exceptional, for the author, Michael Drayton, was at one time a soldier; and, as it has been pointed out, soldiers as a rule are not loquacious. Patriotism, and the fact that in the time he lived Agincourt had become historically a part of the national life, may explain his enthusiasm and recall of war. Compared with this battle scene, "The Charge of the Light Brigade" by Tennyson sounds like a rest cure. Would you ever imagine that the same meter is in both poems? The emphasis on the words in Tennyson's poem shows how mild a man he was. He had only the originality of a rectory and little stomach for fighting. He may have despised war, for all we know "Theirs not to reason why" might be taken as a definition and a denunciation of discipline. He wrote some of the finest poems in the language out of the long Victorian peace. And perhaps the best of all his poems is his scholarly praise of Virgil. On Malory's *Morte d'Arthur* he depended for his joustings and his deeds of arms. As for Malory, he must have been particularly peaceful to have composed such interrupted series of fights.

The English archers have sped their dozen arrows each, charged on the opposing foot; the other Victorians, in spite of their distance from fighting, have sung no battle songs. It was through drawing rooms that Browning marched; Swinburne blew childish bubbles of peevish revolutions; before sunrise Meredith, Matthew

Arnold, Rossetti, and the great and manly William Morris were artists passive and active. We hear nothing about soldiering until Kipling, the Eurasian, gets into the sergeants' mess from which he never emerged. "It's Tommy this, and Tommy that." The only war he was in was carried to him by his brother-in-law Balestier in Vermont, where he managed to make himself as unpopular as he became later in Sussex where he took refuge. The greatest balladist of modern times was almost too hardheaded to be a poet. He wrote neither a love poem nor a convincing battle song. His soul was too small. Shortly before the appearance of this jingoist, the greatest celebrator of imaginary battles, Lord Macaulay, lived and wrote. Why a writer who could make a boy rush about a field shouting his verses and challenging all the heroes of history to deadly combat is not accepted as a poet of England is one of the inscrutable matters of historical judgment. If A. E. Housman judged poetry by the faculty it had of sending shivers down his spine, why is Lord Macaulay not included in the poetic hierarchy? His verse could send more than shivers, it could send raging enthusiasm through every limb. Ah, yes; but so can rhetoric.

I remember trying to persuade the poet Yeats to recognize Macaulay. I quoted:

Pomona loves the orchard,
And Liber loves the vine;
And Pales loves the straw-built shed
Warm with the breath of kine;
And Venus loves the whispers
Of plighted youth and maid,
In April's ivory moonlight
Beneath the chesnut shade.

In vain. There was no response. In vain too, I laid emphasis on "ivory moonlight." The oracular spring was silent. I went away disconsolate, for if Lord Macaulay was not a poet all my fine frenzies were foolish vanities.

It was not until I listened to a fine soldier and a poet to boot, Field Marshal Lord Wavell, quoting a stanza from Macaulay's

Lays of Ancient Rome that some of the explanation dawned on me. At a dinner of the Poetry Society of America, Lord Wavell quoted from Macaulay:

He reeled, and on Herminius
He leaned one breathing-space;
Then, like a wild-cat mad with wounds,
Sprang right at Astur's face.
Through teeth, and skull, and helmet
So fierce a thrust he sped,
The good sword stood a hand-breadth out
Behind the Tuscan's head.

"Nice work," said the Field Marshal. Even I could see the absurdity and enjoy the curt soldierly dismissal of the chief example of those singers of the sword who had never wielded one. There must be something more than intellectualism to make a writer unamiable.

In some obscure way a man's character, no matter what eminence his verse achieves for him, reveals itself and becomes the deciding factor whether he will be accepted or not. You will say, "Style is the man"; and you will be right. Macaulay was too assured. He knew too much until he was confronted with one who knew much more. Yet he was a good man; but of what kind of goodness he was compounded, let Emerson tell us; maybe it will elucidate things: "The brilliant Macaulay who expresses the tone of the English governing classes of the day explicitly teaches that 'good' means good to eat, good to wear, material commodity." This may explain Kipling too. Neither ever wrote out of the subconscious. They were too knowledgeable to be poets.

I am beginning to see now that I made another mistake about Macaulay when I emphasized his "ivory moonlight" to Yeats. It did not affect its author, for he remained unmoved by "the whispers of plighted youth and maid," and died a bachelor. He was "debunked" by the greatest soldier of our time, a man who had a memory equal to that of Macaulay—with this difference: in Lord Wavell's case, Memory was Mother of the Muses.

There is another more egregious example. Macpherson went farther than Macaulay, for he fooled Napoleon and enveloped Europe in a mist of heroic battle songs which he attributed to Ossian. Not alone was he not a soldier, but the songs he attributed to the warrior poet were forgeries. Ossian is described as the Irish Homer; but the fragments attributed to him are more lyrics, and as such anticipate "the return to Nature" of the Lake poets by eighteen hundred years. Ossian was one of the three leaders of the Fianna, a kind of constabulary that "pacified" the wrangling petty kings in Ireland of the second century.

But I do not wish to close on a note of depreciation. Let me call up the poet, Stephen Gwynne, lately dead, who went to the First World War when he was over fifty. Of what does he sing? A paean to the bravery of others. His "Salute to Valour" is nothing less. He could, when the mood met him, describe battles as fierce as those in *The Lays of Ancient Rome*. Take these lines from a description of the fight of the ancient Irish Fianna led by Gull McMorna with a deadly flail against the demons in the Christian hell wherein they were miraculously revealed by St. Patrick to the old hero warrior poet, Ossian:

But in front of all by a furlong,
There in the hell-light pale,
Was the champion Gull Mac Morna
Wielding a monstrous flail.
And still the flail as he flung it
Sang through the maddened air,
Singing the deeds of heroes,
A song of the days that were.

Bird Milligan

This is how he got his nickname, the Bird. He went to a fancy-dress ball at a roller-skating rink dressed in a kind of loose garment or robe. He was supported by two holy women. When the dancing was in full swing, he laid an egg as big as a football, flapped his wings, and chortled. The manager threw him out and the holy women with him. But he was Bird Milligan from that day. He was called the Bird by so many people that his other name was forgotten.

Dublin is not like Paris, where they say that in the garden of the Tuileries knights in armor are to be seen sitting with one-eyed pirates, and nobody takes any notice even of the man with the crossbow who assures everyone that he was the man who killed King Richard Lion-Heart. Nevertheless Dublin has, if not paranoiacs, eccentrics surely. It has Boyle Tisdall Stewart Fitzgerald Farrell, who was called Endymion because he was touched by the moon. He caricatured in his own person anything of which he disapproved. He carried two sabers and wore starched cuffs on his ankles to show that the world was upside down. Sometimes he made a nuisance of himself by going into the public library and entering all his names in the book. That done, he left muttering. Then there was Professor Maginni, Professor of Deportment. His idea of deportment caused him to dress in a dark brown frock coat, striped trousers, brown shoes, top hat, and waxed mustache. He walked mincingly. He walked about for business purposes. His real name was Maginnis. Evidently he thought that Maginni gave his name an Italian flourish all the more useful for business. No one could accuse the Bird of acting for business purposes. It would be very hard to see anything faintly resembling business in the laying of an egg.

The Bird retired for a month to his farm near Dublin. People said that he was engaged in breaking in young horses. He had the reputation of being a good horseman. It is hard to say how these rumors got about. Perhaps because his nose was broken by a horse throwing his head back suddenly. To suffer such an accident he must have spent his time among young horses, and hostlers' talk in the taverns did the rest. He certainly had a buggy with a fine horse in the shafts when he appeared in town. By that two-wheeler hangs a tale. He and a young woman were seen driving up the slope of Portbello Bridge. They were evidently quarreling, for the Bird's voice was raised so that anything the lady said could not be heard. But the Bird's voice was distinctly heard when the buggy reached the crest of the bridge, because it halted for a moment there. "You have been the pest of my life," the Bird shouted, "and it's time it ended." With that he threw her bodily into the canal. A policeman in full uniform plunged, helmet and all, into the water. He swam to the rescue, only to find a dummy from a shop window in a fashionable part of the town in his arms. By the time he came out and looked for the Bird, the Bird had flown.

A complaint was laid, not by the police but by some busybody, with the father of the Bird. The Bird's father was an alderman of the city and a most respectable man. He should curb his son. Perhaps his father had not looked after the Bird with due care. It was known the alderman was a widower, so the busybody argued. His father at last reluctantly consented. He spoke to the Bird, and whatever he said to him, the Bird went to Canada for a while. But the Bird came back.

If you want to look for the counterpart of the merrie men of Dublin, you will have to look at some of the characters in Russian novels—Turgenev, for example. But the characters in those novels tend to do dangerous feats which are meaningless. A young man jumps his horse over a precipice where failure means loss of life. They are not truly counterparts.

The Bird was within his rights, and he should not have been thrown out of the skating rink ball. After all, it was a fancy-dress affair. If the fancy dress represented a bird, it was quite in order to lay an egg. And the manager was in no position to decide how big the egg should be.

During the Bird's absence in Canada, the town depended for its merriment on Endymion; and he did his best. That is doubtless why the Bird's exploits and Endymion's tend to merge, so it is better to know the authors of the different actions that kept the old town amused. Endymion must be credited with the fishing incident. It took place in this way. Dublin has two-decker buses, some of them open at the top. On one of these Endymion stood fishing. He had a salmon rod and a line at the end of which was a fly as large as a sparrow. Solemnly he cast the fly onto the cement sidewalk. He waited until some passenger would try to humor him by asking if he had caught anything. Then Endymion would come into his own. "What, on that?" he would say pointing to the cement sidewalk. "You must be mad!" So that helps us to differentiate between Endymion and the Bird. A further source of confusion comes from the two sabers Endymion carried on occasion to show his disapproval of warfare. The Bird may have borrowed one or provided one himself. After his return from Canada, he went to an Italian warehouse, as the delicatessens were called in Dublin. Hams and flitches of bacon hung suspended from an iron bar high in the air outside the store. One morning before the rush hour the Bird approached the owner of the delicatessen and bought a ham. He got a receipt. After the transaction he asked the proprietor to let the ham hang where it was for a few hours. The Bird had other things to do, and he did not wish to cart the ham around with him. To this the owner consented. At the rush hour the Bird returned. He had a saber in his hand with which he *addressed* the ham, inviting it to a duel. After a few flourishes he transfixed the ham and, putting it over his shoulder, ran off. He was closely pursued by two policemen. Cornered at last, the Bird produced the receipt for the ham and asked was there no liberty left in the country when a man couldn't buy a ham without being arrested?

As a result of this exploit, and probably because of a few others, the Bird was sent to Australia. He pretended that he went willingly, that it was a country that delighted in horses and it was just the place for him. But after a few months the Bird proved to be a homing pigeon. He returned.

Dublin is possessed of a Ballast Office, over the door of which is a clock which tells sidereal time. Promptly at noon the Bird took up his station before the clock. When the clock's hands pointed to the hour, two alarm clocks which the Bird had in his tail pockets went off together. Much mirth attended the Bird. He smiled and went off satisfied. He had the exact time.

All the aldermen of the city, headed by the Lord Mayor, planned to hold a World's Fair. It would be like nothing on earth. It was.

Nations from all parts of the globe were invited to show their wares and to be sure that their national costumes were represented. The Americas were in it; South Africa and the Far East, which meant Japan. It was Japan that caused the most interest. This was largely if not altogether due to a tribe that were never before beheld by Western eyes. They were the hairy Ainus, a very primitive tribe who were reputed to go into dark caves and to fight with bears with nothing but a knife and a bearskin thrown loosely over their shoulders. The bear would grapple with the Ainu only to find that the bearskin came off in the fight, during which he was disemboweled. A whole family of hairy Ainus was displayed, children and all. They were copper-colored, even to the baby in arms. The baby was not long in arms, for it disappeared mysteriously. Whereupon a truly frightful uproar broke out. Nobody knew what the mother was saying. She was pointing to her breasts; but nobody understood. The man of the tribe was desperate. He would have broken loose but for the iron bars behind which the family was ensconced. At last someone, probably a member of the Japanese government, said that the baby had disappeared and that, naturally, the parents were frantic. Would no one search for it? If the Ainus broke out . . .

At last the baby was found in the French pavilion. It was at long last, for nobody thought of searching there. The baby was found smiling, for it was interested in a bottle of warm milk the like of which it had never seen.

The aldermen held a special meeting. Eyes, unfriendly for the most part, were turned on Alderman Milligan. Was he not directly responsible for getting the corporation of the city in such a jam? Had the baby been found anywhere but in the French pavilion, it might have been a different matter. As it was, the French took the placing of the baby there as a direct insult. Obviously, the reference intended was a reference to their falling birth rate, as well as to the fact that the French nation was very high in the scale of infant mortality. An international incident could be made of such an insult. The French consul attended and he took a lot of placating. He forgave the aldermen because it was proved to his satisfaction that none of them was responsible.

The Bird was banished.

Months later, a friend was strolling down a street in Buenos Aires. There was a large hole in the street, at the bottom of which a man was working with a pick. The friend chanced to look down. He thought he recognized the broad shoulders and the red neck, which were out of keeping with the local workmen. "Good Heavens, Bird, is that you?" The Bird looked up. "Get to hell out of that! It took a mighty lot of influence to get me this job!"

He was through with bad companions. It may have been due to the difficulty of securing a job or it may not. But there were no more "incidents" in Dublin.

The first and last I saw of the Bird was in the Phoenix Park, which is said to be the largest park enclosed by a wall in Europe. He must have been pointed out to me, for I never remember meeting him. I saw the nose across his face, the red face and neck, and the well-dressed setup of the man as he came prancing by on a big bay horse. I saw his light brown waistcoat, his riding gloves, one of which fell over his left wrist, the bowler hat, the riding trousers and boots. He raised his whip in an exaggerated salute and cantered off.

That was long after the changing of the Ainu baby: you cannot call it stealing, for it never left the Fair.

The Bird was of a generous nature: he harmed nobody. Dublin is a lesser place since it lost its men of mirth.

Do You Mind the Fourth?

Once I was on my way to Tim Costello's, a pleasant hostelry at the corner of Forty-fourth and Third Avenue, when the elevated was running and Tim's was in its old haunt. I took a taxi and gave the driver the address, "I want to go to Tim's at the corner of Forty-fourth and Third Avenue." The taximan said, "Do you mind the Fourth?" "Certainly I do," I said, "I want to go to Third and Forty-fourth Street." "I mean the Fourth Symphony of Beethoven."

As I said, the el was running in those days, and with the roar of the traffic on either side, and not to mention that the taximan had to keep his eyes on the street, he could hardly hear the Fourth Symphony. His judgment was bad: it was not a time for emotion. All his attention was wanted for his cab.

I arrived at Tim's in spite of the music-obsessed taximan. Then I considered the case of the taximan. He could not hear the music. It was noise he wanted—Noise!

I am far from being a warrior, but when I think of the crooners and other interferers with music, I would willingly become a sergeant of Marines or some equally tough regiment (if there is anything tougher than the Marines) just to get the crooners where I wanted them. How I would put them through their paces! Yes; I very often regret that I am not a sergeant when I hear the crooners on the air. And you cannot help hearing them, for they are omnipresent. You cannot listen in without them interrupting whatever you are trying to listen to. It may be due to the general use of radio sets, it may be due to general and indiscriminate education, or to both; but it is not music any more than that which the taximan thought he could hear.

Then there is the juke box, the lighted coal scuttle. Tim's has no juke box. That is the reason for the crowds, who go there to hear one another talk. I have seen two sailors in a bar put two quarters into a juke box and then walk out. They may have felt that their walking was a reflection on those who listened; but I don't think so. They did not mean anything in particular, yet they left those in the bar to endure the noise. Some of those in the bar liked noise: they could not talk without it. But music, no!

Music is rhythm, that is a succession of sounds pleasing to the ear. At this time, and for all I know in the long history of music, cacophony stood for music. Witness the "composer" who lately wrote what he called music deliberately outside the octaves within which music exists.

There are people who cannot work if they don't hear noise, just as the London street arabs, when they were sent to the country to be out of the way of the bombs, could not sleep because of the stillness.

I knew a very intelligent man who could not work until the gramophone was playing. That he had an interest in it undoubtedly may have led to this, because he was the owner of the paper called the *Gramophone* and the editor thereof. He was also a Scotsman. He wrote many novels, all of them best sellers or very nearly.

I also knew a drunk who had an Eton accent and who took everything in by mouth and eye. In other words, he read the newspaper while he breakfasted on many whiskies and five aspirins; but he did not have a gramophone playing. The very intelligent man did not drink. So you can't have everything. You can't fill all the avenues of sense at once. Something drives out another thing.

Abraham Lincoln said, "The Lord prefers common-looking people. That is the reason He makes so many of them." The common people have debauched music: crooners, wailers, and snouters. They have debauched it particularly in the United States, because in the United States there are so many juke boxes, radios, and television sets. In proportion to these, music is everywhere debauched by those who sing through their noses. That is why they are called snouters. And crooning was invented in the United States. The awful thing is that the common people have not got a say in this outrage. They have it thrust on them. But they "listen in." What they want is noise. What they get is impure noise: music turned inside out. The taxi driver didn't want the Fourth Symphony. All he wanted was noise. Children want noise. Could it be that the common people are children at heart?

That very serious domineering and brusque humbug, Ouspensky, divided people into five categories. In the first class were the avatars, the Buddhas, etc. In the next, Homer, Virgil, Dante, and Shakespeare. The self-conscious in the next. By self-conscious he did not mean men who were awkward in society but men who were aware of themselves. In the next two classes he put the lowest form of human beings, those who lived automatically. Those who reacted to catch words like "O.K.," "No soap," "Do you see what I mean?" and so on. Those who were like the taxi driver or like children who delight in noise. Where Ouspensky got the idea from, don't ask me. He probably got it from some review. As he got most things. He wrote *Tertium Organum;* but Bacon was not displaced.

In New York everything is noisy, or used to be until Mayor Wagner silenced the horns on motor cars. Unlike Mayor La Guardia, who conducted an anti-noise campaign with a siren attached to his car, Mayor Wagner has silenced the city only to make the Fire Department, which wails like all the female tiger cats in the world, more noisy still because the city is silent—more or less. Then there is the groaning of the engines of the Sanitation Department, all of which are more noisy as the city is quieter. And what about the wailing of the sirens that are supposed to herald an enemy attack? They have been trying themselves out so long that if it ever comes to an attack, people will think that it is another trial experiment. Noise is the answer. Noise. Even the letter boxes are noisy in New York. Luckily for the United States, New York is (in places) an island detached from the Levant. It is not America by any manner of means. Then there is the pneumatic drill.

I wish I had within my grip
The inventor of the pneumatic drill.
I'd take good care it did not slip
Till I had shoved it up, until
It reached a place beneath his hat,
And drowned his screams with its Rat Tat.

Noise is a form of life. In the grave all is silence. Do you know, I am beginning to like noise. I have a secret liking for the last two kinds of people in Ouspensky's catalogue, the men who are automatons. They have nothing to trouble them.

There are some noises that are quite pleasant; for instance, "Noises are said to be heard beneath the Long Barrow called Fairy Toot in Somerset."

This example is from England, for England has more influence here just now. Examples from Ireland would have to be fraught with magic as in faery music.

I knew a man who composed operas and was a very accomplished musician. He sometimes walked by the seashore listening for faery music in order to take it down. He was an Irishman, of course, and he well believed that he should hear music playing in mid-air. For all I know, he is still alive; but whether he has found faery music playing by the sea I cannot tell you. This I know: that he believed it and made preparation to record it.

There are banshees in Ireland. They must have been the instigators of the wailers, for theirs is an unpleasant noise. I must say this for the banshees; nobody expects their wail to be pleasant for it betokens death in old families. It is otherwise with the crooners or the wailers, for they have outraged music.

The most noisy place in the city of New York is where there is a notice, "Quiet please." The next-noisiest places are the restaurants. There the guests roar at each other, and if you are known, the head waiter roars a welcome above the din. The talkers are driven to making themselves heard above the shouting, and you are turned into an eavesdropper willy-nilly. Of course there is not anything to overhear. You are lucky if you hear anything articulate above the noise of dishes and the yelling of the guests. I must say that I heard several people shout, "Listen." But what they said was drowned in the general noise.

Now some noises are pleasant. I say this lest you should think that I am against all noises. The sound a cooper makes when he hammers on a barrel. "Soon there will be drinking." The pleasant splashing of water from the wheel of an old mill. The sound an airplane's engines make before it rides the air. The ring of hoofs as horses enter the straight when all the rest is silence. And amongst the merriest noises I have heard is the laughter of girls—when not directed at me.

It is a long call from the sailors with a quarter for the juke box to the tramp of Kylemore Pass in Connemara, who said to a friend of mine as he passed her house, "It's a fine, still place that you have here, ma'am, God bless it."

The average person (I may have hypersensitive ears) finds noises above 140 decibels (a measure of sound) intolerable. Noises above that level may give rise to injurious effects even when not heard. For one thing, they have an injurious effect on the nerves which protect the body, and for another, supersonic noises may do great damage to the brain. That they have been used in this connection I have heard stated; but we don't know enough about them as yet. As for producing cancer, your bet is as good as mine. We as yet do not know the cause of cancer. We do know that cancer given to a mouse or rat can be cured either by injections or by altering the diet; but the fact remains that the cancer was given in the first place. Yes; noise may have something to do with cancer. I have heard cancer blamed on a host of things, among them dogs' defecation. There are, according to statistics, some twenty million dogs in the United States. You can see their traces on any street: they must weigh tons daily. When dry they are sniffed by the nostrils, and this can do no good. When wet, they get on the soles of your shoes and so are carried into the house. It is cruelty to animals to have any dog, especially a hound dog, "room broken" and never permitted to go without a leash. A hound dog or any big dog runs ten times more than you walk when taken to the country—those countries where he is not on a leash. Yet no newspaper, and not even the Society for the Prevention of Cruelty to Animals, will act against this cruelty. Obviously, the newspapers do not want to lose a part of their readers, and the S.P.C.A. possibly have their own reason for taking no steps.

Whatever may be blamed on supersonic noise, it is noise within the range of the human ear that is to me actually painful, so is it any wonder that I minded the Fourth?

Is the Other World a Madhouse?

"FOR THE MIND ASLEEP HATH CLEAR VISION, BUT IN THE DAYTIME THE FATE OF MORTAL MAN CANNOT BE FORESEEN." AESCHYLUS

Water divining, clairvoyance, mediumship are well-established; apparitions and hauntings not so well. Of two of these I have had personal experience, of water divining and of an apparition. The facts about the others were told to me by trustworthy friends.

Water divining I will take first. I was staying in a house in Dummerston Center, Vermont, a few years ago. The water supply ran out for the first time in sixty years. The owner of the house, a practical man, was confronted by the fact that he would have to sink an artesian well, a costly matter, or seek the services of a well-known water diviner, who might find the underground spring from which the house was supplied. The water diviner was sent for. He arrived promptly on a Sunday—I remember it well—and he carried a brown paper bag in which were half a dozen slight twigs or forks about eighteen inches long. Before he entered the field where the spring was presumed to be, he asked us to guess from what kind of tree he had taken the forks. Everyone guessed wrongly. I held my peace because I knew. "Witch hazel," he said. He advanced, holding one of the forks with the backs of his hands turned inward. He had not gone far when the fork began to dip. Presently it broke. "There is water here," he announced. "At what depth?" the owner of the house asked. The water diviner took another fork and walked over the hidden spring. The fork began to dip. "Nine feet six," he said, and so it turned out to be.

In the Middle Ages water divining or dowsing fell into disrepute because it was used to "divine" heretics and witches, who very often were the diviner's enemies. Perhaps witch hazel got its name from such practices.

After his striking demonstration the diviner handed his fork to several of the bystanders. In each case nothing happened. Nothing happened to me. I was disappointed because I had hoped that I was endowed. Of the accuracy of the divination of the diviner, George Harris, there can be no doubt. I was present next day when the spring was found, and its depth was as predicted.

Now for apparitions fully externalized. I was driving my car slowly at the end of a grass-bordered road that went through the Phoenix Park near Dublin. My mind was all but a blank, as near to the "complete indifference" mentioned as a condition favorable to supersensory phenomena by Mrs. Eileen Garrett, the famous medium. If I were thinking of anything, I was thinking of the danger of a child running out of the gate lodge as I passed out of the Park. Along the grass border to my right a horseman came cantering on a large chesnut horse. He raised his whip solemnly, with the jocular solemnity of a salute. He wore a bowler hat, a brown tweed coat, and a striped waistcoat of lighter brown. I could see the four little holes on each button of his waistcoat. He had a red face and a broken nose. I knew that face. I had seen it somewhere. When he had passed, it suddenly occurred to me that he had been dead for months. And yet I saw him riding by in broad daylight. You will say that I was dreaming. Very well; but what are dreams? I should have known that it was impossible to see the little holes by which buttons are attached to clothes at ten yards. But why should he appear to me, who hardly knew him, when there were many dead who were much closer to me who never appeared after death? This purposelessness, this irrelevance, appears to be a characteristic of many apparitions.

There is a tree-darkened country road which goes beside a river in the west of Ireland, which is haunted by an old woman in an eighteenth-century cloak and hood. She gets in the way of cyclists after dusk, but she is never run into because she is never overtaken. This happened to a very great friend, who spoke of it casually because he did not know that the road was haunted. To what purpose is this? You need not ask; but note that meaninglessness is characteristic of them so far as phantoms are concerned.

As for prophecies, clairvoyance: Freud, who was all the rage once and for all I know may be still, attempted to "explain" them by telepathy. According to him, the fortuneteller telepathically and of course unconsciously perceives the unconscious wish of the sitter. In other and honester words, the fortuneteller perceives that which she does not know herself and the sitter does not know! Ignorance calling to ignorance! Apart from begging the question, this is no explanation but a statement. There is something dishonest in the attitude of superiority in talking as if telepathy, which cannot be explained, was an explanation in itself.

The oracle at Delphi employed a priestess of "canonical years," that is, old enough not to cause scandal. Before becoming oracular she fasted for some days, then she inhaled gas which came from a crevice in the inner sanctuary of Apollo. I inhaled it myself, but it was some distance from the ancient site owing to an earthquake. Then with frothing mouth she uttered a prophecy which the priests translated into hexameters. In Italy there was the Sybil. All this is significant: women make the best mediums to the present day. They act on instinct. It is as if we had to depend on frenzied and entranced women to foretell the future. They have to get as far away from reason as possible. The corollary to this is that reason has nothing to do with foretelling but is actually an obstacle to foresight. "For the mind asleep hath clear vision, but in the daytime the fate of mortal man cannot be foreseen."

It is a well-known fact that nitrous oxide or "laughing gas" acts on some people in a manner analogous to prophecy. It acted on me in this way: I seemed to be under a sheet of ice, through which I could see the skaters above me. I felt, I knew, that if I could only get up I would tell them the mystery of the cosmos in two words. The two words would unite the field and explain everything. Note: there was a mystery, and an urge to explain everything in a few words. A friend on whom nitrous oxide had a similar effect put his experience more poetically: "I felt that the mystery of the world could be written on a blade of grass."

The effects of that most fantastic of all sciences, the science of "higher mathematics," are something like those of laughing gas. There is the same intellectual delusion, the same urge to simplify, to unify the cosmos. This is to be done by a formula instead of a blade of grass. Thus in a reputable daily newspaper we are informed that: "In his quest for a new understanding of the fundamental laws governing the cosmos Dr. Einstein has searched for simple unifying principles underlying the multifarious phenomena in which the material universe manifests itself. . . . Dr. Einstein believes that the physical universe is one continuous field like an endless stream." I thought of it as a frozen lake!

It is known that lunatics are revered by certain primitive tribes because their eccentricity and unaccountability are held to be of divine origin. We who consider ourselves more civilized go to oratorios and to readings of poetry because we believe that we are listening to those who are inspired, to those who have had something "breathed into them" from outside, as God breathed into the clay whence Adam sprung. This reverence for genius is an acceptance of the incalculable, of the mysterious, of something outside ourselves, of Revelation in fact. It is akin to our belief in another world; and how much better this is than the belief that man consists of a system of reflexes and of nothing more!

Mystery indeed! The world has no mystery to men who "commute," arrive punctually "on time," keep appointments, rush on business, become go-getters—men who dare not stop to think. These are the real "escapists." They would go mad if they were confronted by a mystery, if they were faced with anything that could not be explained in a rational sense. It is to those who strive to get beyond reason that mystery is ever present; and mystery it is that has caused towns to rise into spires. The mind asleep!

So far we have had apparitions whose appearances are without meaning; we depend on women who froth at the mouth for prophecy; we go for messages to mediums who have the gift of divers tongues of which, unentranced, they know nothing; we employ diviners to find water when the supply runs out; and we admire geniuses whose gift is just as unexplainable as any of these. It is before the unaccountable we bow. Not a hopeful congeries if the other world is to be regarded as anything but a madhouse.

But wait! This is but a catalogue of points rather than a total impression. Before we criticize the other world, what about this one? Great religions have been founded on the belief that this world is all a Maya, an illusion, a veil behind which reality lies. Others present it as a Vale of Tears in which the soul is tested before entering eternity. To some it appears as a kaleidoscope of dreams. Then there is the "I am Thou" of certain religions in the north of India; and the solopism (*solus*, alone, and *ipse*, self), the idealism or subjectivism of Bishop Berkeley, which holds that everything that exists depends on the mind of the percipient for existence. Absurd it may be, but it is irrefutable. Dr. Johnson, who kicked a stone to demonstrate its absurdity, exposed his ignorance of its contention. He did not refute it. The nearest thing to refutation came from my friend George Russell. One day Yeats, the poet who was far from being a philosopher, was reading Berkeley when the idea struck him. He rushed round to Russell. "Everything that exists in this world depends on my mind, Russell." "Thank you, Yeats, I have written your poetry." After all, Russell claimed a share in the subjectivism too.

I am aware that to show that one world is fraught with inconsistencies does not make the other any saner. If you believe, as Bishop Berkeley did, that all existence consists of percepts, you will see that there is no such thing as an other world. The mind is everything. There is but one world, the world of the mind. The net of the mind hampers everything; but there are powers of the mind withheld from the generality of mankind, from the sophisticated as well as from the uneducated. If we have to turn to priestesses, mediums, soothsayers, and poets, we are turning to those who are best suited to deal with things beyond the mind, the parapsychologists. It should not prove impossible to translate the irrational into the rational, though why that is desirable I cannot see. This we know: reason is inimical to investigations of the subliminal. We are dealing with phenomena which are beyond reason and which are adumbrated by such means as are set out above, all of which a rationalist would consider absurd; and yet the greatest minds of which we have knowledge, Aeschylus, Shakespeare, Blake, etc., treated these intimations with awe. Not only did they acknowledge their presence but they were awestruck by their mystery: "For the mind asleep hath clear vision" and "There are more things in heaven and earth." So far from thinking of the other world as a madhouse, we should think of it as the greatest minds have thought of it, and the great religions as well. I should be the last to set myself up as an authority, I who could not divine water, yet I hold by the doctrines that mankind has accepted. Remember the question the little girl asked when the teacher was telling the class that all life originated in the sea: "Who made the sea?"

Whence comes the conviction, the innate instinct that this life is not the only one? In spite of the irrationality of dreams, the rarity of clairvoyance, the unreliability of mediums, and the meaninglessness of apparitions, the conviction still is there.

The mind has limitations: for instance it cannot imagine that which has had no beginning, though it can imagine time without end. It cannot even imagine a new being without combining things already existing or known. The mind cannot get away from itself. That which is unimaginable the churches call mysteries; and the mind is the greatest mystery of all. In the mind are cause and effect; the beginning and the end; time and eternity; the rational and the irrational. It avails nothing to ask what made it, for making is contained in it. Making is a concept of the mind.

Mankind believed once that the earth was the center and that the sun revolved round it. Then mathematicians proved that mankind was wrong. One of the mathematicians has informed me that it is only a question of mathematics to prove the opposite. So mathematics at its core is fanciful. Be that as it may, scientists who go along their own path have found that path to lead to a mystery. Proofs are misleading. It is instinct, the eternal feminine principle in Nature, that leads us on. And instinct feels that there is another world which is not a madhouse but a dwelling place for immortal spirits. The converse proves this: We have only to look at a system which sets its face against such a belief to find that the very life of man is threatened. After all, it is a belief in something beyond that enables us to live. With all respect due to Aeschylus, a respect that, strange to say, deepens with time, and for all Dunne has said on the subject, I cannot see that "the mind asleep hath clear vision." Rather it seems to me that we spend a third of our lives in a madhouse, for who can control dreams?

What the Mikado's Doctor Revealed to Me

When Trinity College, Dublin, was celebrating the second centenary of the foundation of its Medical School, the Board decided to send an invitation to the world's outstanding figures in the realm of medicine. There were so many celebrated doctors and professors of medicine in the world that it was obvious that the College could not house them all. Therefore the medical practitioners of the city were requested to invite as many of the visitors as possible to their homes. A list of the foreign medical men who had accepted the Board's invitation was sent to each potential host. A circular was sent to me. On looking down the list my eye caught the name of Dr. Irisawa, Professor of Medicine in the University of Tokyo and private physician to the Mikado. Being full of an indefinite and romantic curiosity about the East, about China and Japan, I applied for the privilege of entertaining that eminent physician. After a becoming delay, the Board graciously granted my request. By the time I got the Board's consent, the Professor was already on his journey. Eagerly I awaited the day when that fourteen-thousand-mile trip should end.

As time went by and he came nearer and nearer, my curiosity was mingled with anxiety: What would he be like? How would I entertain him? Would he eat rice only? Chopsticks? Would he speak English? Would I make a mistake similar to the one I made when I sipped tea before a Chinese lady, whom I was endeavoring to entertain, had raised her cup to her lips? Little did I realize that in China such an action was tantamount to a signal of dismissal. I was amazed when she rose to leave the room. It took some little time to explain. "You know so much about Chinese porcelain," she said, indicating some Oriental jars in the room, "that I thought you knew something about Chinese politeness." Now such a mistake as that must not occur again. Definitely not. Where could I get a guidebook on the manners and customs and conventions of Japan? I despaired of mastering them in time. I regretted my headlong hospitality. Why did I not leave him to some of my colleagues? They could have housed him and I could have called in and satisfied my curiosity to my heart's content. The Board could just as easily have sent me someone else. Now I had a medical Nipponese round my neck. I was always too precipitate. I had asked for it. It served me right.

The mind, when too intent on anything, sometimes protects itself by forgetting. One day on returning to my house I sensed a feeling of suppressed excitement in the air. At the moment the Land of the Rising Sun was far from my mind. The servant met me in the hall. "They're here," he said. "Who are *they?*" I asked. The man seemed embarrassed. Whether he thought I was serious or not I cannot say. Possibly he did not know what to call the little foreigners. He was afraid, as most Irishmen are, of being unconsciously offensive, or unconscious about anything at all when it comes to that.

Suddenly it dawned on me like a forgotten appointment. "The Jap?" I asked. Inscrutably he nodded. "But you said 'they,'" I reminded him. "There's two," he said. "They came when you were out."

Had I given it consideration, I could not expect a man so eminent and important as the Mikado's physician to travel without his body servant. "Where have you put them?" I asked. "I took up their luggage and showed them to their rooms."

I hastened to go up to welcome them. On my way I looked into the drawing room. There they stood. I didn't know which was which.

The smaller of the pair came forward a pace and, bowing, presented me to the older and taller man. "Professor Irisawa," he said.

The Professor bowed. I bowed and with some temerity I tried to shake hands. It worked. The Professor, who spoke English fluently, introduced his companion. A gong sounded in the hall. Now among the plans and precautions I had determined to take, one of them was that gong. We used it for a dressing and dinner gong. But in Japan it once may have been a temple gong and a summons to prayer when we were really going to a meal. It might be as bad a breach of etiquette as to sip tea before a Chinese guest, if not worse. "A little refreshment after so long a journey?" They accepted. I rang the bell.

It was a relief to think that by offering drinks before dinner I had not fallen into some strange Japanese ambush. Now the thing to do is make some vague conversation, I thought. It won't do to ask them if this is their first trip to Europe; but I can ask with impunity if it is their first trip to Ireland, for in Ireland Japs are as rare as are colored people. (I remembered the colored girl student from Columbia University who in speaking of a trip to Ireland said, "Colored persons must be rare in Ireland." "Why do you think that?" I asked. "Because a little girl fainted when she saw me," she said.)

Dr. Irisawa had been trained in the University of Berlin. He did not bring his companion into the conversation. For the sake of politeness I let it appear that I attributed this companion also to Berlin.

At dinner there was less restraint. They accepted whatever was served. I had not forgotten to tell the cook that there was to be no rice. I may have forgotten about the gong; but I had distinctly forbidden rice because it was too obvious a dish. It would be just too awful if the kitchen were permitted to interpret Japan.

They had come via San Francisco, New York, and the Continent. The Professor, with extreme politeness, suppressed the length of time they had lingered on the Continent, so that it would not appear that their visit had any other object but to attend the bicentenary of our Medical School.

After a few days the festivities were in full swing. The Professor was invited out by the Provost and the various hosts who were co-operating in the hospitalities of the College. The younger Japanese was left with me.

He, it appeared, liked my house, which was somewhat unusual. It had been constructed by an architect who was slightly mad, in that it possessed four bathrooms and there were basins with hot and cold water in many of the rooms. Whenever they passed one of these, my visitors lost no opportunity of washing their hands. We discussed washing and bathing. In Japan they wash with soap and water first before immersing themselves in an oval-shaped wooden tub up to the neck in water of a temperature higher than a European could sustain.

One evening during the absence of the Doctor, I asked the little man about the fatal tricks of jujitsu. I was not quite accurate in calling it jujitsu. It was something else. But whatever it was, its secrets could not be demonstrated, not because of any vow not to divulge them, but simply because speed was the essence of their execution and any adequate demonstration would be fatal. Strange as it may seem, my curiosity languished.

But I tried a test for strength, the old one of trying to force your opponent's arm down against the table. I should say the little man weighed, allowing for his solidarity, about 125 pounds. I was 50 pounds heavier. My arm was forced back with ease. "When I felt a muscular tremor, I knew that your strength had reached its limit. I had no difficulty," he said. But the imminent return of the Professor caused us to decline an invitation to which there could not but have been the same end. I am not exactly "the full of a door," which is the prerequisite in Ireland for a successful physician of strength; but I had considered myself to be pretty useful until then. Whatever strength I had was futile when compared to the compact muscularity of the little athlete from Nippon.

The relationship between my visitors being unknown, I forbore from discussing intimate questions with Dr. Irisawa and confined myself to the mutual topic of medicine. He would like to visit one of the hospitals. Luckily we had an up-to-date one, recently built, of which I happened to be one of the governors. Now unless a medical man is actually assisting at an operation, there is very little to be learned by a qualified doctor from the mere inspection of patients. He asked but one or two questions, which revealed a mastery of modern practice but left me uncertain of the verdict of his opinion. Later, however, his friend revealed the fact that in the short space of our visit he had ascertained how much soap went to each patient and what the cost of upkeep of each bed was per annum.

It was, of course, not polite to begin a conversation with the Mikado's physician, who was half-sacred because he had touched the Emperor, by asking "Well, how's the Son of Heaven doing?" (It would be as shocking as if one inquired about the health of the Holy Ghost.) But I learned some interesting facts about Japan—the freedom from cancer among its women was one thing that stuck in my memory.

One morning about five-thirty I heard the sound of the lawn mower in the garden. I looked out from my bedroom window and saw a strange sight. The Professor was pushing the lawn mower, while his companion, who was crawling alongside it, was telling him how it worked.

The apple trees were in bloom and beginning to take the light. It was a nuisance to get up so early. But then it also was a shame to be in bed. With that to console me, I bathed and dressed. When I at last arrived on the lawn, the investigation was still in progress. They are patient in Japan.

It was scarcely more than 6:00 A.M. It was far too early to wake the servants to serve breakfast. In Dublin the reveille rarely sounds before 9:00 A.M. What was I to do with my visitors? I could not with propriety leave them to the lawn mower and return to bed. I explained its workings. And then I had a sudden idea, born perhaps of the thought of one mechanism leading to the thought of another. I could start my automobile and take them for a ride through the Phoenix Park, whose hawthorn trees would be fresh, while their perfume would fill the motionless morning air. They accepted my suggestion readily.

The town looked strange in its sleep. I was glad of the silence and the space of the streets. I told them that the rose-red houses were built of brick all the way up from the foundations and not faced with a layer. The walls were two feet thick or more. Little does one realize the strangeness of a country's houses. What must the great walled houses 150 years old and more have seemed, compared with the papier-mâché houses of Japan? No, there were no earthquakes in Ireland. There was a good deal of stagnation, but that was not intended for a compensation. They got my feeble sally quite well.

The drive was so enjoyable that we decided to continue it. There is a spa at Lucan, a lovely village about seven miles from the city. It is a medicinal spa of sulfur water. There is a well not far away which bubbles with water faintly charged with radium. I resolved to say nothing of the sulfur spa because it gets its curative effects by permitting its votaries to recover from it when they can stand it no more. The radium water was different. It can give the drinker cancer of the stomach if it is drunk over a prolonged period. Yes. The Professor could well believe that. He knew one case where the continued irritation to the stomach ended in malignancy. And yet the Public! Yes. We were in complete agreement with regard to the public tendency to attribute magical attributes to the latest or the oldest discovery.

As we left the well, the attendant called me back. Would the gentlemen sign the visitors' book? I supposed they would, but he had better ask them himself. This he did with a little hesitation. When he saw the signatures, which went down the page like a column of figures and took up half the sheet, he asked indignantly, "What am I to do with this?" "Add it up," I said, and drew my visitors away, out of earshot.

On the way back the Professor was more expansive. He acknowledged that he thought that Europeans, especially the British, made themselves "sodden" with sleep. "You think we sleep too much?" I asked, with that four-o'clock-in-the-morning effrontery which Napoleon praised. "Five hours is enough," was his professional opinion. For politeness' sake, I must get a touch of insomnia until the visit is ended. Reluctantly I resigned myself to the prospect of that horrible up-in-the-morning habit, which is, if the truth were known, one of the signs of senile decay. At least in Europe.

There was something childlike about Professor Irisawa. His quietness was almost inhuman. He gave me the impression that there was some all-absorbing concept in his mind, some conviction or devotion which he was trying to conceal lest a realization of it by a foreigner would reveal an attitude of assured superiority and a fixed disdain. He never would allow any hostile criticism of our Occidental ways to appear. And he must have thought that we were a heterogeneous collection of distracted humans, with different-colored eyes, variously shaped bodies, prone to disease, and willfully shortening our lives by at least one-sixth by the drug of sleep.

It was my turn to give a party to many of those who, like myself, had overseas guests. I asked the Professor if there were any of his fellow countrymen in the city. I had never seen one. That was not the reason that prompted me to urge him to invite any of his fellow countrymen to dine with us who happened to be in Dublin. Eight appeared, however. What they were doing in the city at the time, I do not to this day know. They may have been unobtrusively guarding the man who guarded the health of the Son of Heaven.

A strange thing happened when they were all assembled in the drawing room. They stood as if in deference to one of their number. When he was seated, they all sat down with hardly a perceptible interval between them as they took their seats. I could not detect who was the person to whom they deferred. I do not believe it was my guest. I noticed one thing, however. The little companion of the Professor sat down last. I left them to talk among themselves behind closed doors for about half an hour. The Professor thanked me for making the suggestion.

One day, shortly before their departure, the Professor gave me some coins of Korea for curios. This led to a discussion of the Japanese policy of expansion. We discussed the recent Russian war, the conquest of Korea, and the richest prize left in the world, the market of China.

I tried to elicit from him, who was an intimate of the Emperor, some information about Japan's future foreign policy. I elicited nothing. The little I knew of the Orient came from the writings of Lafcadio Hearn who, a quarter of a century before, had viewed with grave concern for the survival of the white race the day when the moiling millions of the Orient would become mechanized. I lamented certain shortsighted policies of European statesmen, as they appeared to me. I do not have to recall his remark. It has never left my memory. As I elicited nothing that he did not wish to say, what he did say has all the more import: "In Japan we think in centuries," he said. "And what do we think in? What does the West think in?" I asked. He answered, "Elections."

There is somewhere in Tokyo a statue of Professor Irisawa. When the Marines come upon it, they find the portrait in bronze of a broad-foreheaded, small-faced, non-grotesque Japanese who warned the West that it was too sleepy and who thought in centuries—one of which, I hope, may have been medieval.

After their visit some months elapsed. One morning very early—what influence caused it to be unusually early I know not—a van drew up to the door laden with boxes from Japan. There were presents for all of us, for all the members of the family. Silks and lacquered boxes, ivories exquisitely carved, statues, and pictures on very old silk. I remembered how the little Jap had told me that at the time of the Boxer rising the Japanese had gone to Chinese warehouses and seized century-old silks so that they might later on copy the masterpieces of Chinese pictorial art with little fear of the fraud being discovered, for the touchstone was the age of the silk. Half the room was full of gifts from the Mikado's doctor.

What was I to do? To send a complimentary gift of any of our *objets d'art* would be too obvious an attempt at return. I was in a quandry. Was it the early hour that gave me the idea? I had it!

I sent what I believe were the first two lawn mowers to Kobe and to Tokyo.

The Most Haunted House of Them All

There are haunted houses everywhere. There is that college in Cambridge in which a divinity student lived on the second floor of one of the houses, the back room of which was haunted by something so evil that the student resolved to exorcise it himself. The story, which I had from one of the three who helped him, goes thus: The young man obtained a large crucifix to hold in front of him as he entered the back room. The day came when this was to be done. His friends stood behind him as he entered the room. Suddenly he was seized by something invisible and the crucifix was all but torn from his grasp. He cried to his friends to hold him. The first caught him round the waist, the others held each other likewise. They all pulled together to drag him back. The four of them were rocked and, as they swayed, were violently shaken. The young divinity student collapsed. When they managed to get him out into the open he was found to have lost his reason. The others were bound to secrecy by the college authorities, and the room was walled up.

Everyone knows of the Glamys ghost, for Glamys is the ancestral home of Her Majesty's mother, Queen Elizabeth of England. And there is a ghost that lowers the drawbridge of a moated castle on the border of Wales. But the worst ghost of all is in a castle in the middle of Ireland, which is spelled "Leap" Castle though it is pronounced "Lep."

The old coach road that runs by it is widely margined with

grass borders that are almost as wide again as the macadam. Here the unschoolable tribes of tinkers tether their horses and pitch their black tents. But they never camp in the vicinity of the haunted place.

It is said that the site was inhabited long before Christianity was introduced into the country. There must have been strange rites practiced there, for today it is one of the spots on earth which an unwholesome spirit holds. It is off the highroad, but it would not hinder the spirit if the road passed close by. There are empty houses to be seen standing in prosperous villages, houses that no one dare live in, for they are on a "pass"—that is, they are standing in the way of the faery hosts as they go riding through the night. But the faeries are the "Good People."

The landscape round Leap Castle is bleak enough though the land itself is rich, for its richness depends on the rains that sweep the countryside, making it look desolate and inhospitable.

The owners of Leap Castle are far from being inhospitable, for they used to entertain many guests. From some of these the story comes, for the owners do not speak of it. When I met the present owner he avoided any reference to it. I skirted the subject as closely as politeness allowed, but I forbore to question him directly, seeing that he did not volunteer to tell the story himself.

This is one of the strange things about hauntings: the local people will not discuss them nor mention them at all. This is due to the conviction that to speak of a ghost is to bring him on you; and maybe they are right.

The ghost of Leap Castle is a nightmare thing, the thought of which even on a sunny day makes the air about you cold and charnel and roughens your skin.

The only man of my acquaintance who had any knowledge of such supernatural apparitions was the poet Yeats, and with him I talked of the ghost of Leap Castle and got his conclusions. We had to piece together many stories, only one of which was at first hand; but there were others pretty well authenticated, which gave an idea of the castle's grim history and set the scene, as it were. One of these was the story of some workmen who were working on an ancient part of the house when they came upon some skeletons in armor immured in the thickness of the wall. They were the remains of some of the garrison who had perished during a siege. Their bodies could not be thrown from the battlements to fall into the hands of their enemies, nor could they be buried in the ground. The only thing to do (and it was the practice of the time) was to build them into the wall with stones and mortar until the end of the siege. Evidently the siege had not had a happy ending, for the bodies in armor were forgotten.

There must be many a castle in Ireland whose walls, if they were searched, would yield such evidence of the stormy times of the country's history, for so badly was the country ravaged by war during the reign of Good Queen Bess that only four houses were built in Ireland during her spacious days. But let me return to the subject of the ghostly apparition that so many saw in Leap Castle during the last century or so.

The strange thing is that all who reported seeing the apparitions were guests. Maybe the family had seen it and had grown accustomed to it, though to grow accustomed to such a thing is beyond the power of human self-control.

The first account came from a bishop who with his wife was a guest at Leap. He woke during the night to find a heavy and warm object lying beside him outside the counterpane. At first he thought that his wife had come from the adjoining room, but the atmosphere of his room began to change. It grew cold and foul. He put out his hand, and it sank into a fleece of wool. When at last he was able to rise and to strike a light, whatever it was had gone; but an awful stench remained. This was not seeing a ghost. It was not for some time that a sight of it was caught by a young officer. He must have seen something, for a wardrobe standing against the wall at the foot of his bed was riddled by revolver shots. The young man packed his bag and left at daybreak without speaking to anybody. From him no account was obtained.

We heard of a man who was shaving before a mirror. The sight he saw over his shoulder caused him to draw the razor across his throat. This story was so hushed that no details could be described, and were it to be investigated, a great deal of opposition might be expected, so great that the story possibly would be so garbled as to be worthless.

We got closer to the apparition from the report of another guest. It looks as if the guests felt bound by considerations of hospitality not to gossip about what befell them when on a visit to Leap. However, this leaked out. At dusk, after the candelabra had been lighted, a visitor was ascending the great stair. He felt two weights suddenly laid upon his shoulders, which tended to press him down. He could not turn about; but on looking at his shoulders he saw a hoof on each, and, as he bent, he could see behind his knees the hindquarters of a gigantic black ram. The same story about the smell was repeated; but there was this detail. When at last the mounting animal let him go, he turned and saw no more than the legs of which he had already caught a glimpse; but he heard the scamper of hoofs. He spoke to one of the servants, who could throw no light on the affair. The visitor must have been a stranger to the country, for the idea that you could get an Irish servant to talk about such an apparition showed an ignorance of the established ritual.

This observance of secrecy can be very annoying, even though it is but to be expected. However, it led to my gathering the best account I could of the ghost.

My own curiosity and Yeats' eagerness made me determine to visit Roscrea and try to obtain from friends who lived near the castle some account of the apparition. I knew some people who were not afraid to discuss the supernatural. The place had been burned down during the civil war in Ireland, and this circumstance, strange to say, was a help instead of a hindrance to me in my researches, for it put the ghost, as it were, into the past and people felt freer to speak of it.

The difficulty that lay before me was to get an excuse for a visit, because if I were to go without any other purpose in mind, I might be told nothing. But while I was casting about for an excuse, I thought that there was nothing to prevent me from going to fish the Brosna, which is a little stream nearby. I don't suppose that anyone except those in the immediate vicinity ever thought of fishing in the Brosna, but I was fishing for more than trout, and it would be as good an excuse as another to include the Brosna in some plan. There is no county in Ireland which is without an abundance of lakes or streams. So to Roscrea I went. I am not a fisherman, though I used to be. I will say this: I can cast a line, if not with the best, at least with the best intentions. And the intentions were there and no mistake.

It was not until the second day that I risked making inquiries. I waited until evening, and good cheer loosened the tongue of mine host. I had listened to fishing talk till I realized why fish themselves were dumb, and I could not blame them. They would have to rebut too many misrepresentations if they spoke. When it came to my turn to tell a ghost story, I told of the ghost of my own house, and I told it with such proprietorship that you would think that there was not a ghost to be compared with it in all Ireland. My story disparaged all other ghosts and haunted houses until the implied challenge brought out the welcome question,

"Have you never heard of the Leap Castle ghost?" I had, but it was so little that it was not worth talking about.

"Well, if you had, you wouldn't want to talk of it at all."

"But no one has ever seen it," I said.

There was silence. Evidently my host was debating whether or not to reveal the secret of the Leap Castle ghost.

"It can't be very terrible if nobody has seen it," I said to tarr him on. "I wouldn't be so sure of that," he said. The silence into which he relapsed was discouraging, when to my relief, he continued, "Most ghosts have human form, but the ghost of Leap Castle has only a human face. The rest of it is a great black ram."

I had more than I had bargained for: I felt shocked at the revolting thing; but there was worse to come. I said nothing, for I had nothing to say. It was the best thing I could have done, as it turned out; for, seeing a look of consternation on my face, he proceeded with all the zest of a storyteller to press his advantage.

"There have been people who have committed suicide when they saw its decomposing face."

"Decomposing?" I exclaimed horrified.

"Yes; like something dug up that was buried for weeks and rotting, all but the eyes; they have a piteous look as if they were imploring somebody to set them free."

"Heavens!" I exclaimed.

"You may well say that. The place has been inhabited long before St. Patrick set foot in Ireland, and God knows what devilish rites went on before Leap Castle was ever built. But there's no use talking."

"Tell me," I said, "before you stop. Am I to understand that some poor fellow has been locked up in the body of a ram, all but his head?"

"It's worse than that."

"Worse?"

He nodded and said reluctantly, "It's a woman who has been turned into a ram."

For a long time I remained silent. At last I said, "There are rituals for blessing houses and for exorcising evil spirits." I made the suggestion, thinking of that piteous thing shut up forever in the body of a male beast.

"It's a bit late now," he said. "The castle was burned down during the Troubles." ("The Troubles" is an Irish euphemism for the civil war.)

"So Leap Castle was burned down?" He was silent. Then in an altered voice he said, "It's burning still."

"How can it be burning still if it was burned years ago, after all the rain that has fallen since?"

"So you would think; but you should see it flaming upon the night when the moon is set and the stars give no light. Flames glower behind the empty windows and the whole place goes on fire again, rain or no rain. I have seen it myself."

"But are the stones hot in the morning?" I asked, thinking that the castle might be used to shelter homeless wandering men.

"There's not a soul in the country that will go near it now."

That's a strong haunting, I thought, and I looked forward to telling Yeats what I had gathered during my visit to Roscrea.

On returning to Dublin, I reported. He listened in silence. He did not appear to be horrified by the decomposing face.

"The flames are still there?" he inquired.

I told him that the place had been repeatedly seen to be on fire.

"That spirit is still there, be assured," he said.

"Is it an elemental?" I asked, not having a very clear idea as to what an "elemental" might be. I thought that an elemental was one of the fallen angels.

"It is not an elemental," he said solemnly. "It is not even an evil spirit. It is someone who was partially metamorphosized into an animal body and is seeking release," he said.

But to be a woman, with a woman's sensitiveness, imprisoned forever in the body of a ram. I could not think of any fate more awful. I knew that the place was inhabited long before Christianity. Probably it was the center of obscene rites. Some king perhaps had handed over his wife to be punished by magicians with a fate more horrible than any torture that ends in death. To break the silence, for it was evident that he was concentrated on his own thoughts and that he would tell me no more, I began:

"It reminds me of something distantly similar of a Scots ghost about which there is a little-known ballad." He pricked up his ears when I mentioned a ballad. It tells of a monster in human shape who came to a cottage to ask for work. He said that he was a wonderful worker and kind to little children. He may have been an elemental seeking release from immortality and a share in human death.

"Do you remember the ballad?"

Unfortunately not all of it, I told him. "The Brownie of Blednock" is the title. The name of the ghost or brownie is Aiken Drum, which in itself is a triumph of a name. It tells of how he appeared at the door of the peaceful cottage of a Scots farmer's family to ask for work in return for a cup of meal, and of the consternation he caused, which the poet Nicholson, the author, uses with wonderful skill. The auld wife lost her speech. The guidman seized the Bible. The young farmer's wax end broke as he mended the flail. The young lassies screamed and objected to his being taken in because it would put an end to their young men's visits to the house:

For a foul and a stalwart ghaist is he,
Dispair sits broodin' aboon his ee bree;
And unchancie to light on a maiden's ee
Are the skimes of Aiken Drum.

However, the auld wife comes to her breath and engages him, for workers are short and the crop is out yet and meal is plentiful. She thinks that if he will carry out his promises that he will be cheap at the price.

I'll sheil your sheep in the morning sun;
I'll bury your crop by the light of the moon;
And I'll baa the bairns wi' an unkenned tune,
If ye'll keep puir Aiken Drum.

"That 'unkenned tune' might be a definition of poetry," I suggested. Yeats agreed, and added, "I like the description of a 'stalwart ghaist.'"

Certainly he was a much pleasanter ghost than the horror of Leap Castle; but it is strange that these visitants to the glimpses of the moon should all be abhorrent. This may arise from a pagan criticism of the other world, the world of shades such as Homer knew, an opinion coming from days before a "fairer hope" was held out to men. Another strange thing about ghosts is that they appear only to certain people. Some people are by nature unable to see ghosts, just as I am unable to divine water though a water diviner once handed me his forked witch hazel wand and told me how to use it. The fact that few people are able to see ghosts may account for the fact that none of the members of the British society for investigating haunted places has seen a ghost, and for the consequent discredit thrown on hauntings. It may explain the complacency of the owner of Leap.

Drums

When that hypothetical creature, Primitive Man, gave up his growl and permitted it to be broken and divided into words which crystallized his feelings, his emotional nature suffered a very great loss. He could ring the changes on his deep growling monotone and express the motifs of approval and disapproval, love and hate; and no one could pin him down to facts (in the days before "the record") or use his words in evidence against him. He was a born politician; he could have it both ways. There were no words to swallow then. When he succumbed to words, he lost his organ voice and left the deepest currents of his soul pent up for the want of an outlet. Worse, he cast aside music for the sake of words. By curtailing this important adjunct of religion, he became almost an atheist. Ever since, he has been striving to return to sound. Those who are the most accomplished musicians and can express emotions and imaginations without words in the one art without form are accounted men of genius.

Far into the darkness of the Congo basin went this desire to relieve the feelings by sound, to cleanse the bosom of the perilous stuff. Away back in history, in the canyons of ancient Thrace there was provision for the solemn and mass hysteria of wild women with their hand drums or tambourines. Woe betide those who tried the tactics of Peeping Tom. What could "the Muse herself that Orpheus bore" do to save him from the results of his curiosity?

And so when on the "Twalfth" in Belfast, Orangemen play the drum and give vent by its ritual to the oldest and deepest emotions, when they communicate in spirit with the most unspoiled tribes who live in a state of nature far away in Darkest Africa from the contaminating influences of civilization, the city is made clear for them, the police see to it that there is no eye to peep through the hoardings. And they have the privilege extended to them that we extend to much more complicated ceremonies—freedom to practice. There would be no trouble then. There might be after a lapse of years a little less drumming perhaps, because, if there be no evidence of the presence of evil opposition, the most fervent devotees become lukewarm.

At present the drummers are far from lukewarm. Their souls are like the bonfires they light, on the previgilium of the Twalfth, on the towers of some of the more tolerant chapels. A clergyman who was acting as *locum tenens* for a parson in the Clifton district told me that about ten o'clock at night on the eve of the Twalfth, a party of men wearing orange sashes and bearing a big drum called on him and demanded the key of the chapel for a "rehearsal." He told them that the church could not be put to political uses or made the ark of any party.

"Verra wal. D'ye see yon telegraph pole? We'll soon batter in yon door wi yon."

He yielded up the key. They first ascended the tower and lit a bonfire. Then when that was fairly going, they assembled grimly in the aisle and with bowed heads before the altar and behind the drum waited in deep silence for the coming of the enthusiasm. Slowly the drum began to beat. Slowly it seemed to make the sound "Wullum, Wullum." The invocation continued. Somewhat faster and a little louder now, "Wullum . . . Wullum." Again, faster, louder, "Wullum! Wullum! Wullum! Prince of Orange!" They pounded for their Prince to come! The frenzy caught the drummer and the lodge. They yelled inarticulate cries. The thunder drowned the sound. But drum taps call for action. They could not "march" in the narrow church. Therefore they called it a rehearsal and left it so. The drummer bound his bleeding wrists. There were no personalities about William of Orange. He, for all they knew, might have lived a hundred years B.C. Nor had their ritual become distorted, as inn signs sometimes are from their original meaning. Had they yelled, "Wullum Wullum, Wullum, Pickled Cabbage!" or "Wullum, Palaeolithic!" it would have made no difference to the vintage. This spiritual epilepsy had become after eleven months a physical necessity. The words mattered not. In the sound was the binding back to savage moods. They were dipping themselves in immemorial wells. On the morrow they would arise refreshed. That the true William King of England was a Sodomist who made two of his minions knights of the Garter and raised them to peerage mattered not. It may be the reason that there are no women in the "Big Walk."

That this drum ritual is regarded as fraught with healing and solace will appear from the following dialogue overheard by a student of sociology in a public house in Carrickfergus. On a form sat two friends. Both were dressed in holiday black. The Adam's apple of one moved forlornly up and down as he swallowed his despondency. His friend said, "A know what ye're lacking . . . a large whusky."

"That's not uncommon."

"Well, if it's worse than that, what you want is a swish of the auld Drum."

"Maybe ye're richt. Here's to the Twalfth."

"The Immortal Memory."

And so the whusky!

The reader will have seen that it is rather the Immemorial than the Immortal Memory to which these simple and religion-starved folk are harking back. Beggared by bigotry of ritual, they have nothing left but the Drum. Ritual is popish. The Memory may be of King William, who was subsidized by the pope. The fact remains that these trustworthy workers of the docks and shipyards have not even the color of the Salvation Army to change the drabness of their lives. They have to take their one spiritual holiday fiercely. Their orgiastic celebration depends on an antithesis. Popery, with its pomp, pageantry, choirs, music, and hopes, the Drum defies. It cannot build up. Take the audience away, and it beats without echo. But if you take the Drum away, you will have to substitute for it light and color and something higher than a savage level of life. I do not accuse the employers, the "capitalists" as they are now called, of deliberately leaving these poor Orangemen with neither light, faith, hope, nor charity in their lives. But I do accuse the Protestants because they have not repudiated the orgies of the lithic peoples of Belfast. It must be remembered that the first inhabitants who came to Ireland settled in the northeastern province. They were the lithic men. To and fro they went to Scotia Minor, as Scotland was afterward called, and they remain unchanged under different rulers in different and altered times, devoid of progress, unadvanced from the days when their first ancestor lit the first fire on the raised beach of Larne or Cushendall and growled as he gathered his little clan around the primitive hearth. The Protestants have allowed themselves to be associated with this annual religious orgy. They have never repudiated it.

What advantage do their rulers hope for by leaving this primitiveness untouched? When holding an inquest on a number of the victims of the shootings in Belfast, the City Coroner, Mr. T. E. Alexander, denounced the speeches of men in responsible positions, which, he said, inflamed party passions.

There would be less bigotry, Mr. Alexander said, if there was less public speechmaking of a kind by a so-called leader of public opinion. He expressed the view that, if bigotry could be exterminated, there would be no riots.

"The reopening of the shipyards yesterday after the holidays was not marked by any serious incident. A number of the Nationalist workers remained away, apparently fearing to return until quietness has been restored."

The heads of churches of different denominations send missionaries to China or the Congo; but no church sends a single missionary to Shankill Road, Belfast.

In their Drum revival on every twelfth of July, Orangemen

shoot off a revolver or two for their souls' sakes. But on this occasion it is said that the first shots were fired by the other side. What is the "other side" this time? On one occasion when in the *Evening Standard* I gave a forecast of the way things would go in Ireland, I mentioned communism. The Republican Congress is the armed and active communistic branch of the Republican Army. This has never been suppressed by the President of the Free State. It was permitted to "dump" its arms. It is not even now forbidden under pain of death to carry arms or to have them in one's possession. The "other side" this time is this body of armed and avowed Communists who, keeping their irreligious policy in abeyance for the moment, are masquerading as the opponents of Orange bigots. Meanwhile the Government at Belfast is exploiting this bigotry as if it were loyalty to the Empire. In the Free State "reprisals" are being carried out by the poor dupes of the IRA and the northern government. But both peoples are playing with more than fire. Ignorance can no more be exploited than it can be excused. A drum has emptied a throne before this —"Lillibulero." It may easily cause grave injury to the Empire, or what is left of it. A few hundred hate-inspired ignoramuses set Ireland on fire. They can do it again. The drum can be interpreted both ways by both churches, and both can be wrong. And the fools whom the drum can turn into religious fanatics are hardly removed from the first fools who mesmerized themselves by the boom of a hollow tree.

On Sitting for Your Portrait and Other Forms of Being Sat On

The more I think of portrait painters, especially the "moderns," the more I admire that emperor of China who sat for his portrait backward.

There was a time I thought all Chinese faces were the same, it did not matter whether he sat backward or forward—everyone knew that he was an emperor because the cap of honor he wore stuck out horizontally over his ears a foot each way, like a lady's black folded fan; and because of his magnificent robe, on the back of which was painted the imperial five-footed dragon in gold upon silk of dark blue. But when I lifted up my gaze to the top left-hand corner of the picture, I knew that I was wrong. In that corner I saw a landscape that anticipated Leonardo da Vinci by hundreds of years: a river wound between rocky banks as it came and widened out from a wood of slender trees.

It was his taste that mattered, not his face.

Perhaps it is just as well that nowadays no one asks to have his taste put into his portrait. China had no Abstractionists, no Dadaists, no Existentialists, no Surrealists, and no Futurists. If any showed, their treasonable heads were immediately lopped off. There were thirteen ways of painting a willow or a mist on a mountain; no more.

There was no mystery about art or about what was good taste. The Chinese loved nature and they respected it.

You must be subtle to appreciate "modern" art. I am not

subtle, not subtle enough to appreciate it fully. That is why, instead of recommending myself, I got into the doghouse with the editress of a well-known magazine which displayed photographs of twelve Abstractionist artists. Each artist was photographed in front of his masterpiece. The first one stood in front of a canvas on which a piece of twisty rag was portrayed. The rag ran obliquely across the canvas. It was called "A Garden in Cyprus." The sixth artist stood in front of a canvas which was completely blank. I stared and stared; but I saw nothing. I suddenly realized that the artist was an Abstractionist. I smiled fatuously because, being courteous by nature, I wanted my face to look as blank as the canvas. Then I remarked cheerfully, "He has abstracted everything!" It was of no avail. For all my good intentions I was met by a frown in which there was no pity, and shown to the door.

In a way, I was lucky not to have been confronted by primitive art, which consists of stunted men and women with hideous heads and indecent pudenda, which is the black magic of savages. I have not genius enough to appreciate that. Mesmerists tell me that I am hard to mesmerize, so I am beyond the pale so far as an appreciation of primitive art goes.

These are extreme cases of which the emperor of China was possibly unaware. Perhaps he was too fully aware. Perhaps he realized that a sitter's function is to provide a face on which the artist may execute a reel or a step dance, or, to change the metaphor, act as a crystal in which the artist may see himself. It is said of the painter Shannon that he had a lovely mouth; so had all his sitters. Augustus John had very fine eyes, so all his sitters were endowed with them. And some critics have told me that they could see Leonardo da Vinci with that inscrutable smile of his peeping out from every portrait that he painted. If I couldn't see it, so much the worse for me. I confess that up to the present I have failed dismally.

Toulouse-Lautrec was a cripple. Are you expected to see his stunted legs in his pictures? Sir William Orpen with his high shoulders, long legs, watery eyes, and stunted body was almost a hunchback. Are you to expect signs of these deformities? By no means. The very opposite is what you are to see. These men drew giants. Lautrec's poster of Aristide Bruant, one of the thirty he drew during his whole career, shows a flashing individual who might have been a famous bass with his black cape, huge red muffler, and crystal-headed cane. He casts over his shoulder a fleeting look at the passing show. But Aristide (in spite of his name) was owner of a cabaret. You see in a self-portrait Orpen as a hunter grim and competent, holding up a bird that fell to his gun. There is no need to mention Giorgio de Chirico, who saw himself in the costume of a matador or a sultan with their attributes of course added—in reality he was fat and incapable—to reiterate my point: the painter wishes to depict his dream of himself. Truly, "A portrait is a model complicated by an artist."

That is their way of escaping from themselves, and they did it; which is more than can be said (in a different medium) of that colossal brat who, in spite of his great age, never grew up, George Bernard Shaw. He was a playwright and he endeavored to project characters, but he never projected anyone but George Bernard Shaw. In contradistinction to my efforts to see the inscrutable smile of Leonardo in all his portraits, it is easy to see the red beard of Shaw on all his characters: his Julius Caesar taught Fabianism to Cleopatra and lectured her on the art of love.

No one expects to see the likeness of the sitter. If you are jejune enough to want a likeness you will have to go to the photographers before they too become artistic with their maneuvering of light and shade. You go to see a Sergeant or a John; but the sitter—oh, no!

There are ways of sitting other than that of a portrait painter. I mentioned Bernard Shaw, who was confined for life in his own ego. But there are others who settle on a "master"; first they become his bibliographer, then they collect his manuscripts, then they become authorities on the author, and finally they become the author himself! This may or may not be done consciously; but the same purpose is achieved in the end.

James Joyce affords a present-day example. He has been adopted by expatriates in Paris and over here. First of all they form a Joyce Society, just as in the last century they formed Browning Societies. There are one or two "collectors"; there are half a dozen "authorities" who never met the man. It would seem that to have met him renders you ineligible. There are many "interpreters," who of course interpret themselves and show their ingenuity in so doing. We shall not have to wait long before one of these takes the place of the others, becomes the sole interpreter, and becomes Joyce himself in the end.

These worshipers lose no opportunity of asserting what their adopted author meant. And they lose no chance of slipping into print on the false pretense of clearing up a mistake or of possessing a hitherto unpublished scrap by the "master." They attribute the meanest motives to all who cross their paths, and lose no chance of denigrating anyone whose attitude seems derogatory to their idol. Decency, integrity are cast to the winds: they have about as much honor as the hosts of old who used a banquet as a means to lure their enemies to their death.

It must be noted that there is a difference on this way of being sat on and the way of the artist: the artist never seeks to identify himself with the sitter; the "authority" always does.

The author of a play must be in far worse case when it comes to being sat on. He is pushed so far out of the picture that it is a wonder that he is there at all. But it would seem that he is somehow necessary. First, and more prominent than anyone else, is the producer with his multitudinous assistants, then the assistant producer and his many assistants. The technical adviser is next with his many; and of course the assistant technical adviser and his assistants. Then (I am out of order, I fear) there is the hair stylist and "costumes by. . . ." I forget by whom. I confess that if the characters had to depend on my memory, they would have to act in the nude. By this you see that the costumier is essential.

I saw *Julius Caesar* and a long list of those responsible for its production. Did the name of the author of that drama not come in at all? I think it did. I think I saw his name. The smallness of the print may have deceived me. Nevertheless, I think I read it. "Association of ideas or wishful thinking," you will say, because I read somewhere that one Shakespeare wrote a play called *Julius Caesar*. It was written in the days when there were no producer and his assistants. Of course it never saw the screen until several centuries later.

I have told you elsewhere of my experience with publishers and with agents who wanted to have a hand in the pie of writing, but it is as nothing to what authors have to put up with from ignorant men and from a public largely the creation of ignoramuses. There is room, and more than room, for a chair in some university to say what history was like before Hollywood.

"History largely depends on the historian." Very well: there were historians with imagination when they wrote of battles long ago. At least they were between kings or usurpers of kings. Now we have what may well be taken for the history of our times written by unimaginative men who have seldom been at school. Or, worse still, have been schooled beyond their understanding. The history of our times, judged by the screen, has fallen among thieves. That is bad enough, but what makes it worse is that it may be accepted by nations who can form an opinion of their own. Why should America be judged by what the movies have painted it? This is not the artistic association of which I have written. But for this, it would be an act of dignity as well as of relief to imitate that emperor of China who turned his back upon it all.

Clubs

We were walking early one morning down the Strand; the rising sun whitened the spires of London. Suddenly out of the blue my companion, a Scotsman attached to one of the great dailies, said as if to himself, "They have large ears, they have long feet, they have no fear, they live in secret; but they are known to each other; and they cannot understand defeat." Dimly, I knew that he was talking about the governors of England. I did not take it all in at once. "Where do they live?" I asked. "In their clubs and in the hunting districts." I cannot say why I guessed that he was talking about the men who govern England, men who live in secret and who cannot understand defeat. Probably it was the last description that gave me the dim clue. And "their clubs" decided it. To these men, governments with their prime ministers who are mere puppets may come and go, one thing remains which is permanency.

So they live in their clubs? From that morning I began to take an interest in their clubs. I found out some facts which may be diverting. One is that clubs are very exclusive; another is that their members have no vocations, unless you consider militarism, hunting, and yachting vocations; and another is that everyone who aspires to become a member must be screened, examined, recorded, and have his background gone into thoroughly. He must be recommended: that is, have his name put up for membership by a well-known and accepted member; and this latter fact has a lot to say as to whether he will be admitted or rejected. If he be rejected, the member who nominated him should at once resign from the club.

As every one of those who are likely to become candidates are already known to the members, or their parents are known, it is unlikely that anyone who is undesirable can be elected. Thus is a club protected from "outsiders." It would be very hard indeed for one who is not of the "set" to understand the language that is used by clubmen. Every vocation has its own lingo or technical terminology. This is apparent more in the trades than in the clubs. For example: you could not be a coal miner even if you were so inclined, or a carpenter, a plumber, a bricklayer, a fitter, or a hod carrier. You could not join one of the groups who go down through holes in the street and are privileged to put up notices "Men Working" during lunchtime; nor, most fascinating of all, could you become one of those stout and hardy men who wear visors and who, by skillfully manipulating levers, move inanimate masses from invisible pits and deposit them on trucks. The technical terms of the trade would in each case disqualify you, even if you were found worthy otherwise. These are not clubs in the strict sense; but I mention them to show that even they are exclusive and have a language of their own. So do chemists, psychiatrists, doctors, philosophers, and oil men.

Now the great thing about an English club is its exclusiveness. One might think that it is the duty of every member to make it as hard as possible for anyone else to become a member. I forgot to mention the fact that a would-be member has to be examined by members of the committee of the club to which he aspires on the neutral ground of another club. This may be the cause of a member trying to exclude all others from membership. He feels that he has passed all tests, and has therefore acquired in some mysterious way a distinction which he is not supposed to share. Otherwise it would diminish his club's exclusiveness. A club must be above all things select.

Freedom is another attribute. If one's house, thanks to the Fabianism of the late English government, has ceased to be one's castle, one's club remains inviolable. The story goes—and I do not think that it is apocryphal—that a lady, growing anxious toward nightfall, called up her husband's club.

"Is my husband there?" she asked. "No, madam," was the prompt reply.

"What do you mean, 'No, madam'? I have not told you my name."

"There never ain't no 'usbands 'ere," the well-trained flunky replied. They live in secret.

London is the home of clubs proper. By "proper" is meant the club as described above. White's; Boodles; St. James's; the Travellers'; the Bachelors'; the Beefsteak; the Royal Yacht Club; and Oxford and Cambridge, senior and junior (I have never heard of a senior), are proper clubs. They are oases from the many who make a desert of life. They magnify one's importance and are factories of self-esteem. They are ends in themselves. Therefore they have nothing to do with charities and that sort of thing. They are not formed for the maintenance of hospitals, giving boys annual holidays, or contributing to the cure of disease. On the contrary, they are refuges from the invasion which too much good fellowship brings. That is, perhaps, why they are nodes of silence. Members are not expected to recognize one another in the better-class clubs. You may talk on the stairs; but only when you are entertaining a guest. And you may call "Waiter!" after you have already given your order, not before, for the waiter may be on his silent way to serve a member whose earlier presence gives him a priority. Besides, calling *after* you have already ordered shows that you are suffering from afterthoughts, an affliction which is flattering to the senior members.

Clubs in England are survivals of feudalism. They are founded on class distinction, and they carry on the traditions of their founders. In one of the military clubs, that one which has as an exhibit on the first landing one of the Duke of Wellington's boots in a glass case, the tradition is Wellingtonian; and everyone knows that he was not a gossip. In another, one given over to the law, it is the custom to drink, not to the man directly opposite to you, but to the man diagonally opposite. (To symbolize the indirectness of the law? Maybe.) And in England customs make the law.

If in town it is very hard to become a clubman, what about the country? You have to be born into the Pytcheley or the Quorn, which are fox-hunting clubs exclusively. In vain may you employ an old whipper-in, who will teach you that a fox has a mask and not a face, a brush and not a tail, and no feet, only pads; and above all that there are no dogs—hounds only—in a fox hunt, and that you must never override the hounds nor the Master. In vain will you learn basic English. Fox-hunting colloquialisms are born, not achieved. The suppression of the definite article is not enough—just as it is not enough for a lady who is not "county" to effect a complexion like gnarled oak or a seat like an anvil. At best she may become a "visitor," but at what a cost in looks and language! "They are known to each other."

Contradictory as it may seem, it is bad form to have a better seat than the Master or a redder complexion. The latter is hard to come by, but not the seat. The best seat I ever saw on a horse was that of a professor from Boston. He would have been called a cowboy and treated as such in the Quorn. The worst seat I ever saw belonged to an important citizen of Chicago. As he paid the penalty with a broken neck, I will not allude to it further.

Difficult as it is to become a member of one of the clubs in town, it is far more difficult to be accepted in the country. You may become a member of almost any fox-hunting club; but that does not mean that you have become one of the "county."

You may be well-acquainted with all the terms connected with the sport of kings, you may have enhanced your individuality by some benevolent eccentricity, you may have achieved a curt and clipped speech, your cousin may have fractured his spine when "out" with the Quorn: it will help you not at all. The insurmountable obstacle remains—birth: you have to be born into the best set. And doing your hunting the hard way will not help you. This is a tale that goes to prove my contention; and, as it was told to me by an Englishman, the late John Drinkwater, there can be no suspicion that I am poking fun at the hunting people.

A certain citizen of London, having made a fortune in trade of some sort, decided to retire. He also decided on a house in the country, the real country, where he could have elbow room for miles and miles. He would buy a big house—big houses are easily acquired now that Marxism has impoverished the aristocrats. All went well. He bought the mansion. He bought the best hunters and filled his stables (for of course the most countrified parts of England are in the fox-hunting districts) and looked about him so that he might become acquainted with someone who would put him up for the local hunt. This was not hard to do: the local vicar lent his kind offices. He hinted that the number of horses the retired citizen lodged was excessive "now that money is . . . well, things are not as they were. Do you see what I mean?" He reduced his stable to ten. Even that amount seemed to savor too much of Dives for the vicar. He settled for five. The first day out the citizen was observant. He used short grunts for speech when asked questions, which indeed was rare. He also noticed that the county hospital was the only subject except the going that was discussed. The county hospital? He discovered that it held one Algy, and that Algy had fallen (no fault of his of course—that damned horse) and fractured his collarbone. Flowers were left at the hospital, together with the best wishes of the many donors. The citizen decided that he would endear himself to the best people by breaking his collarbone. This he managed to do by striking a bough, not by falling. He was rushed to hospital; but nobody called. The whipper-in was the only one who inquired, and that by telephone. At last he was well, and hunting was resumed. Galled by the lack of sympathy, he determined to have a thoroughly serious accident. For this he sacrificed his other collarbone and added concussion of the brain. "Unaware of the fact," said Drinkwater, "that the better classes are born concussed."

Another characteristic of a club is its freedom. I am not thinking of the incident of the lady who sought her husband in his club, but of a club's independence within itself, even of the sponsor of an applicant. Sir Thomas Lipton was put up for the Royal Yacht Squadron by the late King Edward VII. He was not admitted. He was blackballed. The King did not resign. A king can do no wrong, even when he tries to have elected a man who has a vocation which is distinctly commercial.

You must be very careful about whom you invite to your club. I invited a man who had a column in the *Daily Mail* to lunch at my club. I must confess that I was not altogether innocent of wishing to "swank" a little, because I knew that my guest could not make the grade and become a member. The first thing he did was to find fault with the celery, and this in the hearing of the waiters. The next thing he did was, when the talk turned on conversationalists, to ask me who I thought was the greatest talker I knew. Next day I found myself reported as saying, "If you include a monologue as conversation, then so-and-so is the greatest conversationalist I know." It took me a long time to make my peace with one of my oldest friends, who was mentioned by name in the column. The moral of this is not never to trust a journalist, but never to use your club for the purpose of showing it off. What goes on in a club should never be repeated outside, as any worthy visitor well knows. Never again shall I ask that celery critic to lunch. I wish that he would seek to become a member of my club so that I might have the pleasure (for it would be a pleasure) of blackballing him. Thus I would exercise my right; keep the club exclusive and feel all the more righteous in doing so.

Clubs are governed by the old school tie. I have stated that they are feudal; and the old school tie represents their social standards, which are the standards of their Anglo-Saxon and Scandinavian ancestors and predate Christianity. Theirs is a grand old mythology, inculcated and reflected in the virtues of the race. "Manliness, generosity, loyalty in service and in friendship and a certain rough honesty . . . a religion of high-hearted gentlemen not overburdened with brains nor troubled about their own souls." I quote this from George Trevelyan, who holds the Order of Merit and is the author of *A Short History of England.*

That "not overburdened with brains" may account for the exhibit of the Duke of Wellington's boot.

It is pretty bad to be blackballed for a club; but it is far worse to be asked to resign. High treason, cheating at cards, or publicity arising from moral turpitude are among the causes which entail this penalty, though bankruptcy is listed as one of the reasons a member should resign. You will notice that the latter is permitted to resign before he is kicked out. I forget whether that eighteenth-century character, Sir William Harcourt, was expelled or asked to resign. I do not know even the name of the club. However, he is reported to have said when he heard the verdict, "It is a nice club only for the members." And that is a remark which could be applied to whole countries nowadays.

Miss Twickenham's Bequest

St. Botolph's-in-the-Fields was in a bad way; but only from a financial standpoint of course. Spiritually, it was in as good a way as when its patron founded his church at Ikano in Lincolnshire almost thirteen hundred years ago. Allowances must be made for certain changes—such, for instance, as the Reformation, and with it the rise of commercial classes, and with them the universal practice of usury. It was this last that caused the present difficulties of St. Botolph's-in-the-Fields Church. It owed money to the bank.

Now when Mr. Stott was alive the bank was far more considerate. Mr. Stott, in addition to being a well-to-do manufacturer of ladies' garments, was a pillar of the church. It was all very well for certain irreverent gossips to say that as his wares supported half the congregation—more than half, for the ladies formed more than 50 per cent of the worshipers—it was good business to support a church which supplied him with a purchasing public of no mean value. Mr. Stott was also a director of the Midland Division of the Ocean Bank and Insurance Corporation. To his devotion to the church must in all fairness be attributed the leniency of his bank.

Mr. Stott was dead of a heart attack in the street. No funeral service, however heartfelt, could alter the ominous fact that the bank was pressing the Select Vestry. Most of Mr. Stott's charitable bequests had gone to the daughters of the Sick and Indigent

Room-keepers' Society's widows. He had overlooked the fact that although the church's holding was free of charges forever, there were certain overheads, not the least of which was upkeep. For these charges the members of the Vestry were responsible. There were arrears too, which during Mr. Stott's lifetime were considered negligible if they were taken into account at all. Whether Mr. Stott had paid them out of his own pocket could not be ascertained, for there were provisions of the will into which his widow did not wish inquiry to be made, so the Select Vestry had to take the figures that the bank furnished as correct and hold themselves responsible. It was calculated that even if the contributions at Christmas, Easter, and Harvest Home were quadrupled, they would be insufficient to meet the liabilities of St. Botolph's-in-the-Fields. So close it brought another problem which was incapable of solution, because an abandoned church is such a reflection on Religion that, although there are unfortunately badly attended churches, there are few abandoned ones. And owing to the terms under which it was held, St. Botolph's could not be pulled down or sold to a movie theater company, as certain churches less well established have been known to change hands, to the eternal discredit of their trustees.

There was just one ray of hope, but it depended so much on the patience of the bank that its ray was dimmed. Miss Twickenham was the richest member of the congregation and the most devout; but Miss Twickenham was alive. To be sure, she was aging rapidly, but not as rapidly as the increment of interest due to the bank. Her mind was wandering, losing continuity as it were; but before she exhibited any signs of mental aberration, she had announced her intention of leaving her vast fortune to her favorite and familiar church. Had she not been baptized, christened, and confirmed in St. Botolph's? And she would have been married in it but for an unfortunate fear of fortune hunters and a *fixation* on the Vicar, who was a married man. On the approaching dissolution of its richest member, discreditable as it was, the present incumbent of St. Botolph's banked. The word is unhappy; but it shows what is meant to be conveyed, and that is one of the functions of speech.

Of late, hope sprung in the breasts of those who would have to foot the bill due to the bank unless a miracle occurred; and miracles, owing to the Reformation, are not as rife as they were in the original St. Botolph's days. What caused hope to spring was far from being a miracle, even though it was misunderstood for a considerable time. One morning after service Miss Twickenham remained seated long after all the congregation had left the aisle. Mr. Slocum, the preacher who was acting as *locum tenens* for the Vicar, at first was inclined to attribute this attitude of Miss Twickenham to the effect of his sermon, which had reached quite unusual heights of eloquence—that is for St. Botolph's, where service had to be conducted in a manner that, if it led toward High Churchism, would lead there very gradually. Mr. Slocum was almost High.

It was not that, however, which kept Miss Twickenham seated. It transpired that Miss Twickenham was beginning to exhibit some of the symptoms of advanced age; she could not use a low seat—that is why the verger afterward provided two hassocks for her when she attended divine service. That is also why Dr. Mudge diagnosed atrophy of the quadriceps, which it was whispered are the muscles on the front of the thigh. True, Dr. Mudge was a general practitioner and belonged to the old school; nevertheless he was unlikely to be deceived by such an obvious disability as old age. In fact some of the old school knew just as much about old age as the modern scientists.

In spite of Dr. Mudge's diagnosis, there were not wanting those who suggested that Miss Twickenham's discomfort was due to the ill-chosen text of Dr. Slocum's sermon. He had preached and preached fervently, "He that trusteth in his riches shall fall." That, they said, was the reason for Miss Twickenham remaining seated. Some thought that the sermon was somewhat pointed, and that Dr. Slocum had been tipped off—to use an unseemly expression more becoming to bookmakers than to clergymen—by the Vicar to preach *at* Miss Twickenham. And that would explain the absence of the Vicar from the parish during the tenure of his coadjutor.

This sign of aging on the part of Miss Twickenham, then, was the tenuous and un-Christian hope that brought consolation to those who were responsible for the church debt. But the very fact that the clergy and the Select Vestry should have come to regard interest due to the bank as legitimate goes to show how far from the times and the spirit of St. Botolph his latter-day Vestry had fallen. The moneychangers had invaded the temple and were threatening to undo the church.

A great fear counteracted the thin hope of the debtors—the fear that Miss Twickenham, for all her bodily fixation, had a wandering mind. The verger—he did not want it to go farther—solemnly assured the Vestry that one morning at matins when Miss Twickenham was passing the white marble baptismal font she had said to him, "It should have been defrosted long ago." Now a wandering mind would make a will invalid. If it could be proved that Miss Twickenham was not compos mentis when she affixed her signature, the will would be invalid; of course, always provided that there was not an earlier will. Now as a matter of fact there was an earlier will, made years ago and deposited in the safe of Dr. Arch, the Bishop who was prebendary of St. Botolph's when Miss Twickenham was nubile.

It gave some satisfaction to the Bishop to let the members of the Vestry stew for a while. It would do them good and teach them not to be too concerned with the ways of Mammon. The difficulties of St. Botolph's were but temporary, while what it stood for was eternal.

Dr. Mudge made no comment; but from his manner it was deduced that the end of Miss Twickenham was not far off.

But Miss Twickenham was far off of late. Nobody knew where she had gone. She might have lost her memory, Mr. Frazer the curate suggested; and Dr. Slocum assented, for he remembered how Miss Twickenham had called on him to apologize for being absent from church on the very morning on which she had remained seated. The concern of the members of the Select Vestry was not diminished when it was rumored that Miss Twickenham had changed her faith and had been received into the unreformed church. The Vicar returned; and Dr. Slocum, who had been granted three weeks' vacation, said he would make inquiries. His inquiries left no doubts. Miss Twickenham had indeed forsaken the church of her parents and joined the Home for the Aging, which was run by an order of nuns. She could not be reached. Dr. Slocum thought that with her faculties failing Miss Twickenham was unaware of what was happening, and that she imagined that she was attending some new and higher form of ritual connected with High Church services in St. Botolph's.

Miss Twickenham was dead.

That was what the papers announced. A religious periodical added that she died fortified by the rites of her lately adopted church, and a short account of her conversion was given.

There were anxious days for the Select Vestry; and prayer failed to dispel anxiety. But prayer, the prayer of those held responsible for the church's debts, was answered. Bishop Arch was to address the congregation after he preached the second identical sermon on the coming Sunday afternoon. Everyone knew that an important announcement was about to be made, and indeed they were not disappointed. The Bishop, who was an eminent theologian, chose for his text a passage from the Book of Ruth: "Blessed be thou of the Lord, my daughter: for thou hast showed more kindness in the latter end than at the beginning, inasmuch as thou followedst not young men whether poor or rich." And then the announcement: "Our late highly respected parishioner, Miss Ruth Twickenham, has left her entire estate and the yield thereof to the church in which she worshiped for more than half a century. Whatever weaknesses beset her at the end of her life—and some of the great figures of history died demented—it is to the years of her labor in the vineyard that we must turn our thoughts; and when we regard those long years she shall not be found wanting."

When, after long legalisms, the will was proven, the bank sent a very nice letter to the members of the Select Vestry. Banks' letters seldom bring messages of good will; but on this occasion the bank wrote that any further accommodation the Vestry wished to have was at their disposal. A note added that the bank hoped for many years' continuance of the cordial relationship that always existed between it and the Select Vestry.

Rivalries, envies, and jealousies are the forms in which Satan disguises himself to foment the skepticism of our day. Of old he could appear in person; but those who believed in such apparitions have long ago passed away. The Devil has not passed away. The forms he adopts are subjective, but nonetheless Satan's for all that. It was murmured abroad that the income of St. Botolph's was derived from the red-light district of the parish. Miss Twickenham's wealth was derived from real estate for the most part. There were numerous investments, but it is with the real estate that the church was chiefly concerned. It could not be denied that some of the property now belonging to the church included slums and some of it included fashionable apartments. The slum areas housed honest, hard-working people, mostly Italians. If there were any truth in the rumor, the houses of ill fame had to be looked for in the upper part of the city. But who was to look for them? Which member would undertake such a quest? If Mr. Stott were alive—but what was the use of making retrospective conjectures? He was not alive. Mr. Flick, the verger, was too far gone in routine to bring back an observant report. It was a matter for the Bishop, who was trustee for the church funds—an urgent matter, as it proved, because an unsigned letter reached the Vestry, and it was written in no veiled words. "Unseemly, disgraceful, shocking." And the Vestry had to agree.

At a convocation, Dr. Arch suggested that the incumbent of another parish might be the best investigator; so the name of Dr. Slocum was brought up. "The very man," His Grace remarked.

During the week following, Dr. Slocum was approached. "Such a thing is out of the question," he said shortly. "Why not acquaint the police?" The leader of the deputation replied, "Don't think, reverend sir, that we have not already reported the matter; but the police say that they find no irregularities or any complaints in the neighborhood involved. Of course they may be paid for 'protection,' and who can blame them if they can point to our interest?"

"It appears to me to come to this," Dr. Slocum remarked. "What you want is somebody with authority to expostulate with whomsoever is running brothels in property belonging to the church, one who can speak for the church. I gather that with leases such as they are and the terms of the will such as they are, you cannot evict or dispossess any of your tenants."

"That is why the Bishop suggested you," the spokesman said.

Dr. Slocum thought awhile. "The Bishop cannot expect a man in clerical clothing to enter a house of ill fame, even with an express order from His Grace. If it is to be done at all, it is to be done in the full light of day and in civilian clothes."

"It's not so hard as you imagine. Only parts of the houses are used for prostitution. The remainders are apartments. Of course—and who can prevent it?—there are black sheep in every fold, and some of the women living alone in these apartments admit lovers. Some two or three a year. Others are more promiscuous. So lax are moral standards that very little scandal arises. And I do not think we would have any scandal had it not been for some ill-conditioned and irreligious occupant of an apartment of such a house."

"Scandal," said Dr. Slocum, surveying the speaker. "Is there not sufficient scandal in the established fact that the church of St. Botolph's-in-the-Fields is receiving money from whore houses? I must put it bluntly."

The spokesman hung his head. But a linesman who was a politician interposed, "All the more reason, reverend, why you should adopt the Bishop's suggestion and do your best to stop this horrid traffic."

The mention of the Bishop seemed to have influenced Dr. Slocum, for his next words were in the form of a question.

"What is the address, if any, of the house from which the letter came?" There was some hesitation before an answer could be given, and before it the speaker, somewhat confused, had to make a little apology: "Don't be offended, sir; but it is only two doors from your rectory."

"Is that so? Then, gentlemen, you may safely leave the matter in my hands. I will send a report to the Bishop in due course." The deputation withdrew.

Dressed rather conservatively, an elderly man with a grave demeanor pressed the bell of Madame Théry's apartment. It was answered without delay. A lady with silvery blue hair dressed à la Pompadour came out on the landing to greet the visitor. She stood back and motioned him into the apartment. In silence, smiling graciously, she indicated a chair.

"Thank you. I don't think I'll sit down."

"Monsieur is precipitate. Please be seated." Dr. Slocum sat down.

"Monsieur has come lately to town?" Dr. Slocum did not reply. In fact he had no chance to reply for Madame Théry went on uninterruptedly, "To whom do I owe the pleasure of Monsieur's visit?"

Dr. Slocum said, "I am here as a layman. I am here as a representative . . ."

"Monsieur is pleased to make a pun? I consider it bad taste on Monsieur's part." Dr. Slocum blushed with anger. He was put in a defensive position.

"I had no intention of making any such thing. I came here on the church's business."

"Then why select me?"

"Because of an anonymous letter which said that the church was enjoying money from houses of equivocal reputation."

"Then, I repeat, why select this house?"

Behind Madame a low, sweet voice asked, "May I come in?" Madame Théry said, "This is Melle. Melle, I want you to meet . . . ? If you gave your name, I did not catch it." "The Rever——" Then, remembering that he had come in unclerical clothes, "Mr. Slocum." Madame Théry said, "Meet Melle, Mr. Slocum." Melle bowed to acknowledge the introduction. Madame Théry continued, "Melle, Mr. Slocum says that some anonymous letter brought him here, of all places. Melle, both of us know the author. Mrs. Little, who hates the sight of any woman younger than herself. But for her letter and her telephonings to the police, Mr. Slocum would not have made this mistake."

Melle said, "I am to blame. Until I got that room on the ground floor, all was well. Then Mrs. Little got ideas. But Dr. Mudge would not let me climb the stairs. He said that it was bad for my heart. Hence all this trouble. It all began when I got the ground floor room. While Mr. Stott was alive there was not a breath of scandal."

Madame Théry said, "Mr. Stott was a very good man. He left most of his money to charity—some to Melle, of course."

The Reverend Mr. Slocum thought, 'Why, of course.' Madame Théry as if anticipating his thought, went on, "You see, Melle's mother belonged to the Sick and Indigent Room-keeper's Society, and when she died any little moneys that came to her dried up, so Melle had no place to go until I, at the instigation of Mr. Stott, took her in, that is, acted as her chaperone. Then Mr. Stott dropped dead just outside the door. The ambulance came and whisked him away. So there was no cause for any anonymous letters from Mrs. Little, or from anyone else for that matter."

The Reverend Dr. Slocum rose.

"Oh, you must not go until you have had some light refreshment. Melle!" Melle left the room.

Dr. Slocum insisted that he did not require any refreshment. But Melle returned bearing a tray on which there was a decanter—sherry, perhaps—and three glasses. Gently Dr. Slocum excused himself.

As he reached the street, the full enormity of his meeting with Madame Théry presented itself. If he had sealed the interview by drinking with Madame Théry and Melle! Thank God he had no intention of doing so. But what kind of fellow was this Mr. Stott? What was he doing . . . why was he interested in Melle? And then his dropping dead in the street, "just outside the door." Looked upon from the most charitable angle (and he hoped he was charitable) women like Madame Théry and most French women had a very different view of sexual matters than Dr. Slocum. And yet the most glorious cathedrals were built in France. "Hearts that believe and build." Who was the author? At any rate, it was said about the French—or about the Middle Ages, which were largely in France. But Dr. Slocum was discretion itself.

His report to the Bishop could not very well recommend discretion, however. That would never do. If he told him all, he would have to bring in the name of Mr. Stott. *De mortuis nil nisi bonum.* He knew that; but why not report the interview just as it occurred? And if he had to name Mr. Stott, well, an account of the interview demanded it. If he had to go to all this trouble on the orders of the Bishop, then the Bishop would expect a report. He should have one. When Dr. Slocum left, Madame Théry made a little gesture which looked as if she were brushing crumbs off her lap. "What are men?" she said.

Dr. Slocum's report to the Bishop ended with the words, "In the great hotels in the city supervision is impossible to some extent, whereas in a village everyone's conduct is open to the light. St. Botolph's-in-the-Fields is independent. With great humility I venture to suggest that scrutiny be confined to St. Botolph's parishioners only." That takes care of Mr. Stott, thought Dr. Slocum drily.

The Bishop sent for Dr. Slocum and thanked him for his inspection and for his report.

"I heartily agree," said the Bishop. "Large towns shelter vice; and as for your suggestion that we should look after our parish, does it mean that we should look after it only and ignore the city?"

Dr. Slocum hesitated. "Well, you are in-the-Fields," he said, "and removed from the congestion of the denser parts of the city. Your parishioners are a community and as such can attend to services, for they are mostly retired businessmen and women of independent means."

"I agree: it is easier to look after a flock in a village than in the devious ways of a town. The lives of the parishioners of St.

Botolph's are an open book, an open book; and their example may well compensate for the backslidings in other parts of our property over which, owing to the terms of the donor's will, we have no control; nor can we resign it. It is a problem to be faced with fortitude. If we cannot extirpate Evil from the face of the earth, we must confront it and confound it and counteract it by good example whenever and wherever we can. Providence has placed St. Botolph's in the fields. It is still, though a suburb, self-contained and almost separate from the city. St. Botolph's-in-the-Fields must become an example of good conduct and a reproach to those other parts of our estate which have the misfortune to be mixed up with what is nothing less than paganism. By the irreproachable conduct of each and every one of its parishioners, St. Botolph's must bear and compensate for the iniquities of the town. We must make our parish exemplary."

Dr. Slocum gazed with astonishment not unmixed with admiration at the Bishop. He had brushed aside difficulties, with more dignity it is true, but with an ease equal to that with which Madame Théry had brushed men off her skirt. Never had he realized so clearly that the function of the Church was to set an example of goodness that would lead stray sheep back into the fold. Never had he realized that safety lay in the fields—that is, in the country, as opposed to the vicious town. Oh the simplicity of it! Not for nothing had Dr. Arch been appointed and consecrated; his worldly wisdom was wide and profound. Evil was there to beget Good. It was there to be counteracted by upright conduct. To the Bishop that was evident, and he saw clearly the way out. In a way, Evil was necessary. Was it not Plato who said that we must go to Heaven with our black and white horses? There must be two poles to a battery. The problem was to keep the positive pole well charged.

A Plain Tale When You Know the End

Frank Lloyd and I were walking by the hanging gardens north of Trafalgar Square. We could not have been talking about a serious matter. Whether we were or not, it was obliterated from my mind by the sight of Marjorie Mellows coming toward us. What was she doing so far from New York, where she was connected with a prominent fashion journal; and why was she hastening now that she had seen us—or me, rather, for she had yet to meet Frank Lloyd?

"The very man!" she said. And, when I had explained the paper that Frank edited, she repeated it with the variation, "The very men!" Then she said, "Let us grab a cab. I will tell you the emergency when we are on our way."

"Where?" I said.

"To the Savoy, in the Strand. Mr. Parsons has run out of churches, and he sent me out hurriedly for a brain trust to help him out." I had little assurance of Mr. Parsons' sanity. But then I thought that he could not have made Marjorie go out on a wild-goose chase. "Run out of churches?" "I'll tell you when we arrive," she said. Then she turned her charming smile to Frank. Frank is a bachelor, and I knew how he felt under that smile. I caught some of the conversation, and it was not about Mr. Parsons' predicament at all. I remember she asked Frank how long he had been in London. That was pretty smart, for hardly anyone would know that Frank was not London-born. As a matter of fact he was a Welshman.

Presently the taxi swerved from the stream of traffic and pulled up before the hotel. I forget who paid the taxi, I was so anxious to meet the man who had "run out of churches." We entered the elevator and were shot up to a suite that overlooked the Thames. There were six or seven girls busy taking down the dictation of a man who sat in a chair. He rose when he saw Marjorie and Frank behind her, for though Marjorie is tall, Frank is much taller. He is over six feet. "Girls, dismiss," said Mr. Parsons. Then he greeted us. I must say that he got our names mixed. He called Frank by my name. But then he had a weight on his mind, or rather the absence of a weight, because he had run out of churches.

We were seated and Mr. Parsons had turned from the tube into which he had spoken. Now he settled himself, and said, "Well, well. I can trust Marge. She has told you that I am in a fix. Up against it, in fact. I have gotten only two and I want at least three. Four of course would be better. I could do with a few in reserve, but no time. I am up against a deadline. Just got back on the Flying Scotsman this morning. I am worn out." He picked up a telephone. "Room service! That speaking tube does not work. The refreshments should be here immediately. What kind of a joint is this?"

I tried to get a look of sympathy into my face instead of the look of wisdom which had failed to register. Frank assumed his editorial air. Mentally he blue-penciled the fatigue of Mr. Parsons.

"Yes, sir, worn out. Just gotten back from Maxwelton where the braes are, as I was saying, and what do I find? What have my assistants done? Taken tickets for some show. They should have had the country covered by this time. I am up against distractions on every side. Obstructions! Lack of teamwork."

I could see the barges sliding on the Thames beneath the large windows of Mr. Parsons' sumptuous suite. I wondered what compliments were being paid by the bargees to one another. Then I heard Mr. Parsons again:

"Let me explain. I've gotten Annie Laurie's church; affidavit signed by the rector. Same stone from the same quarry and wood from the same wood, as far as he can trace it. Oak? Right. Measurements to a millimeter. Got them right here . . . Where's that girl?"

Instead of his stenographer, the floor waiter appeared, followed by the wine steward with an elaborate chain round his neck and in his hand a bucket of ice in which slanted two magnums of champagne.

"Ah, that's better!" exclaimed Mr. Parsons. "We can relax. Now, Mr. Oliver." Frank undid the wine a little too expertly for an amateur. He poured for the four of us, beginning with Marjorie's glass. I could see that he was revising his estimate of the sanity of his host.

Annie Laurie's church was the second. Mr. Parsons did his best to recall the name of the first, but evidently the fatigue of his journey interfered with recollection. "Oh, you know the fellow that came home with mud on shoes after they put out the fire?"

"The plowman homeward plods," I suggested.

The leap was not so great as it looks, for I had already deduced that the churches he was collecting had more to do with literature and romance than with religion.

"Got it!" he shouted.

"Stoke Poges," I added, "where Gray wrote his 'Elegy in a Country Churchyard.' "

"The very place. I had to reduce the spire ten feet to make it do. That was a great one. What about another steer? I am still a church short."

"Have you thought about 'Lead Kindly Light'?" I asked.

"Girls, come back!" yelled Mr. Parsons. "Get this!" Then to me directly, "Where is it?"

"If you want the church connected with him who wrote the hymn, it's at Littlemore near Oxford. The poem was written by Cardinal Newman when he was at sea—I am not speaking figuratively—in the Mediterranean. The church his mother gave him is near Oxford. There you can see the lich gate on which he wept when overcome by emotion at the step he was about to take in changing his religion."

"This fits the picture all right. Marge, you were not far wrong when you said you'd bring me back some bright boys. Take it all down, girls. I like the lich gate. What is it?"

I did not like to take away the enthusiasm to which he had worked himself. I knew that when I had explained the lich gate he'd be disappointed.

"Lich gate, what is it?" he repeated.

"It's a roofed gate outside the church where they used to put down the bier."

"Beer! They must have been regular fellows."

"Ah, no," I corrected sadly, "not beer, but bier for the corpse."

"Well, your church sounds fine. Let's go. Girls, dismiss!"

He took up the telephone and ordered a car. Frank's expostulations—late editions, etc.—were of no avail.

"A well-run newspaper publishes itself."

The large Daimler had revolving armchairs and a man in livery who drove. He was outside a glass partition. A speaking tube went to him. There was also a footman. The footman was ordered to stay behind. I was the guide, and what a guide! The chauffeur knew every village in England. "Wantage," I ordered.

Mr. Parsons' fatigue had vanished. He was in excellent form. Marjorie chatted on subjects that were not religious.

After half an hour threading our way through traffic we reached open country. Soon Bray appeared with its Anglo-American inn. Maids went about bare to the elbows with skin like cream tarts. Oaken pillars obtruded at every corner and flaunted deep hackings intended as evidence (for American clients) that the wood bore the authentic marks of an ax in times out of mind when the inn was built.

"The beer here is as good as any in England," Frank announced. "Don't listen to those who say that you can't get English beer cold. And that applies to the remarks about our women."

"What are the remarks?" Marjorie asked.

"And the proprietor throws out anyone he does not like."

So impressed was Mr. Parsons with the last remark that Marjorie's question went unanswered. Mr. Parsons felt himself complimented by implication. I thought of my favorite tavern in Dublin, where the customer is always wrong. Only the proprietor is right.

Mr. Parsons ordered whitebait. It was said to go well with beer. As I also go well with beer—that is, it agrees with me—I declined any concomitants to thirst.

When at last it was time to leave, Mr. Parsons seemed loath to go. It may have been that out of politeness he was waiting for his guide to give the signal, or it may have been that he was considering adding ancient inns to his collection of churches.

We went to Wantage in something over an hour. And then I, the guide, fell down. I could have brought forward an excuse or a number of excuses. Mr. Parsons could not have known what a bump supper was like. It was due to one of these in the days of yore that I mistook one side of Oxford for the other. That is why I placed Littlemore thirteen miles to one side instead of three to the other. It would not have made much difference in the long July evening but for the fact that we had to go with Mr. Parsons down the High. It was with difficulty that he was restrained from leaping out and inspecting the colleges which lined each side of the street. I calmed him.

"Take no notice, they are not churches."

"Then what the hell are they?"

"Examples of domestic Gothic and Baroque; just dormitories."

"But the one with the square tower and the pinnacles?" He swung his chair round and eyed Magdalen Church longingly as the car left it behind. Firmly Frank held him.

"There's one with a lich gate."

"That's only Tom Tower. It's a curfew tower, not a lich gate."

"That would do damned well!"

He struggled until we got him safely over Folly Bridge.

"Wait until you see Littlemore," I said.

At Littlemore Mr. Parsons showed his mettle. He showed himself a man of action, and the action was direct. He looked at the lich gate, but he did not permit it to divert him from the church. We entered and paused before a tablet on the left wall. We read:

THIS CHURCH WAS PRESENTED BY JEMINA NEWMAN TO HER SON JOHN, AFTERWARDS CARDINAL NEWMAN, IN THE YEAR 1852.

Mr. Parsons disappeared. We found him in the graveyard kicking the nettles aside in an endeavor to find any interment that would antedate the date of the gift. Apparently he was satisfied. He went to the car for his movie camera and came back in the best of humor. To me he said, "Just lean over the lich gate while I take a picture. Look a bit down in the mouth."

This was asking too much. Far be it for me to refuse to cooperate in a religious observance if the call came; but to imitate a Cardinal, oh no!

"My torso is on the burly side, and I am out of the wrong century," I said. "Nobody could mistake me for Cardinal Newman, who was ascetic; and, as for weeping, on a day like this I feel more inclined to turn upon the toe."

"Well, well, have it your own way." Then he turned to Frank.

"Now, Frank, take Marge by the arm and I'll do a shot of a wedding in the Gothic door."

There was more than a hint of embarrassment as one waited for the other in the hope of distracting Mr. Parsons.

Mr. Parsons went away, probably to interview the sexton, who was absent during our proceedings.

On the way back he relapsed into silence. Silence was so unsuited to him that I became anxious. When we got to half a mile or so outside Henley he was asked what was biting him, and he said, "I have been thinking about Cardinal Newman and his church. I don't like a man who switches, and there's too much religion about that church!"

Frank, who was writing a leader probably, started to mutter something. When asked to speak clearer, he said, "Have you never thought of Lorna Doone's church?"

Mr. Parsons raised the speaking tube and was about to give an order to the driver when Marjorie, to whom he always listened, said, "It's two days away. And we have not eaten yet."

Distracted as he was by the church at Henley, he let himself be led into the inn.

When we assembled again before dinner, which greatly to my relief Mr. Parsons ordered, he said to Frank, "You were talking about Lorna Doone's church. It seems a very good idea. I'll go there tomorrow."

This, I said, was a plain tale if you knew the end. I'll let you in on the end.

Mr. Parsons was the architect for a great cemetery, which was then only a dream and a matter of organization. Many morticians organized themselves to make the cemetery possible. Among the first things they did was to give Mr. Parsons a free hand and the run of England and Scotland.

I do not know if Annie Laurie's church graces the burial ground, and I do not know if they have a replica of the church at Stoke Poges; but I do know that there is a chapel called The Wee Kirk of the Heather, and it is enough to make any wedding guest stand still. It may be Mr. Parsons' final rendering of Annie Laurie's church. You can be married in the Wee Kirk (marriages are not prohibitive; but the doves loosed cost money) or buried between the buttresses at a thousand dollars (or whatever the cost is) per foot. There is another church called Recessional. There is nothing too religious about this. It is called after Rudyard Kipling's poem. There are cops with bowed heads on every corner and corridor after corridor of vaults, clean, ventilated, dry, and "on easy terms"! But why ventilated? Are the people of that neighborhood like those mentioned by Chesterton—"They haven't got no noses?"

Kipling and Queen Victoria are there to give it the necessary dignity that is associated with death. And nobody, no matter what his religion, is offended. And for those with no religion, surely a man is provided who can disbelieve twice as much as the doubter for fifty cents.

Not a gravestone is visible, and that is exactly in keeping for two-dimensional people. When they forget that they are only two-dimensional and try to get off the screen, they come to grief: separations, divorces, and murders all ensue, all through endeavoring to be real and not in a world of shadows. The cemetery suits the shadowy people, and the churches that are but shadows of real churches suit it. They have done away with death. In some sarcophaguses they say that the voice of the occupant can be heard if a gramophone is provided.

"Death, where is thy sting?"

Mr. Satterthwaite's Conversion

Some famous men, Oliver Cromwell and Dr. Johnson for instance, had an inordinate fear of death. Fear of death is a measure of the relish for life. Think of the reverse: what confessed failures suicides are.

Mr. Satterthwaite, though not as famous as the men above, easily outdid them in their obsession. I will admit that he was helped in this by living in the age of advertisements. Cromwell was unaware of the respectability of funeral parlors, and Dr. Johnson was not coaxed into cremation by the cheerful glow of an open furnace. Mr. Satterthwaite suffered from both. One day inadvertently he took a bus. What did he see over the heads of the passengers opposite to him? An advertisement for vaults. Beside it was another for Planters' cooking oil; and then unabashed, one for a funeral parlor. So bad was Mr. Satterthwaite's obsession that he could not bear any hint of his last end. "Vault," in spite of the fact that a bank was concerned, suggested interment; and as for "Planters'," he recognized in that (for he was a well-read man) a slang word for burial, as in the song, "For when we plant Matt Hannigan's aunt, We won't be too put out." To him the word "cooking" was less associated with domesticity than with cremation. And as for the last advertisement, we won't go into that! Suffice it to say he never entered a bus again.

Mr. Satterthwaite had purchased his apartment in a co-operative building. In it he kept his books and his bric-a-brac. It was his home. He began to fear that the district was not as fashionable as when he took up his residence in it some years back. His daily stroll to the avenue, where he would hail a taxi, gave him visual evidence of some slight falling off in the social amenities of the place. The last straw, or to be exact the second-to-last straw, was provided by the office of a mortician who had established himself right in front of the building in which Mr. Satterthwaite dwelt. He could not take his daily walk, nor at night could he rest because of a pink neon light which blinked in and out and admonished all and sundry to "GET DEAD." You could no more keep the thing out than you could keep out lightning. The pink glare pierced his window shades.

What was to be done? Of course he could move to another part of the city; but he had bought his apartment and was loath to leave. To pack all his bric-a-brac and perhaps lose some in moving was not to be thought of; it would be nothing less than an upheaval.

Mr. Satterthwaite had a brain wave: he would send his man of business, Mr. Shattock, to interview the mortician and prevail on him to remove the sign and, better still, himself to a less salubrious neighborhood.

Mr. Shattock was a shrewd man; but though he was shrewd, Mr. Satterthwaite always found him reliable. He regarded him as a mentor, for his advice was sound and, if followed, left no room for regret.

Before calling, Mr. Shattock went to considerable trouble to find out the mortician's name. That of the firm was written in large letters, "LOAM, Inc.," but the mortician's name was moot. At last, from a woman who worked in the building on the ground floor of which the funeral parlor was situated, Mr. Shattock learned that there were two partners, one of whom was a Mr. Tuck. The name of the other was unknown to her; he was usually away at funerals, or rather interments.

He called on the mortician by appointment. He met a suave little man with an unctuous voice. His professional pose was touched by melancholy, for his outlook on life appeared overcast.

This was as it should be, for life is the enemy of the mortician; and though we are assured that in the midst of life we are in death, the latter is not as frequent as those who live by death would wish. This is becoming somewhat confusing. It is likely to end in a paradox, so let us drop the subject and turn to Mr. Shattock's interview with Mr. Tuck.

When Mr. Shattock entered the office, Mr. Tuck offered him a chair. He regretted that, owing to a temporary absence in the course of duty, his partner could not share the pleasure of making Mr. Shattock's acquaintance. He inquired what he could do for Mr. Shattock, and assured him that all the resources of the firm would be gladly put at his disposal. Mr. Shattock said, "I have come to see you about a friend."

Mr. Tuck bowed, as one who should say "Naturally," and sighed gently. Then he added, "I am glad that it is not a relative."

Mr. Shattock said, sensing cross purposes, "Not about a dead friend, but one who is alive. In fact, I have been instructed by him to call on you and discuss this business of yours."

At the word "business" the mortician's manner sensibly became cold. You might think that a spot of *rigor mortis* had set in, so chilly was his reply:

"Before you go any further, I would have you know that ours is not a business: it is a profession."

Mr. Shattock was not slow to recognize that here was an Achilles' heel. He decided to humor Mr. Tuck: "I beg your pardon." Mr. Tuck bowed. Mr. Shattock took the bow for an acceptance of his apology. He continued, "Surely in this profession of yours you must have had many moving experiences?"

He was sorry that he said "moving." Mr. Tuck might think he was making his profession a butt for ridicule. However, it was too late to change it, and it would never do to apologize twice. Evidently Mr. Tuck, oversensitive though he was, saw no concealed sarcasm in the word "moving," for he adopted it:

" 'Moving,' " he exclaimed. "I should say that I have had! I can give you an instance that occurred only the day before yesterday. You remember that accident on the elevated railway? Well, we had a basket case. All I had was a few photos of the poor fellow and 168 pounds of wax. He was well known to my partner, who unfortunately was away in the country, so I had to rebuild him all alone. I had nothing but a toenail to go upon. I worked for hours, thirty-five without end, without a letup. The relations and friends were already filling the parlor. You know how diffident an artist feels before an exhibition? I was about to admit the relatives when in comes my partner—and this I consider the peak point of my career—I turned to my partner and pointed to my handiwork. 'What do you think of that?' My partner went over to the casket, stretched out a hand, and said, 'Speak to me, George!' My heart leaped up. Art, as the poet said, is its own exceeding great reward."

At that moment the door opened and a tall, merry-eyed, red-faced man in a black frock coat, black kid gloves, and a tall silk hat entered the office. He took no notice of Mr. Shattock. "That's that!" he said, and went over to the window breathing relief. Mr. Tuck called, "Let me introduce you to Mr. Shattock. Mr. Shattock, this is my partner, Mr. Ashe."

"Pleased to meet you, excuse my gloves," said Mr. Ashe as he extended his hand. "I'll be out of uniform in a moment." He left the room and returned quickly, without hat, gloves, or frock coat. Instead he wore a light alpaca sports coat of grayish blue. He had doffed his manner with his "uniform." He was in a merry mood.

"The two fifty at Woodlawn and the six hundred with canopy. The one at Trinity is still to be checked. Well over a thousand bucks a day. I could do with a boilermaker. Where's the bourbon?"

Apparently the question was not rhetorical, for Mr. Ashe at the window lifted the window seat and produced a bottle and two glasses, which he placed on a table. "Tuck, we'll want a third tumbler."

When Mr. Tuck found a third tumbler, Mr. Ashe proceeded to pour the bourbon into the glasses with an experienced hand. At the third glass he turned to Mr. Shattock and said solicitously, "Say when." When the glass was about half full Mr. Shattock nodded. Mr. Ashe handed him the glass. "Neat or on the rocks?"

Mr. Shattock asked him if there were a chaser. Mr. Ashe went to the window and produced a can of beer. He tossed off his liquor while his partner was toying with his.

"We are giving a dinner on Saturday with a client in the chair. Perhaps you could join us? Couldn't Mr. Shattock join us, Tuck?"

"By all means; by all means. Nothing would give us greater pleasure." Then he added as an afterthought, "I am sure."

There must have been an icebox under the window, for when Mr. Ashe politely opened the can for Mr. Shattock, the beer in it was cold.

"That's settled, then. Here's mud in your eye." Mr. Shattock winced at the toast. In some respects he was almost as bad as Mr. Satterthwaite, to whom "mud" would suggest interments, etc.

While the mood was cheerful, he thought he would broach the object of his visit.

"I am representing a Mr. Satterthwaite," he said.

"Bring him along. Bring him along. The more the merrier, eh, Tuck?"

Mr. Tuck inclined his head till it reached the rim of his glass.

"Does your friend play or sing?" Mr. Ashe inquired. Mr. Shattock shook his head.

"A pity. A pity! Perhaps he can recite?"

The thought of Mr. Satterthwaite reciting at a morticians' musicale was overwhelming. Caution fell from Mr. Shattock. He laughed immoderately. Mr. Ashe took the laughter for an assurance of Mr. Satterthwaite's power as a reciter.

"I suppose he can give us 'I learnt about women from her?' Talking about women, you should have seen the blonde at the second interment. None of your jokes, Tuck, about an Ashe blonde. She was all in black. She must have been the daughter of the dear departed. She was too young to have been his wife. She was under the canopy near the grave. I'll check on her when I get through with my arrears of homework."

When Mr. Shattock entered the large cellar under the mortuary parlor, the band was in full swing. Every musician played on some sort of bottle, jar, or jug, which he used as a wind instrument by blowing into it. One or two used ash trays for cymbals. The din was terrific. Mr. Ashe stood behind an improvised bar and kept the musicians lubricated. He hailed Mr. Shattock with "Where's your friend?" Mr. Shattock explained that owing to a slight indisposition his friend was unable to attend. The fact was that Mr. Shattock had resolved not to inform Mr. Satterthwaite until he had something definite to report.

"Indisposition. That's bad. What height is your friend?" Mr. Ashe asked. Mr. Shattock, who failed to see the connection, said, "About your height." "That," said Mr. Ashe, "would be six feet and a half in my stocking feet. Weight two ten."

The place continued to fill. Mr. Ashe was kept busy behind the bar. An old gentleman entered. Two of the musicians began to cheer. Mr. Shattock found Mr. Tuck and asked who the newcomer was.

"That's our chairman tonight. He's well over seventy. He had a lot of money at one time, but he spent it all in nylons and mink. Now he is reduced to traveling for a stocking factory. He says that he does not regret it one bit. He says that if he had his money back, he'd spend it the same way again. He insured himself long ago for three thousand and he is engaging us. Mr. Ashe is presenting him with a gold pencil at the dinner. You must meet Mr. Kinsey himself."

The band blared again. Mr. Kinsey greeted his host behind the bar. He was handed something in a glass. Mr. Shattock sat beside Mr. Ashe. Mr. Kinsey had the place of honor at the first table head. Mr. Shattock looked at the second table, but not too closely, for he wished to smother the suspicion that it was a trestle. On Mr. Shattock's right were two policemen in plain clothes. One of whom invited Mr. Shattock to a pistol competition which would be held at the station house in the following week.

"If my book is out next week, we'll all go." Mr. Shattock was interested. He inquired what was the subject of the book.

"What do you think?" Mr. Ashe asked, winking. "I call it

After Death . . . What? If that is not an intriguing title, I'll eat my hat."

Mr. Shattock ventured to say that there might be some misunderstanding: the religiously inclined might buy it with the idea that it solved the great problem. When the contents, which Mr. Shattock took to have something to do with interments, were disclosed, Mr. Ashe might find himself in trouble.

"*After Death . . . What?* A decent funeral, of course. I have no religious scruples. Anyhow, I don't want to take sides. I have my job to do. Ain't that enough?"

"I don't know how you find time to write," Mr. Shattock said, impressed.

"Write?" said Mr. Ashe. "I provide the title. My publishers do the rest."

Somebody, probably Mr. Tuck, rapped on the table. Mr. Kinsey was about to speak. The old gentleman at the head of the table rose. At first his voice was feeble, but it gathered volume as he spoke. He raised his champagne glass:

"Don't take my toast amiss. I know that I am, in the eyes of Loam, Inc., a case of delayed burial. Nevertheless, here's to our next merry meeting. Then ashes to Ashe."

Prolonged cheers and laughter followed Mr. Kinsey's speech. The musicians, who were seated at the second table, cheered loudest. Mr. Ashe, still laughing, rose and struck his glass for silence. He held a gold pencil in its case.

"Gentlemen, my friends, I have here a present from our firm to one of its firmest supporters. I have known Mr. Kinsey these many years. As you are aware, it is not often we have the opportunity to talk to one of our customers beforehand; and I am sure that none of you would like to talk to them afterward. Mr. Kinsey, I am glad to say, though I say it myself, is far from being a ghost. Mr. Kinsey, on behalf of Loam, Inc., I present you with this gold pencil, with the hope that you will not use it to write your memoirs, which are known to us all, and which are an envy of the old and a caution to the young—Mr. Kinsey!"

With raised glasses, all stood and drank to the oldest man in the room.

When Mr. Shattock saw Mr. Satterthwaite, he had more than a missionary's task; he had not only to cure him of his obsession, but to convert him. No easy thing to do; but it would not be said of him that he had failed because of lack of enterprise.

"Not only did I see the partners of the firm but I dined with them." Mr. Shattock decided that shock tactics were the best approach.

Mr. Satterthwaite regarded his agent with suspicion. Had he betrayed him? Fraternization with the enemy looked very like it.

"I dined with them," Mr. Shattock continued, "and I came to this conclusion: They have found a means of making the common enemy work for them. They make Death pay. They have blunted his scythe—or what have you? Behind the black glass of their window there is revelry and joy. I have never had a more amusing time than when I went under the parlor to an extensive cellar to a dinner given in honor of a valued and prospective customer. I am bold enough to suggest that you put some money into the firm, obtain if possible a controlling interest, become a partner, and get out once and for all from the state of fear which every suggestion of mortality puts you into. Take your courage in both hands. I have asked the partners if they required capital. What money they have invested in it is increasing a hundredfold. I am joining them. I advise you to do likewise. Put your money into a mortuary and make Death pay. Get behind it. Drive it in front of you. And as for art; your artistic nature will not be blighted. There is wax to be sculptured into the semblance of flesh. There is death to be made lifelike. What more is the aim of art?"

And that is why if you cross the city you can read on a discreet pane of dark glass, "Ashe, Tuck, Satterthwaite, and Shattock, Morticians." There is no neon light. Only the words "After Death . . . What?" in golden letters on a background of black.

William Spickers, M.D.

The auspices under which we met could not have been more favorable. The house where I lived was next to his at a distance of about a quarter of a mile. He had a tennis court, and what was more to me, a swimming pool.

The Ramapo Mountains form a horseshoe at the base of which runs Ewing Avenue in Bergen County, New Jersey. At the angle made by this avenue and Franklin Lakes Road stands the house of Dr. Spickers, with its short drive off the road, a drive lit at night by a ship's lantern. It was his habit to keep a light burning all night by the door of his house for the convenience of night callers and because he liked a friendly light at the entrance of his home.

The daughter of the owner of the house which was put at my disposal was one of the loveliest girls in America, which is saying something, as the phrase goes. I say it nevertheless. And because it was she who introduced us, my friendship with the doctor could not have had a happier beginning, as I have already stated.

Many a time during the summer, when the sun was cooling and the doctor's round of hospitals was over for the day, I would take a racket and go down the slight incline that led past a few fields to his tennis court, there to sit under a bright yellow umbrella and look at the players until our turn came. Bill Spickers was tall, with a fresh complexion. His eyes were clear and China blue, witnesses to his Teutonic ancestry.

He had the younger generation always about him, the friends

of his sons and daughter. When they were not playing, they sat on the seats beside the tennis court or swam in the blue pool under aged willow trees. The court was made of sand and bounded by a wire net at each end. Wild woods rose beyond, and at one end sprang a fountain which served the swimming pool.

To judge by the size of the great trees that overhung it, there must have been a little pond there originally, before it was gathered in by cement to form a pool. The perennial overflow made a tiny waterfall and a stream that wandered through the lawns to a little lilied lake where large carp glowed down between the floating leaves. Beyond, the valley lay filled with purple mist. A man might bring his heart to rest in worse places than Wyckoff in Bergen County.

The doctor played a skillful game. His serves had a swerve and a break when the ball bounced. He kept at the back of the court and played to protect himself from undue running. I am a bad player, with a style which might deceive a casual onlooker who judged by a few spasmodic shots and did not watch until the end of the game, which I seldom won. I wondered why the doctor failed to exert himself. He would let shots go by that an older man could have played. Little did I know at the time how great was the handicap against him. Had I known, I would not have aimed at putting the ball so often out of his reach.

After a set or two (for he tired easily) he and I would go and float in a rubber ring in the deliciously cool spring water. I remember how often I reminded myself to set down those hours to the credit side of life, so that if I were ever depressed and tempted to denounce my lot, I should have the memory of Bill Spickers and his tennis parties to revamp the mood.

Mrs. Spickers came from California; but her ancestors came from Ireland, from the well-known Waterford family of de la Poer. She was literary and musical, talents which she passed on to her daughter, who was the only brunette of a family of four. The boys were all athletes, well built and nearly as tall as their father. Albert, the youngest, devoted himself with extraordinary tenacity to the study of music; and though his mother, a gifted musician, was aware that in spite of his talent he had not the endowment to become a first class pianist, she was careful to refrain from any comment that might discourage him. Hour after hour when I was near the house, I could hear the piano and see in my mind's eye the timekeeper oscillating on the instrument as he practiced.

The doctor's house was at the disposal of his family's friends. They came late and early, often so early that they appeared soon after breakfast in time for lunch. Their late hours gave us long periods of quiet in the evenings, when the doctor would sit by the radio which he turned on from time to time when any subject of interest was on the air.

Very often evenings passed when he did not use the radio at all. He loved to explain to me the latest surgical practices and to recount the cases on which he had operated during the day. From this I got much information and the impression that surgery in the United States, advanced as it was, differed from surgery elsewhere by being more enterprising. I felt all the time we talked that I was in the presence not only of a great surgeon but of a remarkable human being, a humanist, a man devoted to the service of his fellow men, a man whose life was consecrated to saving others from pain. I looked at the long fine wrists that slid into his hands without displaying the bone beneath, wrists that showed the sensitive surgeon that he was famed to be. His knowledge of internal medicine was unusual in one who you might think had little time to devote to study; but he was an unerring diagnostician, and many an interesting evening passed in discussing points that were new to me. One trait that did not accord with his power of diagnosis when applied to the moral field was his avoidance of judging persons who happened to be the subjects of criticism. Even those who were known to be generally reprehensible passed without comment before his tribunal. This is a roundabout way of emphasizing his aversion to causing pain. His was the sweetest nature I have ever known. You could deduce his kindness from his voice, which was low, with a kind of echo in it. I never heard it raised in all the years I knew him. If he were pressed to agree with an unkind comment, he detached himself from comment with a smile and a quiet laugh that had the effect of disarming insistence.

If he could be said to have specialized in any branch of surgery, eradication of malignant disease held great interest for him. I learned that he had been a victim of such a condition in the large intestine and that he had undergone a most successful operation at the hands of Leahy of the Leahy Clinic in Boston. Then I realized why his movements on the tennis court were restricted; and I became full of remorse remembering the way I had played against him. Perhaps he did not wish his disability to be known; but that was little consolation to me.

It would be unfair to explain his sympathy with suffering humanity by fellow feeling. The natural sweetness of the man and his loving kindness sufficed to make him a benefactor long anterior to his experience of the pain before an operation for cancer and the anxiety and fear of recurrence after it. Years before he had any suspicion that he himself was affected, his unremitting labors and long hours in the operating theaters were witnesses to his disinterested devotion to all whom his skill could relieve.

Never was the nobility of the profession of medicine borne in upon me until I came in contact with Bill Spickers. Often I had repeated the truism about the self-sacrifice of doctors without feeling it as an ingrained conviction. Here was something tangible: the living proof of a devoted life. Unwearied when his body craved a moment's respite, his spirit urged him far beyond his physical capacity. He would sit down with a weary sigh to enjoy an hour's talk or music, when the telephone would ring and a house surgeon confess that an emergency had cropped up with which he found himself unable to cope without help from his principal. Without a word of impatience or a gesture of exasperation Bill Spickers would rise, leave the room and put on his coat, and away with him to Paterson, regardless of the lateness of the hour or the weather. I have seen such things happen time and again; and for those who were not what are known to the profession as "paying patients."

He had one diversion which was more than a hobby: he loved painting. At the top of his large house there was a studio where he painted on Sundays and on occasions when an opportunity arose and the spirit moved him. These occasions had to be snatched from his daily round. I have seen him return at two o'clock in the morning and go upstairs, not to bed, but to his studio. Sometimes he would invite me up to it, so that we might talk while he painted. I never saw him painting out of doors, yet the studies of his that I liked best were outdoor scenes: trees and vistas. Painting is one of my blind spots. Of its technique I know nothing. I am (and I believe it is a heresy) inclined to permit my liking for a scene to affect my judgment of the technique of the painting. I liked the way he painted trees, the great willows beside the pool or red trees along some road. I could feel the bursting life within them; and his palette with its strong colors and assured light appealed to me, even though I knew nothing about the drawing. When I was with him in his studio he used to paint still life, bunches of grapes, oranges, apples, and flasks of wine in greenish glass. He would labor at his art until he realized that he was keeping me up. Then he would send me to bed while he remained at work. I could see the light in the roof of his house from where I slept; and it often burned on into the dawn.

About this time, a month before the war, there came from England a refugee artist, a quaint fellow who was known for his extraordinary technical skill as both a draftsman and an etcher, as well as for his eccentricities. I introduced him to Bill Spickers, and they got on well together. The artist was an excellent teacher, and he, in spite of being somewhat self-centered, was generous enough to help amateur artists. There was a bevy of them in the neighborhood at the time. A studio was placed at their disposal; and there on Sundays they all would meet to benefit by the advice and the demonstrations of the professional. Bill Spickers was foremost among these students. So quick was he to learn that the teacher took a personal interest in him, and some of his canvases bear marks of the brushwork of the master. Through his readiness to help amateurs, the artist was more or less accepted among the rather closely walled community of Wyckoff; and his quaint proclivities were attributed to the "artistic temperament." The man with the most charity was Bill Spickers.

One day I saw Albert the musician sitting in a garden chair sunbathing and reading a book. I wondered why he was not grinding away at the piano, as he had done for months without any letup. He told me that he was studying mathematics, for a knowledge of mathematics was indispensable for any candidate for the Air Force. Albert was about nineteen, and his mathematics had been allowed to become rather rusty during the long days at the piano. I asked him how he could bear to study mathematics, knowing that for one who had at least the temperament of a musician, mathematics must be distasteful, to say the least of it. I spoke with understanding and real feeling, for the thought of a cosine acts on me like an emetic.

Albert had scrapped his music. He was all set on getting into the Air Force, and he had hardly time to make up mathematics before he would be twenty. With that power of devotion to his job which he inherited from his father, Albert worked on day and night. Surely such will power would get him into the Air Force, I thought. Albert had a magnificent physique. His body shone like gilt bronze from sunbathing, and the muscles on his young limbs flowed like an unbroken stream.

One morning Bill invited me to see some surgical results.

"I think that you will find that the treatment of tuberculosis has undergone a considerable change," Bill Spickers said, and he said it gently, so as not to correct my outmoded theories too authoritatively. "I think that you will find . . ."

He was about to start for a hospital that had recently been built for tuberculosis in the neighborhood, and he asked me if I cared to accompany him. We started off, and within half an hour arrived at what was evidently a quite new building standing in grounds that were just planted with young trees. After giving my name to the secretary, who owed his appointment to politics, as I learned afterward, we went upstairs. In Ireland it is religion and not politics that influences hospital appointments, as it was in the days before Hippocrates. But, because politics cannot be wholly expelled from any form of human activity, in hospitals it assumes the form of hospital politics, which is manifested by tensions and rivalries and even calamities between opposing members of the hospital staff. This is the way in nondenominational hospitals, of which there are but few extant; whereas in hospitals run by religious orders, precedence comes from observation of church ceremonies. For instance, when the allocation of an important operation on an important person is in the hands of the reverend mother, the case will go, as a wag put it, to him who showed the greatest prowess in the church and not the theater. Thus in Ireland we are a little before Hippocrates. In New Jersey politics is extrinsic to hospitals and is satisfied with making appointments from without. Thus it came about that the secretary to the hospital represented the vicarious philanthropy of Boss Hague.

Four young women were in bed in a small room. Each of them had been operated on for tubercular cavities in their lungs; each was an example of modern treatment of what is known as surgical tuberculosis. In order to obliterate cavities in the lung, cavities which cannot close while the lung is held open either by adhesions to the inner surface of the ribs or merely by the negative pressure maintained by the thorax, the ribs on the affected side are removed to permit the lung to collapse and obliterate its cavities. It is of primary importance to get rid of cavities, for in them infected sputum can collect and unsupported blood vessels rupture. None of the young women was emaciated, nor had any of them the classical hectic color I had been taught to expect in advanced stages of the disease. They were plump and pink-faced, in spite of the fact that the American complexion is not pink. They were free from disease. The doctor asked one of the women if she had any objection to letting me inspect her thorax. She sat up in bed and removed her nightdress until her back was exposed. On the left side was a long curved wound that began near the junction of the neck and curved away from the spine to her waist, the mark of the incision over the site of ribs removal or thoroplasty. The doctor called her by name and said, "That was very kind of you,

Annie. Put on your clothes again." She was all smiles and proud of herself. The others seemed to me to be disappointed that they were not called as living examples of their doctor's skill.

"The old ideas of fresh air and sunlight are superseded," the doctor said. "Provided that the lung can be made to rest, you can cure tuberculosis in a cellar if the worst comes to the worst."

I looked at the splendid hospital as we drove away and thought of how much more favorable to recovery it was than a slum in Dublin, where there is much more money for hospitals and sanatoria than in any country in the world. And none for prophylaxis.

The doctor was a silent man. I had noticed how much his patients were attached to him in spite of the few words he exchanged with them. He had a language which was older and more effective than any words; and this was his gentleness "and that cometh from the very fountain and spring of all courtesie and humanity, which should never dry up in any manne living." The qualities of his heart explained his power and endowed him with powers of healing that all too seldom accompany surgical dexterity.

This explains why he permitted people to call him "Bill." In England a certain pomp hedges a great man. Here, in the United States, pomp is regarded as pomposity, and instead of making a man more respected, it tends to make him absurd. In England a surgeon calls himself "Mister" to distinguish himself from "Doctor," which means an internist or inner medicine man. Here a very expert surgeon and a born healer such as Dr. William Spickers can be addressed without detriment to prestige as "Bill."

There was good news when we returned. Albert had obtained a commission in the Air Force. I do not know how his father felt. I do know that he said in his quiet way, "A man must fight for his country"; but at heart he, whose vocation was to save life, must have been averse to all that made for its destruction. There was rejoicing in the family—more for Albert's success, perhaps, than for that which it involved.

Occasionally on evenings in the half-light Bill Spickers would drive quietly along the many lovely lanes that led through the Ramapo range. One evening we climbed up the eastern slopes and reached a point from which the George Washington Bridge, Amann's marvel of geometrical simplicity and engineering mastery, could be seen. Beyond, the topless towers of Manhattan actually seemed to be topless in the afterglow.

"There," he said, "lies New York. It never lured me, though there may be more money to be made there. I am quite satisfied to remain where I am. When a man has all he wants, why should he strive for more?" I agreed; and I am afraid that I turned to quotation, a trick that reveals a certain shallowness, because when you quote you do not speak for yourself but allow another to represent you; but as it happened to be apposite, the offense may be mitigated to that extent. It was Longfellow I quoted; Miles Standish recites a saying attributed to Julius Caesar,

"'Better,' said he, 'to be first in a little Iberian village than second in Rome.' And I think he was right when he said it." But as it implied that the doctor might be only second in New York, it turned out to be less happy than I had intended.

"What is that thing that looks like the last piece left of some gigantic city wall?" I asked. "Rockefeller Center," he said.

We gazed until the sun went down behind us and the lights like sudden stars came out in the vertical streets which are the skyscrapers of New York. It was dark as we turned and descended past lakes seen white through fringing pines.

Meals were on a sliding schedule in the doctor's house, thanks to a wife who understood and welcomed any relaxation the doctor allowed himself.

On our way home he told me of a consultation he had that morning, a differential diagnosis between colitis and diverticulitis. His preoccupation with the lower part of the intestine was the only indication, or hint rather, I got of what must have been ever present to his mind: recurrence of his own trouble. What a sword of Damocles to have over you day and night: more than day, night, when you can be possessed by the dark things that range in the stillest hour.

"Multiple diverticulitis. The best thing to do surely is to have it out," I opined. "There are objections to that," he said. "Talking again of Rockefeller Center, that reminds me that a prominent man in the Rockefeller Institute told me that, so far as a cure for cancer has been discovered, the towel's in the ring. It will be discovered some day suddenly, and possibly turn out to be some quite simple law of growth that has been overlooked, just as the penicillin mold was overlooked until Fleming came along."

"Necessity was the mother of that," I said. "The Army sent out an SOS to the research men to get something quickly that would arrest gas gangrene. Somebody remembered a paper by an anonymous student of the University of Vienna, and that led to Fleming's beneficent discovery."

I went into a reverie about molds. Why is one of the lowest forms of life the most efficacious in preserving the highest? I knew that the premises were more or less invalid, nevertheless I liked propounding to myself a mystery probably as corrective to the assurance of science. Scotsmen were certain to be assured. A little inorganic thing like a milligram of copper or a grain or two of iron, stuff that is found in stars, is more essential to life than a lung, a leg, or an arm.

"It's a strange thing," I said, waking up, "that the late poet laureate of England, Robert Bridges, put researchers before poets. He acknowledged that he had not the gifts necessary for a great discoverer in the field of physics. He writes:

Thrice happy he, the rare
Prometheus, who can play
With hidden things, and lay
New realms of nature bare;
Whose fearless feet have trod
Hell underfoot, and won
A crown from man and God
For all that he has done.

That highest gift of all,
Since crabbèd fate did flood
My heart with sluggish blood,
I look not mine to call . . .

He confesses that the researcher who discovers a panacea has a higher gift than the poet. And I am inclined to agree with him."

"I am afraid that I am not up in literature; but if I remember rightly, the poet laureate was a doctor. And that would naturally account for his preference."

"You are right," I said. "The poet, however, attends to the spirit of man by means of his inspiration. Few poets, if any, nowadays show any signs of inspiration. What breathes into them would do mankind little good. Poetry is addressed to the healthy in body. Penicillin restores the diseased body to health. Dr. Robert Bridges was a master of metrical technique. He never quite dispensed with the micrometer when writing verse. It was the humanitarian in him that measured and judged his own case rightly. It seems to me to be only a matter of time and diligence before the scientists will discover anything on which their minds are bent: but no amount of discipline and diligence will discover a Shakespeare. The two, penicillin and poetry, are non-comparables, and the fallacy lies in comparing them. With Bridges it was different: he was an indifferent doctor but a distinguished poet. This he knew; but nevertheless, the regret lingered that he had not 'that highest gift of all.' So don't you regret that you 'are not up in literature' when the best literary man of his time preferred to be a good doctor."

The winter kept Bill Spickers away from home, busy in his hospitals for most of the twenty-four hours. I too was busy trying to keep the large room in which I worked heated. It had been converted from a squash racket court, and the lofty ceiling with its lantern, as well as the great fireplace, carried away most of the heat. At the end of March the thaws set in, and with them the sudden spring burst in field and wood; then April came and with it blighting news. Albert, who was training in Texas, flew with a friend, Lieutenant Kennedy, to lunch. After lunch Kennedy took over the controls. The plane crashed in flames shortly after taking off. The Army sent Bill his son's charred pocketbook.

I was away at the time. I hurried to Wyckoff. The household was resigned. I did not refer to the tragedy. I remembered asking a friend who lost a son how many years it was before you got over such a bereavement, and his answer, "You don't." So I merely remained with Bill and said little.

Some months later, Bill and his wife came to rest in a private hotel in New York. Bill put a proposition to me. Would I write a poem in memoriam of Albert? It was to be a business matter. That was Bill. To me it came not as a matter of business, but as a chance to show an affection for him and his family that long lay unexpressed.

At Bay Head, on the New Jersey coast, Bill Spickers had two houses. The larger, a block away from the smaller, which stood beside Barnegat Bay, was nearer to the Atlantic. I went to stay with him in the larger house. There was but a row of houses between us and the sea. The bathing, to judge by the number of lifeguards, must have been quite dangerous, yet Margaret Spickers went far out to sea of a morning. Bill and I collected driftwood or sat on the beach watching the breakers come ashore after their long journey.

One evening as we were going back to the house I carried a balk of timber on my shoulder. I thought that I was going slowly, but Bill was distressed in his breathing as he tried to keep up with me.

"I wish I could do that," he said, referring to the load I was carrying. "I am supposed to have a mitral murmur. That excellent Dr. Shapiro, to whom you introduced me, when he examined my heart before operating, said, 'Mitral murmur, fully compensated. What can you expect at your age?' I must say that was the first I heard of it; and it came as a surprise. Now I am trying to live up to it, though it lacks humor. I would hate to die drowning, with my lungs flooded through cardiac insufficiency, as I am likely to do some day."

I stopped and turned. "I never knew you had heart trouble," I said.

"For years I have been painfully conscious of every beat of my heart."

"And you never said anything about it?"

"It would not help," he said.

That set me thinking. How much suffering, apart from the mental anguish of his son's awful death and his fear of a return of the malignant disease for which Dr. Leahy had operated, had he been bearing without a complaint? Now he confessed that his heart was not compensating, and yet he never ceased to drive himself.

"For the future you must go easy," I adjured him. "Why must you work?"

"It keeps me from thinking," he said.

I remembered how little time he allowed himself for sleep. He must have known the consequence of insufficient rest; but, bad as that was, it was not as bad as the sorrow-laden dark. His life had been devoted to the work of easing pain. Now he utilized that work to ease his own pain in death.

One evening, as we were walking in silence by Twilight Avenue, he asked out of a reflective mood:

"Do you think there is a life after this?"

I pondered long before I answered, for I realized that the study of medicine tended to make men atheistical. I did not know much about his early religious conditioning. Whatever it had been, it was evidently returning to him now. His end was in sight and he knew it. I would be loath to dampen any comfort that might come to him from religion.

"Honestly, I do not know. How can anyone know, seeing that knowledge depends on consciousness and consciousness depends on our being born? Reason, an outcome of life, is asked to beg the question and to explain that of which it is a part. Obviously it can't be done in terms of reason anyway. That is well put in the story of the angel who was found trying to put the ocean into a hole he had made in the sand as a lesson to some saint or philosopher who was trying to work out an answer to the mystery by reason. Reason cannot supply the answer. It is strange that it takes reason to tell us this and, by so doing, to invalidate itself. But so far as conduct is concerned, and religion emphasizes the importance of conduct as a means to life everlasting, you have nothing to worry about. I may tell you to your face, you are the most devoted man I have ever met in any walk of life. If I had your record I would take your leaky heart."

Silence fell on us; but I felt his grasp tighten on my arm.

At length, "You are honest . . . and kind," he said, but he brooded still. I felt that my words were but cold comfort to a man who knew that he had not long to live. The thought of James Stephens' test of a successful life came back to me: "How many *men* have loved you?" He was not talking of sex.

Here was a man, perhaps the only man, who loved me, and I was failing him when it came to facing death. I was neither kind nor candid. I was not putting my cards on the table. I was permitting pessimism to darken the outlook. I was not a pessimist. If not, why not try to impart a little of my own philosophy, if I could call it philosophy, and do all in my power to cheer him up?

"The way I look at it," I began, "is that death is universal. With things as they are, it would be worse to be left old and derelict, bereft of contemporaries and friends, old and alien in a world of youth, a chatterbox with no one to chatter to about the good old days. Goethe said, 'Death cannot be an evil because it is universal.' Even though that is insufficient because there are many things universal that are evils, such as disease and pain, yet the fact that, whatever happens, we are in the same boat as all mankind, is comforting.

"When I think that my grandmother got by with it and myriads more, I am braced up. Surely I can go the way a woman went. It is the thinking about it that gives death its terror. Placid and unintelligent people are resigned to death. Now if its terror depends on thinking, it may be said that the intellect invented death. But there is something in us that can look beyond death and regard it as from a pinnacle fixed above life. Something above and beyond ourselves, a place whereon to stand, a point of view. The same thing as that which enables us to laugh at ourselves. Something that informs us that our reason is inadequate. Something that can regard the pessimist and the optimist alike and ask, 'Is Life a dance or dirge?' And answer that it depends upon the point of view. All this means that the terror of death depends on the fear in ourselves. Once that fear is out, there's no sting; and a little overplus of sugar can obliterate all."

"Coma, you mean?" he asked.

"Yes," I replied. "Coma is one cure; another is advanced age which, according to Metchnikoff, can come to desire death as a man desires rest."

I should have said nothing about old age, for it was not for Bill Spickers. Few of us can expect to escape disease and reach an age to which death will be as welcome as rest.

After all, if we regard it from a medical point of view, we realize that fear is necessary to the continuance of life. If people had no fear of dying, they would be chucking away their lives the moment something disagreeable cropped up. Fear, then, is the counterpart of enjoyment, a measure of the value we set on life. When life becomes unendurable, fear vanishes and death becomes welcome. That's the way I look upon it. But, nevertheless, like Caesar, I hope for a sudden death. He got his. Meanwhile I dismiss all forebodings.

I had done my best; but I could not help wondering how much comfort my philosophy would bring me when it came to my turn. Foreknowledge of death cannot be combated; and Bill was condemned to that. Hence he avoided sleep, and he used work to distract him and bring the longer sleep.

The glow over Barnegat Bay faded and night came on. The slow sea boomed behind us as we walked down the road and entered the house by the long, open garden at the back. His short holiday at Bay Head came to a close. He had to go back to his work and to the nights in which he could not sleep. He lent me his house and I stayed on for a week alone. Then I returned to New York.

I met the doctor every few weeks when he lunched at the Russian Tea Room in West Fifty-seventh Street or in Sardi's somewhere in the theater region of Broadway. Bill held occasional lunch parties in Sardi's while his daughter and her husband were studying for the stage.

One morning I answered the telephone. When I laid it down I was bereaved: one of the few men who loved me was dead.

The end, I learned, came suddenly. He was painting in his studio on the top of the house. Against advice, he had climbed the stairs as fast as a friend whom he had invited to talk to him while he painted. He painted for a while and then said, "Will you excuse me, I think I must lie down." He stretched out on a couch. His appearance and his labored breathing alarmed the friend, who rushed downstairs to Mrs. Spickers. They came into the room just in time to see the doctor press his hand over his heart.

"Oh, the pain!" were the last words he said.

If life is a jungle or a slaughterhouse in spite of its distracting decorations, a valley of tears and of trials as they who preach a religion of suffering tell us, Bill Spickers was a knight who spent himself in warding pain off from others. He was a champion of humanity.

Long before the first symptoms of his own malady appeared, he had made the alleviation of pain his lifework and had founded his philosophy upon it. Those who can make phrases might call his life a life of kinetic compassion. He was at the call of all who suffered. Alleviation of pain was his reward. His love of his fellow men sustained him in his unremitting fight against pain. When he found himself a victim to one of its most terrible manifestations, he faced the grim remedy fearlessly and went on the more resolutely with his work.

Why it should be such a man's lot to suffer not only the loss of his health but the appalling tragedy of a beloved son's death is beyond the domain of reason to justify. It is linked with the problem of why the best should suffer most. Bill Spickers' bad fortune, bad as it was, cannot be contrasted equally with his good nature.

I affirm, without fear of contradiction by anyone who knew Bill Spickers, that in him medicine reached its noblest personification in our time. He saw the world as an arena of suffering (he had little chance to see it otherwise), and he, suffering, devoted himself to relieving others. I hope that the consciousness (which an expert must feel) of his skill may have been some satisfaction to him. It must have been, seeing that it made him pre-eminent as a surgeon.

I owe him much. When with him, I felt myself in the shelter of a soul at peace. His presence ennobled his friends. While in his company, it was impossible to entertain ignoble sentiments. One characteristic of his which must not go unrecorded was his courtesy. Courtesy is a gift which is rarer than genius. The courtesy of William Spickers was of another age than ours. It came from the great period when there were great persons in the world. He was one of those great persons out of his day, gazing about him at a world distraught. His largesse turned to the service of his fellows. He was a great surgeon, and his work restored to the profession of medicine ideals long submerged in the struggle of our time. There are many of his ilk scattered over the United States, laboring devotedly, who want no praise for their devotion, all members of the great brotherhood who wage a war that permits no intermission against the viewless enemies that menace mankind.

These men seek no applause. They want no crown. Their work is their reward. It is well that such men exist. They are literally and metaphorically the saviors of humanity. Of each it might be said, and William Spickers would wish that it were said of each equally, though from what I know of him it applies to himself particularly:

"A rare man and nobly given in all things."

Generalissimos

Somewhere I read that to be fair meant to be like the fair-haired people who conquered that part of the known world in their day. They were conquerors—they had to be—to make the conquered people look up to them and to say, "Let us be fair." The reverse of this thought strikes me (it always does): Suppose we were to be conquered by the black people or the yellow, would we say "Let us be black" or "yellow" where "fair" was?

It must have been brunettes that the fair people conquered to change the values so.

Instead of suggesting Gaels or Scandinavians, "fair" comes from the Anglo-Saxon *faeger*. The Anglo-Saxons may have been fair. I have seen men in the north of England, Lancashire to be exact, whose hair was so fair as to be almost white. They were remnants of the old Saxon stock, I was told. They may have been conquerors once, but they didn't look like it at the time.

This is an article on Generalissimos. I had better get on with it.

"Generalissimo" is a Spanish word. The only genuine generalissimo is General Franco, who warred against the Communists and for a while had his head in a noose. That was not necessarily so of the other generalissimos, Stalin, Tito, or the generalissimo whom for the moment I forget. They were politicians, dodgers, and of course, scoundrels. There was a regular outbreak of them. Apparently they thought that the title "generalissimo" meant the highest that could be achieved in the military line. And what achievement! There was a time when a leader saved his nation and was honored for it. Then there came a time when leaders went to war for war's sake: to conquer fresh lands or to uproot the neighboring tribes. Alexander the Great went to war and it was endless. He wanted to "fix his frontiers" and finally his troops mutinied somewhere in India. Genghis Khan made war ruinously. One good thing he did, though; he became the grandfather of Kublai Khan, who built a "pleasure dome" for each of his mistresses, and he had one for every day in the year! So the legend goes. In Ireland they allow only twelve hens to a cock; otherwise, a lady told me, it would be cruelty to the *hens*. If this be so, what must it have been like in the days of Kublai Khan?

Napoleon after his escape from Elba had one hundred days in which to convert French boys into soldiers, only to be defeated at Waterloo by Wellington (aided by Blücher), an "amateur." Wellington set the fashion for high-grade stupidity, which is the affectation in the military clubs of London to the present day.

The question remains unanswered: Why is it that generalissimos and their ilk regard soldiering as the highest profession? Why should they be admired at the expense of better men? It looks like a remainder from the days when men were herded and took their overlords at the value they set upon themselves. This speaks badly for mankind as a whole. Why should they be herdable? They are herdable in the majority of countries still.

Or is it, as the psychiatrists say, that men worship death? The very fact that psychiatrists say it is proof that it cannot be right. Boys we know are cruel, destructive and military-minded; and girls go for a uniform. Mars was not noted for his brains—still he got on with Venus very well.

If the betterment of mankind is the object of life, then Alexander Fleming, and before him Pasteur, should be honored. But no; generalissimos still hold it.

The fact is that there will always be wars—followed, of course, by Leagues of Nations or, in our own day, by the UN, the United Nations, that is. And they will last until mankind is ready for the next war.

"We, the people of the United Nations, determined to save succeeding generations from the scourge of war which twice in our lifetime has brought untold sorrow to mankind . . ." etc., etc. The United Nations has not only advocated the use of force but applied it (see Chapter VII, article 42). It may take such action by air, sea, or land forces as may be necessary to maintain or restore international peace and security. Even the United Nations recommends war as a means to peace! War to end war! We had it before. No wonder there are generalissimos! I am reminded of Cromwell's major-generals; and of the absurd knighthoods in Dublin in the days before and after Lord and Lady Aberdeen, two Scotch people who were made respectively Viceroy and Vicereine of Ireland. A picture dealer who sold a dud Corot to the King was knighted—not because he was Lady Gregory's nephew, as I thought, and not, as Walter Sickert the artist said, "for admiring Manet"; but for no reason except that he had the necessary money. Another was knighted for keeping things quiet in Mount Jerome cemetery, of which he was manager. It is quiet to the present day. Sir Andrew Percy was knighted for recruiting for the Royal Navy. He did his recruiting from land and from the Masonic Hall. He was presented with a sword of honor. "Join the Navy and see the world." Some wag added the word "next" before "world." Sir John O'Connell was knighted apparently because he was so small. When the Viceroy commanded him, "Arise, Sir John," no one knew if he was still kneeling. So serious did this knighting become that one Dubliner wrote to Lloyd's in London to ask what the premium was against being knighted. Of course he got no answer, for all honors are supposed to flow from the Throne.

Knighting became so ridiculous in Dublin that it is no wonder that they called Dublin "The City of Dreadful Knights." It was as ridiculous as the knighting of an Indian, Sir Tej Bahadur Sapru. Yet there was a time when knighthood meant prowess on the field of battle!

I used to wonder why Churchill, who made the serious mistake of letting himself be thought of as the savior of England, did not use the title "generalissimo." With two potential generalissimos beside him, he must have thought that it was too much for the English to swallow. He became a "naval person" instead. He was First Lord of the Admiralty, a position usually held by a civilian; but he could not keep in his place.

If Mussolini had only stopped at making the trains of Italy run on time and at clearing the Mafia out of Sicily, and Hitler had stopped at getting Germany back for the Germans, what a different picture it would have been! But they had to go on: they became generalissimos; they got control of the army—we know with what disastrous results.

Stalin—his own people don't like his memory—was a generalissimo. He had control of the army. The army will have control now that he is gone.

Tito is another generalissimo, one who is trying to fool the United States.

I had almost forgotten the greatest generalissimo of them all, Chiang Kai-shek. Five times he promised to clear the Reds out of China. Five times he did not succeed. But obversely, he caused the greatest march in history, that headed by Mao Tse-tung across China to the borders of Tibet. Just as Churchill was saved by Hitler, Mao was saved by Chiang. Mao dominates China now. Once he had only ten thousand men; that was in the time of Chiang. He has millions now. Chiang is shut up in Formosa. The latest news is that Chiang Kai-shek has been invited by Red China to join some league or other in the heart of Red China's capital, Peking! Generalissimo!

I am as far off as Herodotus was when he guessed why the Nile had its inundations when I set myself to discover why generalissimos exist. Maybe it is because three fourths of men's lives are combative: the remaining fourth is old age with its serenity and the wish to be let alone and to let others alone. But that doesn't answer why the masses put up with them. The masses are very plastic and they hate responsibility. That is why they readily—I almost said "welcomely"—tolerate generalissimos and such-like. For instance, for seven hundred years the kindly people of England have until quite lately been used by an implacable aristocracy. For seven hundred years this aristocracy dominated the people of England successfully, and Europe as well. The aristocrats gave the people pageants—the English love pageants and pageantry—witness a Coronation parade with its glass coach, etc., and the ceremonial connected with any order from the Order of the Garter downward to (even to) knighthood. They are surrounded by the emblems of armory; their country's patron saints; the coins bearing the royal arms; letters from government departments bear the royal insignia on their tops. The very inns of England have old signs, immemorial signs, whose significance has been long forgotten; tombs and memorials in their churches; and of course their armies' uniforms and standards are heraldic. They have made more wars than any people in Europe—and, of course, their occasions of state down to the changing of the guard are heraldic. There were a few rebellions in the course of England's long history; but it was not until the aristocracy began to fail, when cunning no longer counted and the pseudo aristocrats so messed things, that England lost its dominance in the world. Too many pseudo aristocrats tried to fool the masses of England, with the result we see at the present day. The Cecils and the Salisburys are in the background—so, in spite of the Lloyd Georges and the Atlees, England may recover by and by. No generalissimo has set himself up there.

The generalissimo is like the bad boy at school: everyone concedes that he is great, because he would cause such a stink if he were to be crossed; so, to hide their cowardice, the generality of boys called him great. So we get generalissimos. We know that they are anything but great, yet we put up with them. Yet there is not a generalissimo outside of Spain that is not a rogue, and above all a humbug.

It comes to this, then: generalissimos are more than deplorable. They are schemers and scoundrels. War on the other hand is not to be deplored. What is to be deplored is the enthusiasm of the members of the United Nations. I suppose it was just the same at the island of Delos, the Council of Vienna, the League of Nations. And why shouldn't it? If those connected with war to end war were insincere, they would not be tolerated for an instant. Much less than to the next war. I wonder why nations insist on getting into the United Nations. I think that at least there would be one nation who would have seen the farce of the UN preventing war, and would have stayed out.

On the other hand, if we had only Pasteurs and Alexander Flemings, how pedestrian life would be! And there would be no way of getting rid of the surplus population; and lives would get longer and longer until the world would be full of dotards; and insurance offices would go out of business.

Instead, there is a balance between wars and wars, UN's and UN's. Both need great sincerity, even among those who believe that a good battle justifies any cause.

Compared to wars and the United Nations, how spurious generalissimos are! The fact that they assume the title is quite sufficient to mark them down. There's something insincere in that and in the fact that they never turn out right. They are always found out even if we have to wait for the death of them—Stalin, for instance.

For my part, I would like to become a Kentucky major, if there be such a thing. Something that would keep me hidden while the colonels were in the limelight. Something the opposite to a generalissimo. Besides, it is obvious that, while there are no non-commissioned officers or men, an army consisting of colonels only cannot move. So, though I am unwilling to accept a lower rank than that of major, I want to pave the way, as it were, to getting men of a lower rank together and getting a move on. Let us be fair!

Are Americans All Morons?

Judging by those critics that England sends over here, they are.

Two men come to my mind, one of them a fellow who wanted you to think that he had that implacable "implied superiority" about him. But when he mispronounced Callimachus, calling the name Kali Machus, he aroused the suspicions of those who heard him. Then he gave details of his "tummy ache" by which he thought that he was inviting sympathy. He was in the wrong quarter when he expected sympathy from the people to whom he made the blunder of bad taste; and very much in the wrong when he mispronounced Callimachus. Both were evidence of his want of a background, even of common sense.

The other is a colonel in the British Army. It is said of him that he rose from the ranks. His behavior makes this obvious. It is a sign of what the English think of Americans that the colonel should have "risen from the ranks." It is what they think is a sop to democracy. The colonel certainly "rose from the ranks," especially in one story he told.

Now why does England send such men over here? For one thing, she cannot get any better in her peacetime secret service. They are usually men who have evaded conscription (the draft) with their tummy aches, or men whom England has no use for at home, men who have risen from the ranks. So she turns them loose on this country. You meet them in the best houses. People who own the "best houses" little know (or care) that they are entertaining the dregs of England. They put the eccentricities and bad manners down to the difference that exists between the two peoples. They may be all right in England, that is, modern England; and even those who never give it a thought otherwise know that modern England has changed mightily.

The fellow who complained of his tummy ache started denigrating the Irish. That meant me. He did it in the usual superior way. He thought that his superiority was unanswerable and that therefore he could get away with it. He was sadly mistaken. Even the most shanty of the Irish are superior to him. They don't evade the draft, for one thing, and they never funk a fight. All the better if the fight is for personal freedom. And they never go in for colonization, particularly of superior peoples. They are loath to ape people, and that is what the very superior was doing or trying to do. He was trying to imitate the Englishman of the higher class to impress his hostess.

When I heard him mispronounce the name I knew him for a man who, for all his pretense, had no education or, worse still, was one of those self-educated ignoramuses, so I wrote to a friend in England about him. This is the reply: "The fellow you refer to has written a number of sentimental books about life in a country cottage. In one of them he says, talking of the kitchen (a very different affair in England from an American kitchen), he says that he came into the kitchen with his boots on; and he gives you the impression that he was brought up in a kitchen." Yet he lived on the fat of the land over here. And he went to Florida for the holidays. A friend complained of him to the English Ambassador in Washington only to learn that the English had never heard of him. The usual procedure in the secret service.

A little laughter would undo the fellow, who never laughed. He took everything, himself included, seriously. Why should I take him seriously? you may well ask. I do not. Even though these men are a menace. If laughed at, they cease to be. So let us laugh at them. Otherwise they will cause a split between the nations, and Russia will be blamed for it, not them.

Then there are Englishmen who do not belong to the secret

service but come over here under their own steam apparently. Everything is aboveboard with them. Even their table manners. Their contribution to this "colony" is to vomit in their hosts' bathrooms or to exceed the speed limit as if they were still drunk. They usually belong to "the ruling classes," such as they are. That is why you find them in the best houses owned by snobs who think that everything English is to be admired. There is more snobbery here than in Buckingham Palace, and these men are cashing in on it. Their hosts get what they deserve.

So effective is the implied superiority that you do not want to burst it, because by bursting it you would cause pain and the owner of the implied superiority has no resources behind him. He can do nothing if he is not allowed to be "superior," except to show that he is insulted and in pain because you do not see eye to eye with him—because you do not share his superiority.

As I say, he and his like are to be found in the best houses, and the best houses are those in which you do not laugh or make a scene. He never appears in taverns, where his measure would be taken right away.

Then there is the American pity for the underdog. With it to protect him, he can count on not having his bluff called. It is this feeling for the underdog that makes possible the existence of these humbugs, because if you break them they become underdogs. I remember that once I was invited to India by Maharajah Alwar. He invited me so that I might put his medical service in order. That is, bring it up to date with Western ideas. Now I did not know what his medical service was like. It might have been run by witch doctors for all I knew. So I consulted with Tim Healy, who was Governor General of Ireland at the time. He had a cavernous voice, which he adopted in order to get people's attention at once. Some speakers take ten minutes or so before they can get the attention of the public. Tim Healy got it at once because of his voice. Maharajah Alwar was his guest at the time. I met him in the Governor General's house. His visit caused somewhat of an upset. He could not use shoe leather. His shoes were made of felt. He couldn't sit on chairs of leather, so chairs with tapestry seats had to be put under His Highness.

I took Tim aside. I put the invitation to him plain. I asked him should I go. I waited for his reply. "Oliver, don't go. First of all, there is no assurance that you will get the lac of rupees; and secondly, there is nothing to prevent the Indian doctors from putting powdered glass on your food."

It seems that an independent prince could not owe you money. Nevertheless, the English put civil servants into his exchequer—his "independence" consisted of anything except money! Then I had learned from Dick Berridge, the owner of Ballinahinch Castle, a place afterward acquired by another Indian prince, Ranji Singh, that an Indian prince became very different in India. Berridge was invited by Ranji to shoot tigers. He accepted with alacrity, only to find that the prince never appeared while he stayed as a guest of his, so he had to pack up and go home without meeting the prince or a tiger.

Afterward, in the Hyde Park Hotel, which Alwar took over for his visit to London, I asked him if he recalled his offer to me. And if he did, why did he choose me instead of many more fitted to accomplish his purpose? I remember his reply very well: "I wanted to get somebody who spoke English without that implied superiority that you cannot escape." Implied superiority. I have borrowed the phrase. It must be very galling to educated Indians to have the implied superiority come from the sons of parsons and the others that passed into the Indian Civil Service, especially as these Indians could trace their pedigree back far farther than most Englishmen.

Ranji Singh suffered from it all his life. He told me so—not in the words Alwar had used; but his meaning was evident for all that.

There is a third class of exportees: "cultural aspirants." They adopt homosexual practices because they think that such activity denotes a superiority of mind and the possession of cultural and artistic tendencies. Lest you think that I am biased (of course I am, and stubbornly biased) I quote from "A Memorandum of

Evidence Prepared by a Special Committee of the Council of the British Medical Association for Submission to the Departmental Committee on Homosexuality and Prostitution." It was published in December, 1955, in London, by the British Medical Association. So we see where these men of whom I have been speaking got their implied superiority. But it is more. It is far worse because in England "the existence of practising homosexuals in the Church, Parliament, Civil Service, Forces, Press, radio, stage and other institutions constitutes a special problem." What is worse still is that public standards have fallen to a lower level and that the law condones the lower standard of morality. Witness the actor who was arrested for suborning half a dozen men in King's Road, Chelsea, and was fined only ten pounds, the equivalent of twenty-seven dollars. And when he next appeared on the stage he was called before the curtain six times.

Here, on the other hand, the church, the House of Representatives, the civil service, etc., cannot be affected to the same extent as in England, for there have been stringent steps taken to remove the rotten ones from public life. And the United States has sufficient public opinion founded on decency to do it.

This country (I quote a Greek journalist so that you won't have to take it from me) depends for its strength on its virtue, that is, all that becomes a man and conformity to law—on its moral character, in a word. It has a Puritan background without any of the Puritan humbug. Whereas the British Empire is at an end. It has failed.

Short of preaching, I think that Americans are all morons in the eyes of the people I have characterized above and they should be proud of it. Suppose it were the other way round and Americans were to have their approval. How would you feel?

Dickie Martin

"I often drove a bus to Cricklewood and back," said Dickie Martin. It was in the days before motor cars. In those days buses were pulled by horses. Sometimes three, if there were a hill. Those were legendary days compared to these. There is a legend about the Cricklewood bus, not necessarily the one that Dickie Martin drove, but a bus that went over the same route. The legend goes like this:

An American sat with the driver, and as the driver's pal hove into sight, the first bus driver said, "Excuse me." He dipped down and drew from under the seat a foot of rope and waved it at his pal. His pal's eyes nearly dropped out of his head. He was speechless for a moment, and when the expletives came, the bus had passed out of sight. The bus driver who wielded the rope said to the American, "He ain't got no humor. His brother was hanged this morning."

Dickie Martin was a chronic medical. Now what, you will ask, is a "chronic" medical? It was a medical who took all the lectures without passing an exam except, of course, the preliminary exam, which was easy. Those were the old days. There were chronic medicals in Dublin University, the College of Surgeons, and even the Apothecary's Hall, whose degrees were looked down upon by all the chronics except, of course, those of the Apothecary's Hall. Now they tell me that you cannot be a chronic because you have to pass your exam before you can go on. They tell me too that the procedure is reversed. Instead of Dublin's chronics going to Edinburgh, Edinburgh sends its chronics to Dublin. So does London; but London did not exist in our day.

We used to drink at Golly's in Crow Street. Dickie was somewhat before our time. He was evidently cut off by his outraged parent when he had to drive the Cricklewood bus. It was in England. How he got there is a mystery. It looks like being stranded after a race meeting. He must have been a great chronic to have been before our time.

Weary Mack was a chronic, so was Barney. John Elwood, whom we called Giddy for he was always talking about Gideon Ouseley, was one too. Vincent Cosgrove was a chronic; so was I.

Some of us preferred to drink Jameson and some preferred Power, which was known by three swallows round the neck of the bottle. I remember one morning I remarked fatuously in Dickie's presence, "One swallow does not make a summer." "They often made a Martin," said Dickie.

As medicals we were immune from attacks in the Kips, the red-light district of Dublin. The reason for this was obvious: there would be no treatment for the ladies who lived there if a medical were attacked, not to say a medico.

The word "Kip" seems to be the way Dublin in the eighteenth century pronounced "keep." It was so intent on imitating London. The word "kip" is found only once in literature, in Goldsmith, who has somewhere, "tattering a whore in a kip."

In a way it was very convenient for Dublin to send its chronics to Edinburgh, at least up to the European war that began in 1914. It meant the establishment of friendly relations with another capital. In the European war an awful thing happened—to the chronics. They lost their status. They were qualified! This is the way it is supposed to have happened. An order came from the higher brass of the war to the examiners to qualify anyone who could handle an ambulance. Because of the shortage of doctors, troops were dying of gas gangrene. So the Edinburgh examiners qualified them all.

I knew one chronic to whom this happened. He took it very badly because an uncle had left him three hundred and fifty pounds a year until he became an M.D. of Dublin University. That was cause enough, but he had another grievance: he thought they did it in order to conscript him. He was right in a way. Dickie Martin on the other hand volunteered. No Irishman could be conscripted, owing in part to Kitchener's damping down the Irish spirit that dreamed that the war was to save little nations.

Dickie Martin volunteered. In his uniform he was a great success with the ladies. He was good-looking; but that goes for very little with women. Before he left for the front his father announced that he was going off for the week-end. So Dickie took advantage of the fact and, as probably he was pressed for time, brought two women into his house in Harcourt Street. Meanwhile his father doubled back—on the Sunday I think it was—and found Dickie in bed with extra company. "Dickie, it doesn't grieve me so much to see your turning your ancestral abode into a common stew as your want of a sense of proportion. One woman is enough for ten men. Look at the wreck your mother made of me!"

Don't think that there was no hope for a chronic. Ireland is full of beliefs, and one of its beliefs is that a chronic "took the long course." Which hints that the course of seven years is too short, and that those who pass it are none other than smart alecks. Another of its beliefs is that a doctor is judged by his size. If he is "the full of a door," he must necessarily be better than something smaller. Now Dublin has two or three doctors who, to say the least, are not the full of a door; but these are foreigners.

Some of the chronics have done well when once they got qualified. It probably is the way with examinations: those that are apt at examinations are apt at little else. Dean Swift had to get a degree *exempla gratia* as a special favor, and there are a host of other famous men who may spring to your mind. One only is necessary to start the train.

Armies are run by stupidity; so Dickie was put probably on

duty that suited him least. Instead of handling an ambulance and taking care of the wounded, he was sent to the front or the rear.

Perhaps, perhaps, he was driving an army bus! Whatever he did, he never came back.